# Gardens and Green Spaces in the West Midlands since 1700

# Gardens and Green Spaces in the West Midlands since 1700

Edited by Malcolm Dick and Elaine Mitchell

*Foreword by Timothy Mowl*

West Midlands Publications
an imprint of
University of Hertfordshire Press

First published in Great Britain in 2018 by
West Midlands Publications
an imprint of
University of Hertfordshire Press
College Lane
Hatfield
Hertfordshire
AL10 9AB

© the individual contributors 2018

The right of Malcolm Dick and Elaine Mitchell to be identified as the editors of this work has been asserted by them in accordance with the Copyright, Designs and Patents Act 1988.

All rights reserved. No part of this book may be reproduced or utilised in any form or by any means, electronic or mechanical, including photocopying, recording or by any information storage and retrieval system, without permission in writing from the publisher.

British Library Cataloguing in Publication Data
A catalogue record for this book is available from the British Library

ISBN 978-1-909291-55-3

Design by Arthouse Publishing Solutions Ltd
Printed in Great Britain by Hobbs the Printers Ltd

Frontispiece: Detail from Jacob George Strutt's *The Great Oak at Moccas* from *Sylva Britannica* (1826). Reproduced by permission of the Cadbury Research Library: Special Collections, the University of Birmingham.

# Contents

List of illustrations — vi
Acknowledgements — xi
Notes on contributors — xii
Foreword • *Timothy Mowl* — xv

Introduction: Gardens and green spaces in the West Midlands since 1700 • *Malcolm Dick and Elaine Mitchell* — 1

1  A landscape of 'ravishing varieties': the origins of picturesque landscaping in Stuart and Georgian Herefordshire • *David Whitehead* — 10

2  Exploring a landscape garden: William Shenstone at The Leasowes • *John Hemingway* — 40

3  Coalbrookdale: more than an eighteenth-century industrial landscape • *Harriet Devlin* — 56

4  Duddeston's 'shady walks and arbours': the provincial pleasure garden in the eighteenth century • *Elaine Mitchell* — 76

5  Enterprising women: shaping the business of gardening in the Midlands, 1780–1830 • *Dianne Barre* — 102

6  Manufactured landscapes: Victorian public parks and the industrial imagination • *Katy Layton-Jones* — 120

7  'Almost in the country': Richard Cadbury, Joseph Chamberlain and the landscaping of south Birmingham • *Maureen Perrie* — 138

8  Care in the countryside: the theory and practice of therapeutic landscapes in the early twentieth century • *Clare Hickman* — 160

9  Finding my place: rediscovering Hagley Park • *Joe Hawkins* — 186

Index — 209

# Illustrations

**Figures**

| | | |
|---|---|---|
| 1.1 | Cartouche of Taylor's *New Map of the County of Hereford* (1786) | 11 |
| 1.2 | Herefordshire orchard | 13 |
| 1.3 | *The Great Oak at Moccas Court*, Jacob George Strutt (1784–1867) | 20 |
| 1.4 | Eywood in *c*.1900 | 22 |
| 1.5 | Richard Payne Knight besmirching the memory of 'Capability' Brown | 26 |
| 1.6 | *A Wooded Landscape with Travelers on a Path through a Hamlet*, Hobbema (1638–1709) and Storck (1644–1708), *c*.1665 | 29 |
| 1.7 | Holme Lacy, in the Wye valley below Hereford | 31 |
| 1.8 | Detail of a map of Herefordshire from *The British Atlas of England and Wales* (1810) | 32 |
| 2.1 | Detail of a map of Worcestershire from *The British Atlas of England and Wales* (1810) | 41 |
| 2.2 | The main features of William Shenstone's landscape garden at The Leasowes | 42 |
| 2.3 | William Shenstone, memorialised in Robert Dodsley's *Works in Verse and Prose of William Shenstone Esq.* (1768) | 43 |
| 2.4 | The wooded landscape of Virgil's Grove at The Leasowes, from Robert Dodsley's *Works in Verse and Prose of William Shenstone Esq.* (1768) | 47 |
| 2.5 | Obelisk at the entrance to Virgil's Grove at The Leasowes, in David Parkes' *Sketches in Shropshire* | 49 |
| 2.6 | Excavation of the Dripping Fountain | 50 |
| 2.7 | Maria Dolman's urn at The Leasowes, in David Parkes' *Sketches in Shropshire* | 51 |
| 3.1 | Detail of a map of Shropshire from *The British Atlas of England and Wales* (1810) | 57 |
| 3.2 | *Cast Iron Bridge near Colebrook-Dale* (1782) | 58 |
| 3.3 | Abraham Darby's reward for information regarding the theft of fruit trees from his garden | 60 |
| 3.4 | The cottage in the woods (photographed *c*.1870), on Lincoln Hill | 67 |

| | | |
|---|---|---|
| 3.5 | The Temple (photographed c.1870), on the Workers' Walks, Coalbrookdale | 68 |
| 3.6 | Joseph Farington's *Pencil Sketch of Coalbrookdale* (1789) | 69 |
| 4.1 | 'The Road to Vauxhall', in Samuel and Nathaniel Buck's *East Prospect of Birmingham in the County of Warwick* (1753) | 79 |
| 4.2 | Advertisement from Bisset's *Magnificent Guide* (1808) | 81 |
| 4.3 | Detail from Pedley's *Vauxhall Gardens, Saltley, 1850* | 85 |
| 4.4 | Advertisement for a concert in *Aris's Birmingham Gazette*, 2 May 1748 | 86 |
| 4.5 | Advertisement of cockfighting in *Aris's Birmingham Gazette*, 2 June 1746 | 87 |
| 4.6 | Detail from Pedley's *Vauxhall Gardens, Saltley, 1850* | 88 |
| 4.7 | Bradford's *Plan of Birmingham Surveyed in 1750* | 89 |
| 4.8 | Sherriff's 'Plan of Birmingham' from Bisset's *Magnificent Guide* (1808) | 90 |
| 4.9 | *Birmingham from the North-East*, from William Hutton's *The History of Birmingham* (6th edn, 1836) | 91 |
| 5.1 | Francis Spinks' Spar Ornament Manufactory on King Street, Derby | 103 |
| 5.2 | Restored late nineteenth-century grotto in Derwent Gardens, Matlock Bath | 104 |
| 5.3 | Detail of Brunton and Forbes' *Catalogue of Seeds, Forest-Trees, Fruit-Trees and Flowering Shrubs* (17[76]) | 107 |
| 5.4 | Lithograph of Ashbourne Hall, Derbyshire (1839) | 108 |
| 5.5 | *Pineapple (Ananas comosus) with metamorphosis of bamboo page (Philaethria dido) and twice-stabbed lady bird beetle (Chilocorus cacti)*, Maria Sibylla Merian (1647–1717) | 111 |
| 6.1 | Detail of Walter MacFarlane No. 249 bandstand (1896), East Park, Wolverhampton | 125 |
| 6.2 | An iron bridge (1880) by Bradney and Company, West Park, Wolverhampton | 126 |
| 6.3 | Cast-iron fountain by Macfarlane and Co. at Hickman Park, Bilston (c.1911) | 126 |
| 6.4 | Carriage bridge (1875) crossing the south lake at Cannon Hill Park, Birmingham | 129 |
| 6.5 | Engraving of Wolverhampton's 1871 Royal Agricultural Show, *Illustrated London News* | 131 |
| 6.6 | Picture postcard (c.1910) of West Park, Wolverhampton | 132 |
| 6.7 | The Industrial Hall, Wolverhampton Art and Industrial Exhibition of 1902 | 132 |
| 7.1 | Map showing small landed estates on the outskirts of late nineteenth-century Birmingham | 139 |
| 7.2 | View from Moseley Hall in a photograph from Richard Cadbury's biography (1906) | 142 |
| 7.3 | Highbury, Joseph Chamberlain's Venetian Gothic house at King's Heath, c.1906 | 144 |
| 7.4 | Landscaping at Highbury | 145 |

| | | |
|---|---|---|
| 7.5 | A terraced platform at Highbury | 147 |
| 7.6 | Oak Tree Pool, Highbury | 147 |
| 7.7 | Uffculme, where Richard Cadbury designed both house and gardens | 149 |
| 8.1 | Sleep-time garden for children at Cropwood Open-Air School, Blackwell | 160 |
| 8.2 | Cluster of open-air institutions in the Blackwell area close to Birmingham | 161 |
| 8.3 | Therapeutic institutions in the Blackwell area funded through philanthropy and patronage | 162 |
| 8.4 | The south aspect of Blackwell Sanatorium, showing the conservatory and gardens | 163 |
| 8.5 | A postcard of Blackwell Sanatorium, showing additional glassed areas | 168 |
| 8.6 | Burcot Grange, Blackwell | 170 |
| 8.7 | Children's garden Cropwood Open-Air School, Blackwell | 170 |
| 8.8 | A class of schoolgirls having lessons in the open air, *c*.1925–35 | 173 |
| 8.9 | A postcard of Blackwell Sanatorium | 177 |
| 9.1 | Key features at Hagley Park, from Jeremiah Matthews' 1826 survey of Hagley | 187 |
| 9.2 | *A View in Hagley Park, belonging to Sir Thomas Lyttelton Bart*, Francis Vivares after Thomas Smith of Derby, 1764 | 188 |
| 9.3 | Section of Jeremiah Matthews' 1826 survey of the Park at Hagley | 191 |
| 9.4 | The ruined Palladian Bridge at Hagley | 193 |
| 9.5 | The Palladian Bridge, shaded by a backdrop of yew, at Hagley | 196 |
| 9.6 | Wooden bench on the Palladian Bridge at Hagley | 196 |
| 9.7 | Brick culvert and stone rill at Hagley Park | 197 |
| 9.8 | The source of the 'rude cascade' at Hagley Park | 199 |
| 9.9 | The 'rude cascade' fully restored at Hagley Park | 201 |

**Plates**

1.1 Pollard willows on the Lugg Meadows, from David Cox's *Treatise on Landscape Painting* (1813)
1.2 *Beech Trees at Foxley*, Thomas Gainsborough (*c*.1760)
1.3 *Goodrich Castle on the Wye*, Thomas Hearne, *c*.1785
2.1 Watercolour by William Shenstone of his ferme ornée at The Leasowes
2.2 The South Cascade at The Leasowes, in a watercolour by Shenstone
2.3 The Ruinated Priory, The Leasowes
3.1 *A View of the Upper Works of Coalbrook Dale, in the County of Salop*, George Perry and Francis Vivares, 1758
3.2 *The South West Prospect of Coalbrook-Dale, and the Adjacent Country*, Thomas Smith and Francis Vivares, 1758
3.3 *Afternoon View of Coalbrookdale*, William Williams, 1777

4.1 *Vauxhall Gardens, Saltley, 1850*, by J. Pedley
5.1 Illustration from Jane Loudon's *The Ladies Flower-Garden of Ornamental Bulbous Plants* (1841)
5.2 Illustration from Curtis' *Botanical Magazine* (1787)
6.1 Bricks moulded to emulate Italian terracotta (1894) at Burslem Park
6.2 Pulhamite cascade and rockery (*c.*1894) at Burslem Park
6.3 A Lion Foundry No. 23 cast-iron bandstand, Handsworth Park, Birmingham
7.1 The grounds at Moseley Hall depicted by Humphry Repton before his suggested improvements
7.2 Repton's suggested improvements for Moseley Hall revealed
7.3 A postcard showing the tall palm-house at Richard Cadbury's Uffculme
8.1 Plan of *Cropwood Open-Air School*, Blackwell, by Bernard Sleigh (1922)
8.2 Illustration from *The Secret Garden*, by Frances Hodgson Burnett (1911)
9.1 Views from Milton's Seat of the parkland and country beyond at Hagley Hall
9.2 George Lyttelton, 1st Baron Lyttelton, the creator of Hagley's landscape
9.3 The restored Palladian Bridge at Hagley

## Publication grant

Publication has been made possible by a generous grant from the Marc Fitch Fund.

# Acknowledgements

The editors of *Gardens and Green Spaces in the West Midlands since 1700* are indebted to many individuals and organisations for contributing to and supporting this book. The chapters are based upon a number of papers delivered at the Annual Conference of the Centre for West Midlands History at the University of Birmingham in March 2014, entitled 'Landscape and Green Spaces: Garden History in the West Midlands'. We are especially grateful that Professor Timothy Mowl, who provided the keynote lecture at the conference, has agreed to write the Foreword to this book.

The authors' enthusiasm, patience, willingness to accept advice and positive response to requests for images to illustrate their chapters has been much appreciated. Jane Housham and Sarah Elvins at the University of Hertfordshire Press have been encouraging, helpful and approachable guides throughout the project from the planning stage to the final publication. We are extremely grateful for the generosity of the March Fitch Fund in providing a grant to cover the costs of illustrations and copyright clearance and to two peer reviewers for reading the chapters and supporting the application. Many archives, institutions and individuals have supplied images and authors have also created maps or diagrams or taken photographs to enhance their chapters. We are grateful to Jenni Dixon for her assistance in formatting a number of images.

*Gardens and Green Spaces in the West Midlands since 1700* reflects the knowledge, skills, efforts and expertise of many people. We believe that the publication justifies their commitment and not only provides a history of individual landscapes in the region but also throws light on aspects of local, global, economic, social and cultural history. We also hope that the book adds to the rich historiography of both garden history and the West Midlands.

Malcolm Dick and Elaine Mitchell<br>
April 2018

# Notes on contributors

**Dr Dianne Barre** took early retirement from the University of Birmingham in 2005 and in 2006 was awarded a PhD on the subject of the formal gardens of Staffordshire from 1690 to the 1750s. She continued her research on historic gardens in Staffordshire for Tim Mowl's volume on that county in his *The Historic Gardens of England* series (published in 2009). Dianne then turned to Derbyshire to look at historic gardens and parks in that county. Her book *Historic Gardens and Parks of Derbyshire* was published by Oxbow in April 2017.

**Harriet Devlin, MBE** studied Anglo-Saxon, Norse and Celtic as well as Archaeology and Anthropology at Cambridge, but went on to become a museum consultant, creating a number of rural museums for, among others, the National Trust. She worked for the Ulster Architectural Heritage Society in Northern Ireland during the 1990s and between 2003 and 2014 ran the MA in Historic Environment Conservation at the University of Birmingham's Ironbridge International Institute for Cultural Heritage in Coalbrookdale. Harriet now leads the MA in the Conservation of the Historic Environment at Birmingham City University. The landscape of Coalbrookdale and the link to the Quaker industrialists is a particular research interest.

**Dr Malcolm Dick** is Director of the Centre for West Midlands History and Lecturer in Regional and Local History at the University of Birmingham. He managed the Revolutionary Players Digitisation project on the history of the West Midlands (www.revolutionaryplayers.org.uk) and is editor of *Midland History* and History West Midlands Ltd (www.historywm.com). Malcolm's research focuses upon the history of the Midlands Enlightenment in the eighteenth century and the development of regional industry, towns and local communities from 1700 to the present. He has published books on the history of Birmingham, Joseph Priestley, Matthew Boulton and John Baskerville.

**Joe Hawkins** was led by a love of nature into the world of historic gardens with a career-start tending the landscape at Shugborough Hall in Staffordshire. After 14 years with hands in the earth, promotion to head gardener awakened a fascination with the development of the English landscape garden, which led to an MA in Garden History at the University of Bristol. After completion, events brought Joe to his post as Head of Landscape at Hagley Hall, where he is tasked with overseeing the restoration of this Grade I registered park. Joe continues his research with a PhD at Birmingham City University on 'Thy British Tempé: Elegy and Association in Hagley Park (1693–1773)'.

**Dr John Hemingway** became interested in William Shenstone in the early 1980s when, teaching poetry, he discovered Shenstone's pastoral poems. He subsequently worked as Archaeological Officer at Dudley Metropolitan Borough Council, where one of his earliest investigations was to survey the landscape at The Leasowes for a Heritage Lottery Fund bid. John discovered that the poet and the creator of the garden were one and the same. He has been studying the man and his landscape ever since and completed his PhD, 'The Origins, Development and Influence of William Shenstone's Landscape Garden Design at The Leasowes, Halesowen', at the University of Birmingham in 2017.

**Dr Clare Hickman** is a Lecturer in History at the University of Chester, where she works on the intersection between designed landscapes and medical practice. In 2013 she published *Therapeutic Landscapes: A History of English Hospital Gardens since 1800* with Manchester University Press. She has held a Wellcome Fellowship in Medical History and Humanities at King's College London and was previously the Research Fellow on the Leverhulme Trust-funded *Historic Gardens and Landscapes of England Project* led by Professor Timothy Mowl at the University of Bristol. In 2005 she won the first *Garden History* Essay Prize.

**Dr Katy Layton-Jones** is contributing editor for the Cirencester volume of the Victoria County History of Gloucestershire. She was Research Associate on 'Liverpool Parks and Open Spaces' at the University of Liverpool and co-author of the resulting book, *Places of Health and Amusement* (English Heritage, 2008). She completed the *National Review of Research Priorities for Urban Parks, Designed Landscapes and Open Spaces* (English Heritage, 2013) and the *History of Public Park Funding and Management* (Historic England, 2016), and was an expert witness before the Parliamentary Select Committee on Public Parks. Other publications include *Beyond the Metropolis: the Changing Image of Urban Britain* (Manchester University Press, 2016), *Uncertain Prospects: Public Parks in the New Age of Austerity* (The Gardens Trust, 2016) and articles on public parks.

**Elaine Mitchell** is a PhD student in the Centre for West Midlands History at the University of Birmingham, where her research focuses upon urban gardens and gardening in eighteenth-century Birmingham. She is editorial assistant for *Midland History* and was managing and picture editor of *History West Midlands* and *Fortunes of War: The West Midlands at the Time of Waterloo* (Andrew Watts and Emma Tyler, History West Midlands, 2015). She was picture editor for *Birmingham: the Workshop of the World* (Carl Chinn and Malcolm Dick, Liverpool University Press, 2016) and is a member of the Centre for Printing History and Culture (www.cphc.org.uk).

**Maureen Perrie** is Emeritus Professor of Russian History in the Centre for Russian, European and Eurasian Studies, University of Birmingham, and has published extensively on Russian history from the sixteenth to the twentieth centuries. In retirement, while continuing to work on seventeenth-century Muscovy, she has developed an interest in the history of Highbury Park, which is close to her home in Kings Heath. She has given talks about the history of the park to various local community groups and published an article in the *Agricultural History Review* (2013) on hobby farming by the Cadbury and Chamberlain families on their suburban estates in south Birmingham.

**David Whitehead** is a retired schoolmaster. He is honorary secretary of the Woolhope Naturalists Field Club; assistant editor of the Herefordshire VCH, as well as its vice-chairman; and founder-member of the Hereford and Worcester Gardens Trust. For the last-named he wrote the *Survey of Historic Parks and Gardens of Herefordshire* (2001). He has written extensively in periodicals and journals on aspects of the historic countryside, its gardens and buildings. In retirement he has been kept busy writing a number of Higher Level Countryside Stewardship Schemes for Herefordshire parks. He lives in the city of Hereford and has a large garden, characterised by 'counterfeit neglect' (R.P. Knight, *The Landscape*, 1794).

# Foreword

*Timothy Mowl, Emeritus Professor in the History of Architecture and Designed Landscapes, University of Bristol*

In the keynote lecture delivered to the Annual Conference of the Centre for West Midlands History in March 2014, from which these chapters are derived, I stressed the need for a multi-disciplinary approach to what is still a burgeoning academic subject. It is only when budding garden historians realise that they must become polymaths – experts in landscape, garden, architectural, art and botanical history, not to mention aesthetics, iconography and hydraulics – that the true nature of the garden history of this country can be charted. In my view this historical narrative can be achieved only by close site investigation combined with directed archival research.

It is heartening, therefore, to see that such an inclusive approach has been taken by the contributors to this volume – academics, landscape practitioners and gifted garden history aficionados alike – whose work is guiding us towards what has been termed the 'new garden history'. Their researches are making a significant contribution to the wider subject and to an understanding of the varied landscapes and gardens of the West Midlands in particular. The chapters presented here cover an impressive range of new research methodologies, from straight garden and landscape history through industrial, urban and suburban history and the history of science, medicine and health to cultural, class and gender approaches. The overriding aim of the conference was to move beyond a narrow focus on celebrated practitioners and elite spaces to a more holistic approach celebrating local and regional history. In this the conference was a resounding success, and the publication of its papers will make a significant contribution to garden history studies.

There is not space enough in a short foreword to point up the many insights and new revelations presented here, merely to state that all the chapters break new ground, whether on well-known subjects such as the origins of the

Savage Picturesque in Georgian Herefordshire, expounded with meticulous scholarship by David Whitehead, and the enlightening exploration of William Shenstone's intellectual titivations at The Leasowes by John Hemingway, or with fresh discoveries such as Dianne Barre's exposition of Widow Spinks's extraordinary grotto-making in Derby and Clare Hickman's fascinating account of gardens as open-air institutions on the west side of Bromsgrove. Harriet Devlin charts deftly the social philanthropy of Quaker ironmasters at Coalbrookdale, who gardened for themselves as well as providing allotments and housing for their workforces, while Katy Layton-Jones continues the industrial theme by focusing on the use of industrial materials and manufactures which gave regional identity to public parks across the West Midlands. Maureen Perrie considers the creation of small estates in the Birmingham environs, particularly Joseph Chamberlain's Highbury, for which there is surviving family correspondence and photographs, and Elaine Mitchell retrieves the Vauxhall Gardens, contrived to give the Georgian manufacturing town some desperately needed social and cultural tone. The book reaches a fitting climax in the brilliant restoration of the eighteenth-century landscape at Hagley Park, masterminded with informed scholarship by Lord Cobham and his infectiously enthusiastic Head of Landscape, Joe Hawkins.

# INTRODUCTION

## Gardens and green spaces in the West Midlands since 1700

*Malcolm Dick and Elaine Mitchell*

Garden history has been a dimension of historical study since the early twentieth century, but only in recent years has it begun to move away from a focus on the well-known landscape architects, including William Kent and Lancelot 'Capability' Brown, and the gardens of the elite, such as Chatsworth and Stowe. There has also been a retreat from a concentration on the aesthetics of design towards seeing gardens and the activity of gardening within wider social, economic, political and cultural contexts. Gardens can be understood as part of the shaping of urban and rural landscapes and are influenced by scientific, technological, industrial, medical and intellectual developments. Social class and gender also affect their creation and development. The role of gardeners and lesser-known designers, how women were involved in the creation of landscapes and the gardens of the working classes deserve rescuing from the 'enormous condescension of posterity'.[1] Methodologically as well, studying garden history involves a multi-disciplinary approach that includes insights from geology, archaeology and horticulture, art and architectural history, philosophy, poetry and novels, material culture and archival research to throw light on the creation, meaning and impact of green spaces at particular times and in different locations. This combination of approaches has been called the 'new garden history' by Tom Williamson.[2]

This volume explores current research into landscape and gardens in the English West Midlands and builds upon recent published work on the region.[3] It contains edited papers delivered at an academic conference, 'Landscape and Green Spaces: Garden History in the West Midlands', held at the University of Birmingham in March 2014 under the auspices of the Centre for West Midlands History. The conference deliberately moved away from the 'great men' approach to history and avoided an overtly celebratory approach towards individuals and their creations. It showed that much remained to be uncovered, even about the well-known designers, as the research and exhibitions that accompanied the tercentenary of the birth of 'Capability' Brown in 2016 revealed. This is the first regional study to explore analytically the application of the 'new garden history' in the West Midlands. As the chapters reveal, it also applies insights from scholars drawn from other disciplines, such as urban, industrial and medical history. Within the contours of the historic counties of Derbyshire, Herefordshire, Shropshire, Staffordshire, Warwickshire and Worcestershire the book brings a range of methodological approaches to bear on the region's landscapes. Boundaries, of course, are porous, especially when exploring intellectual, commercial and cultural networks, and this is reflected by some of the authors. Chronologically the book concentrates on the eighteenth, nineteenth and twentieth centuries, but, as the last chapter reveals, the theory and practice of garden history is being applied to the re-creation of an eighteenth-century landscape in the twenty-first century. The contributions recognise the diverse nature of garden history and show that independent scholars as well as academics in universities are contributing to advancing knowledge and understanding.[4]

The West Midlands has been portrayed as a region of significant manufacturing innovation, industrial enlightenment and urbanisation in the eighteenth and nineteenth centuries, a period christened by Maxine Berg as 'the age of manufactures'.[5] It was also a site of gardening innovation. The entrepreneur Matthew Boulton was one of the area's leading players and the landscape garden that he created at Soho, on the outskirts of Birmingham, was laid out not only to project his status as a gentleman but also to provide a classical setting for his manufactory.[6] Similarly, the region has also come into view as an important centre of Enlightenment thought and practice, investigation focusing on the activities of the group of men who formed the Lunar Society, a network of industrialists, scientists, doctors, inventors and philosophers.[7] At Lichfield one of the 'Lunaticks', Dr Erasmus Darwin, created a botanical garden near to his home and wrote about plants and planting in his poem *The Botanic Garden* (1795), while another, Dr William Withering, began to classify native British plants according to the new Linnaean system.[8] In the nineteenth century the Birmingham Botanical and Horticultural Society enlisted the well-known horticulturalist and garden writer John Claudius Loudon to design Birmingham Botanical Gardens, while Britain's first municipally owned public park, Derby Arboretum, was also laid out by Loudon.[9] Innovation in glasshouse design at Chatsworth in Derbyshire by the gardener and architect Joseph Paxton led to his creation of the Crystal Palace in 1851.[10] The contribution of women to landscape design and horticulture has been largely overlooked: increasingly, however, women are being recognised for their creative work in shaping green spaces. Both Ann Shteir (1996) and

Catherine Horwood (2010) have drawn our attention to the contributions of women to gardening: Henrietta Knight (Lady Luxborough) at Barrells in Warwickshire and the writers Maria Jacson in Derbyshire and Birmingham-born Jane Loudon, for example.[11] The skills, careers and achievements of a variety of individuals show the interconnection between the advancement of botanical knowledge and the development of gardening practice on the one hand and industrial, scientific and cultural history in the West Midlands on the other. As this volume reveals, there are diverse and multi-faceted garden histories to discover.

The first chapter, by David Whitehead, on the beginnings of picturesque landscaping in Stuart and Georgian Herefordshire, reveals the importance of the intersection of both time and place for understanding how landscapes were created. He explores both visual representations and printed and archival primary sources to build a cultural and intellectual history of the distinctive Herefordshire landscape. Two late eighteenth-century local landowners, Uvedale Price and Richard Payne Knight, challenged the accepted canons of the English landscape movement. They attempted to destroy the reputation of 'Capability' Brown and his self-proclaimed successor, Humphry Repton. From the 1770s Price and Knight's estates at Foxley and Downton attracted the attention of the *cognoscenti* interested in prosperous farming with an aesthetic bonus. In place of the Brownian park they recommended a 'natural' style of estate management, which epitomised the Picturesque. Whitehead argues that Picturesque ideas were embedded in the distinctive agricultural history of Herefordshire from at least the late seventeenth century. The county emerged from the medieval period with a predominantly enclosed landscape, managed by small tenant farmers who engaged in both industrial and farming activities. In character this landscape had a varied texture of narrow lanes, high hedgerows, small woods and plenty of water, all of which made Herefordshire different from the open-field countryside in other Midland counties. Price and Knight articulated a defence of their vision of a distinctive county landscape that separated Herefordshire from Wales and Midland England beyond the Malvern Hills.

John Hemingway applies a cross-disciplinary approach to an investigation of the origins of an important eighteenth-century landscape garden. At The Leasowes, near Halesowen, then part of Shropshire, the poet William Shenstone (1714–1763) fashioned a ferme ornée (ornamental farm) that was seen and described by visitors from Britain and overseas. By making subtle improvements to the natural landscape, erecting classical and medieval features and adding reflections from classical Roman poets and his own verses he conjured up pictures from an imagined past and created an environment that aimed to stimulate the senses. The Leasowes promoted Shenstone's reputation as a landscape gardener, but little remains of his original work in what is now a public park. Both fieldwork and archaeological investigations, however, allow Hemingway to explore how Shenstone creatively managed local geology, topography and water to transform a simple hill farm into a setting that was picturesque, sublime and unique. These findings provide additional insights to those derived from written primary sources, revealing both how Shenstone translated his ideas into reality and his practical skills as a visionary landscape gardener.

In her topographical analysis of tourism and philanthropy Harriet Devlin explores green spaces in eighteenth- and early nineteenth-century Coalbrookdale in the Severn Valley, a location that has traditionally been perceived only as an industrial landscape. The Quaker ironmasters, including the Darby and Reynolds families, who were responsible for creating this 'birthplace of the Industrial Revolution' had private gardens, provided housing and allotments for their workers and, most dramatically, created a hillside of public walks now known as the Sabbath Walks. The chapter explores the extent to which these topographies were influenced by religious and moral motivations, a desire to demonstrate engagement in a 'polite' culture or, pragmatically, the need to provide leisure facilities for the growing number of tourists and potential customers visiting the Iron Bridge. How influential were the Bristol Quakers, especially Thomas Goldney, on how the Darby and Reynolds families shaped their green spaces? Why did the ironmaster Richard Reynolds create the serpentine walks through the woodlands in the 1780s? Utilising evidence from, for example, letters, paintings, prints and archaeology, the chapter adds to our understanding of a landscape that was more than a site for mining and manufacturing.

Elaine Mitchell examines the Vauxhall provincial pleasure garden in Duddeston, now part of Birmingham, which has almost entirely disappeared, both on the ground and from the page. In so doing, she re-evaluates the ways in which we perceive the eighteenth-century manufacturing town. In historical writing the pleasure garden of the period has been associated with either metropolitan leisured culture or that of the 'polite' town. Where London led towns in the provinces, such as Bath, followed, and pleasure gardens became part of an urban environment that developed to attract and entertain visitors. It is novel for historians to explore the pleasure garden within the industrial town. Birmingham's Vauxhall was established during the 1740s: a landscaped setting as a commercial site of entertainment, which provided concerts, firework displays and cockfighting. In 1850 'old Vauxhall' closed and the site disappeared beneath the residential streets of the expanding town. Mitchell traces the history of Vauxhall, its establishment as a commercial venture, how it was used, the events that formed part of its activities and its sudden closure.

Birmingham's Vauxhall was a significant social and cultural space in which the urban landscape was adapted to promote the attractions of 'the city of a thousand trades'.[12]

The activities of women, especially those who were not members of the aristocracy and gentry, have traditionally been hidden within garden history. While newspapers have not been widely used by garden historians, electronic access has dramatically improved our ability to search for local evidence online and Dianne Barre gathers evidence of the enterprising activities of 'Widow Spinks', who took over her husband's business selling fossils in Derby and advertised her sales with a tourist attraction: an elaborate grotto in her garden open to customers and paying visitors. Using the *Derby Mercury* as her main source of evidence, Barre reveals how women were active players in the wider expression of garden creation through, for example, the exercise of financial management and the ownership of businesses and land.

Conventionally, urban public parks in late nineteenth-century Britain have been explained as compensatory landscapes, atoning for the sprawl and pollution that surrounded them. In a topographical sense this claim has some validity, as parks provided a spatial interruption of industrial and commercial premises and working-class housing. Katy Layton-Jones, however, re-evaluates our perception of nineteenth-century parks. They were environments that celebrated rather than denounced the materials, scale and socio-economic conditions of the industrial age. Bandstands, water fountains and shelters constructed from cast iron, as well as tea rooms and ornamental bridges built from red brick and decorated with Minton tiles, were creations of modern manufacturing. From the Pulhamite rockery in Burslem Park (c.1894) to the Glass House in Wolverhampton's West Park (1896), industrial materials shaped (and continue to shape) the design and function of public parks.[13] Using examples taken from the West Midlands, Layton-Jones examines the ways in which the aesthetics and architecture of public parks were informed by the principles and processes of industrial production.

The upper and middle classes of nineteenth-century Birmingham, like those of other industrialising cities, frequently invested their growing wealth in landed estates, in imitation of the gentry and aristocracy. Birmingham industrialists, to a greater extent than their counterparts elsewhere, preferred to acquire small properties within commuting distance of the city centre. Maureen Perrie's chapter on small landed estates on the southern outskirts of Birmingham before 1914 focuses on the landscaping of three holdings on the boundary of Moseley and Kings Heath: Moseley Hall, owned by the Taylor family and then leased to Richard Cadbury; Joseph Chamberlain's Highbury; and Richard Cadbury's subsequent estate at Uffculme. Of these, Highbury is the best documented, by Chamberlain family correspondence and photographs, as well as by articles in the press and specialist gardening magazines. Perrie examines how the transformation of agricultural land into parkland by Edward Milner and his son Henry reflected the aesthetic principle of 'natural picturesqueness' expounded in Henry Milner's book *The art and practice of landscape gardening* (1890).[14] Perrie also explores the social anxiety suffered by the Chamberlains as the expansion of speculative building on the outskirts of the city made their estate appear suburban rather than rural.

Clare Hickman marries garden history with the history of health and medicine in her chapter on 'therapeutic landscapes', which focuses on a range of sites and individual experiences in early twentieth-century Bromsgrove, Worcestershire. '[I] have spent most of the time sitting in sun lounge and walking or sitting in the grounds', wrote a patient to her relatives in 1959 from Blackwell Convalescent Home. Access to the open air as described by this patient was an important therapeutic approach in the early twentieth century and a range of institutions employed this method in the West Midlands region. For example, an Ordnance Survey map of 1937 indicates a cluster of open-air institutions on the west side of Bromsgrove, Worcestershire. This chapter places these institutions within the open-air movement in England during the late nineteenth and early twentieth centuries. Often associated with sanatoria for patients suffering from tuberculosis, the open-air treatment (literally being placed in the open air as much as possible) was also taken up by convalescent homes, orthopaedic hospitals and schools. Hickman also considers the importance of place, in this case Bromsgrove, and explores the influence of the Cadbury family on open-air provision in the area. Finally, she considers how the same underlying beliefs affected the planning and design of the Bournville estate.

Historical sources not only broaden our understanding of the creation, nature and importance of gardens but can also have practical relevance, as Joe Hawkins reveals in the final chapter, on the restoration of Worcestershire's Hagley Park. In May 2012 an invitation from the owner, Lord Cobham, to oversee the restoration of the long-since declined but once much-celebrated eighteenth-century landscape at Hagley enabled the author to apply historical knowledge and investigation to the project. A special edition of the Garden History Society's journal in 2007 had presented a diligent historiography of Hagley Park, which formed the foundation for a Conservation Management Plan. Additional overlays of archaeological, architectural, hydrological, ecological and arboricultural reports further informed the park's restoration. In his restoration work, Hawkins tried to avoid preconceptions of what the landscape originally looked like from these reports. He harvested evidence from the primary sources and walked the landscape accompanied only by such descriptions. This approach paid dividends in recovering the reality of the landscape. His chapter details the strategy, discoveries and initial phase of restoration at Hagley.

*Gardens and green spaces in the West Midlands since 1700* represents the effervescent nature of scholarly research in and about the region. The contributions are not only revealing as scholarly exercises but also assist in seeing landscapes in new ways; they illuminate the intersections between public history and heritage, reveal how academic inquiry can influence landscape restoration and build an awareness of place. Green spaces are multi-sensory environments that appeal to both emotion and intellect. The editors believe that, collectively, the chapters provide diverse ways of seeing created landscapes, show the interpretative potential of varied sources and demonstrate the value of different methodological perspectives. There is more to be done. The history of women, the working class and minority cultures as agents of change in shaping green spaces is still in its infancy. The material culture of created landscapes offers huge possibilities for investigation. There is also a global garden history to consider that charts the ways in which local gardens were shaped by international developments and, in turn, how places and spaces overseas were influenced by what happened in the West Midlands. There will be new questions to ask, different insights to make and fresh conclusions to reach. We hope that the book not only stimulates further research into the garden history of the region but offers models for investigative work elsewhere, in Britain and beyond.

## Notes

1   The phrase was originally used by E.P. Thompson to condemn the neglect by historians of the lives and experiences of ordinary people: E.P. Thompson, *The making of the English working class* (Harmondsworth, 1980), p. 12.

2   T. Williamson, *Polite landscapes: gardens and society in eighteenth-century England* (Stroud, 1995), p. 4.; For examples of this approach see: T. Mowl, *Gentlemen and players: gardeners of the English landscape* (Stroud, 2000); T. Longstaffe-Gowan, *The London town garden, 1700–1840* (New Haven and London, 2001); A. Wilkinson, *The Victorian gardener: the growth of gardening and the floral world* (Stroud, 2006); M. Laird, *A natural history of English gardening* (New Haven and London, 2015). Recent contributions to the historiography of garden history include: E. Harwood, T. Williamson, M. Leslie and J. Dixon Hunt, 'Whither garden history?', *Studies in the History of Gardens and Designed Landscapes*, 27/2 (2007), pp. 91–112 and B. Elliott, 'The development and present state of garden history', *Occasional Papers from the RHS Lindley Library: the History of Garden History*, 9 (2012), pp. 3–94.

3   T. Mowl, *Historic gardens of Worcestershire* (Stroud, 2006); T. Mowl and D. Barre, *Historic gardens of Staffordshire* (Bristol, 2009); T. Mowl and D. James, *Historic gardens of Warwickshire* (Bristol, 2011); T. Mowl and J. Bradney, *Historic gardens of Herefordshire* (Bristol, 2012); S. Spooner, 'The Midlands', in Spooner, *Regions and designed landscapes in Georgian England* (London, 2015), pp. 100–136.

4   Important work has been pursued by The Garden History Society (now The Gardens Trust), which has acted as a bridge between the research of individuals within and outside universities through its journal *Garden History*: <http://thegardenstrust.org>, accessed 2 November 2017.

5   M. Berg, *The age of manufactures, 1700–1820* (London, 1985), p. 23. See also P. Jones, *Industrial enlightenment: science, technology and culture in Birmingham and the West Midlands 1760–1820* (Manchester, 2008).
6   P. Ballard, V. Loggie and S. Mason, *A lost landscape: Matthew Boulton's gardens at Soho* (Chichester, 2009).
7   J. Uglow, *The lunar men: the friends who made the future* (London, 2002).
8   P. Elliott, 'The garden: Darwin's gardens: place, horticulture and botany', in Elliot, *Enlightenment, modernity and science: geographies of scientific cultures and improvement in Georgian England* (London, 2010), pp. 48–76; E. Darwin, *The Botanic Garden. A poem in two parts*, 3rd edn (London, 1795); W. Withering, *A botanic arrangement of all the vegetables naturally growing in Great Britain*, 2 vols (Birmingham, 1776).
9   P. Ballard, *An oasis of delight: the history of the Birmingham Botanical Gardens*, 2nd edn (Studley, 2004); P. Elliott, 'The Derby Arboretum (1840): the first specially designed municipal public park in Britain', *Midland History*, 26/1 (2001), pp. 144–76.
10  K. Colquhoun, *A thing in disguise: the visionary life of Joseph Paxton* (London, 2003).
11  C. Horwood, *Gardening women: their stories from 1600 to the present* (London, 2010); A. Shteir, *Cultivating women, cultivating science: Flora's daughters and botany in England 1760–1860* (Baltimore and London, 1996).
12  The phrase was allegedly used by Edmund Burke to describe late eighteenth-century Birmingham: M. Dick, 'The city of a thousand trades, 1700–1945', in C. Chinn and M. Dick (eds), *Birmingham: the Workshop of the World* (Liverpool, 2016), p. 125.
13  Pulhamite is an artificial stone patented by James Pulham (1820–1898), which is made from a mixture of sand, Portland cement and clinker on a rubble and crushed brick core.
14  Henry Milner, *The art and practice of landscape gardening* (London, 1890).

## Bibliography
### Printed primary sources
Darwin, E., *The Botanic Garden. A poem in two parts*, 3rd edn (London, 1795).
Withering, W., *A botanic arrangement of all the vegetables naturally growing in Great Britain*, 2 vols (Birmingham, 1776).

### Secondary sources
Ballard, P., *An oasis of delight: the history of the Birmingham Botanical Gardens*, 2nd edn (Studley, 2004).
Ballard, P., Loggie, V. and Mason, S., *A lost landscape: Matthew Boulton's gardens at Soho* (Chichester, 2009).
Berg, M., *The age of manufactures, 1700–1820* (London, 1985).
Colquhoun, K., *A thing in disguise: the visionary life of Joseph Paxton* (London, 2003).
Dick, M., 'The city of a thousand trades, 1700–1945', in C. Chinn and M. Dick (eds), *Birmingham: the workshop of the world* (Liverpool, 2016), pp. 125–58.
Elliott, B., 'The development and present state of garden history', *Occasional Papers from the RHS Lindley Library: the History of Garden History*, 9 (2012), pp. 3–94.
Elliott, P., 'The Derby Arboretum (1840): the first specially designed municipal public park in Britain', *Midland History*, 26/1 (2001), pp. 144–76.
Elliott, P., 'The garden: Darwin's gardens: place, horticulture and botany', in Elliot, *Enlightenment, modernity and science: geographies of scientific cultures and improvement in Georgian England* (London, 2010), pp. 48–76.

Harwood, E., Williamson, T., Leslie, M. and Dixon Hunt, J., 'Whither garden history?', *Studies in the History of Gardens and Designed Landscapes*, 27/2 (2007), pp. 91–112.

Horwood, C., *Gardening women: their stories from 1600 to the present* (London, 2010).

Jones, P., *Industrial enlightenment: science, technology and culture in Birmingham and the West Midlands 1760–1820* (Manchester, 2008).

Laird, M., *A natural history of English gardening* (New Haven and London, 2015).

Longstaffe-Gowan, T., *The London town garden, 1700–1840* (New Haven and London, 2001).

Milner, H., *The art and practice of landscape gardening* (London, 1890).

Mowl, T., *Gentlemen and players: gardeners of the English landscape* (Stroud, 2000).

Mowl, T., *Historic gardens of Worcestershire* (Stroud, 2006).

Mowl, T. and Barre, D., *Historic gardens of Staffordshire* (Bristol, 2009).

Mowl, T. and James, D., *Historic gardens of Warwickshire* (Bristol, 2011).

Mowl, T. and Bradney, D., *Historic gardens of Herefordshire* (Bristol, 2012).

Shteir, A., *Cultivating women, cultivating science: Flora's daughters and botany in England 1760–1860* (Baltimore and London, 1996).

Spooner, S., 'The Midlands', in Spooner, *Regions and designed landscapes in Georgian England* (London, 2015), pp. 100–36.

Thompson, E.P., *The making of the English working class* (Harmondsworth, 1980).

Uglow, J., *The lunar men: the friends who made the future* (London, 2002).

Wilkinson, A., *The Victorian gardener: the growth of gardening and the floral world* (Stroud, 2006).

Williamson, T., *Polite landscapes: gardens and society in eighteenth-century England* (Stroud, 1995).

# 1

## A landscape of 'ravishing varieties': the origins of picturesque landscaping in Stuart and Georgian Herefordshire

*David Whitehead*

In the seventeenth and eighteenth centuries Herefordshire acquired a strong sense of cultural identity that was reflected in the unique development of its countryside: a radical alternative to the manicured landscape gardens that were to be promoted by 'Capability' Brown and his disciples. Only one estate in Herefordshire – Berrington, near Leominster – can be firmly credited to Brown, although he made unsuccessful approaches to other estates, such as Moccas and Eywood. Explicit resistance to Brown and his 'system' was made a few years after his death by two members of the county gentry, Richard Payne Knight (1751–1824) and Uvedale Price (1747–1829).[1] In 1794 they published, respectively, *The Landscape: a Didactic Poem* and the first *Essay on the Picturesque*, which laid the foundations for picturesque taste and made life very difficult for Brown's perceived successor, Humphry Repton (1752–1818).[2] However, Herefordshire's cultivation of the Picturesque movement had deep roots, which can be detected in the changing management of the countryside in the Stuart and Georgian periods, when the county's agricultural development was distinct. Herefordshire was bypassed by the rapid social and economic changes that occurred nearby, to the east of the Malvern Hills, in South Wales and in the West Midlands. In part this was the result of poor communications with the rest of England, which encouraged a culture of individuality and self-sufficiency in the county. The social structure of the shire was also different from many other areas insofar as the great nobility were absent from the affairs of Herefordshire following the collapse of the marcher lordships in the early sixteenth century, which led to the political and social advancement of the gentry. From the late fourteenth century it was a land of enclosures and smallholdings, which meant that there were fewer landless labourers than in other areas.[3] The poor were settled on marginal lands or employed in rural

Figure 1.1 Cartouche of Taylor's *New Map of the County of Hereford* (1786), indicating the legendary fecundity of the shire. Stages of cider-making dominate the scene and 'Vaga', the deity representing the River Wye, gushes forth water which nurtures the salmon and underpins many other aspects of the rural economy. Reproduced by permission of Herefordshire Libraries.

industries, including ironworking, that were located in the ancient woodlands on the northern and southern fringes of the county.

The enclosed countryside of Herefordshire was different from that in most of Midland England. As the eighteenth century progressed the 'champion' or open-field landscapes of the Midlands and the Home Counties were affected by enclosure, which created a labouring class whose production was geared to urban markets and a landowning elite who took advantage of enclosure to retreat into belted and private parkland.[4] Herefordshire's contrast with other areas was noticed by visitors who came as tourists in the late eighteenth century.[5] They observed that, until the advent of Napoleon's blockade in 1806 during the French Wars, few people in Herefordshire went hungry. Indeed, there was a shortage of labour, so Welsh men and women were employed to bring in the grain harvest. It seems that in the early modern period Herefordshire was the only Midland county that regularly produced an agricultural surplus, thus confirming William Camden's assessment in 1584 that the shire was fruitful for the 'feeding of Cattel, and produce of Corn' (Figure 1.1).[6] As in other highland regions, there was a spirit of independence and improvement, led by the middling gentry.[7] Sources for this study include the family collections for Price, Knight, Foley and Cornewall deposited in the Herefordshire Archive Centre at Rotherwas, journals kept by tourists who came in search of the picturesque experience, guide books produced by locals who noticed there was a market for these publications and the newspaper the *Hereford Journal* or *British Chronicle* (1770).

**The making of a rural idyll: water meadows, orchards and hop gardens**
The Herefordshire landscape was epitomised by water meadows, which involved the deliberate 'drowning' of waterside grassland either in late winter or, less frequently, late summer (Plate 1.1). They became widespread in the late seventeenth century to sustain the fattening of Welsh yearlings for the Home Counties. The cattle could be provided with an 'early bite' on the water meadows before they were passed to dealers via the many village fairs held in the shire in the summer months.[8] A natural spin-off from the water management required for the meadows was the fashionable canal-garden. The most famous was at Hampton Court, on the Lugg to the south of Leominster, which was created by Lord Coningsby and celebrated in a series of late seventeenth-century paintings.[9] At Freens Court the Lingens also had a canal and an orchard planted around six rectangular 'moats', which are depicted on an estate map of c.1720 and still visible in the twenty-first century when the river floods.[10] On the river Arrow to the west of Leominster there are two recently restored water gardens at Court of Noke and Westonbury and at Brampton Bryan on the Teme. The Harley family owned extensive water meadows at Brampton Bryan, where they developed a canal garden below their mansion in the late seventeenth century.[11] At Moccas Court, on the upper Wye, a similar system installed by Francis Vaughan in the mid-seventeenth century, on an area of wetland called The Meres, has recently been restored. Via a long underground conduit, which also dates from the seventeenth century, the canal feeds an ornamental pool in the Little Park, close to the mansion. It continues underground to provide a spectacular cascade at the climax of the promenade at the Court, above the river Wye, which still works today.[12]

Water meadows were actively promoted by John Beale (1608–1683), a correspondent of John Evelyn (1620–1706) and William Hartlibb (c.1600–1670). Beale's ambition was to turn Herefordshire into one great orchard. He

Figure 1.2 In John Beale's view an orchard was an earthly paradise, both productive and beautiful. During the eighteenth century every farm and cottage in Herefordshire acquired an orchard. Cider became the staple drink but great quantities were also exported to the industrial Midlands. © David Whitehead

recognised that planting orchards and hops and making cider provided further opportunities for the small Herefordshire farmer, who could provide fertile soil and shelter from late frosts.[13] Beale also found a site for Evelyn's idealised garden-estate, 'Elysium Britannicum', which would bear comparison with the villa gardens of the ancient Romans. Beale's recommended site was on the slopes of Backbury Hill overlooking the confluence of the Lugg and Wye, the vale of 'ravishing varieties', where a brisk *fons* (spring) emerged out of the limestone rocks at Old Sufton. Evelyn was charmed and soon he was planning his ornamental water garden of 'Fountains, Jettos, Rivulets, Pricina and Baths'. But Beale poured cold water on Evelyn's enthusiasm and said that the spring was too precious to be wasted on a 'narrow mimical' garden (a copy of a classical garden) but should be free to turn the wilderness into a productive paradise. Evelyn never completed his *Elysium Britannicum* – the book of the project – but Beale's stream still runs past the medieval mansion at Old Sufton, below a brick summerhouse-cum-dovecote set at the apex of a walled garden and tilted up to look over the water meadows fed by the stream.[14] Beale's sympathies lay with schemes that had practical purposes but also an aesthetic bonus. He recounted the story for Hartlibb of the poor woman, left a widow by the Civil War, who, falling on harder times, found solace when she discovered a small spring 'gushing out of the side of a hill. She conducted water from east, west, north and south across her large garden, and in the summer heat with "besomes scoupes" [presumably broom-like implements] she scattered the stream in alleys between her crops'.[15] For Beale there lay in the ever-running springs of Herefordshire an endless source of fecundity and well-earned pleasure. A 'true paradyse', he stated elsewhere, was rooted in utility and especially in an orchard, where in the late Spring the 'bloomed trees' created a transcendental experience, beautifying the villages and 'continu[ing] their changeable varietyes of ornament' until the end of autumn (Figure 1.2). Fruit trees, he added, 'purifie the ambient aire' and 'harbour a constant aviary of sweet singers'.[16]

This mixture of profits and pleasure persuaded the poet Alexander Pope to celebrate the life of John Kyrle (1637–1724), the 'man of Ross'.[17] Kyrle embellished his Wye-side town with features that were both ornamental and practical, set within a working urban landscape. The centrepiece was the Prospect, a cliff-top annex to his own garden, which was laid out with tree-lined walks approached by classical gateways. An elaborate fountain played here, which also conveyed piped water to the town. From the Prospect a walk was created southwards along the river cliff to a summerhouse, while, across the Wye meadows, where the middle ground was filled by the ruins of Wilton Castle, a causeway was raised above the floodwater which was also planted with trees and provided with well-spaced seats. On the Elizabethan bridge over the Wye he erected pinnacles carved with sundials. In the town the spire of the parish church was restored and almshouses repaired. Pope used Kyrle's tasteful philanthropy to castigate the expensive frippery used in contemporary formal gardens, epitomised by 'Timon's Villa', in his *Moral Essay of the use of Riches* (1732), a probable comment on the estate of the duke of Chandos at Little Stanmore, Middlesex.[18] Pope's message was clear: true creativity could be found in Kyrle's 'poetic gardening', which was set in the real countryside and was useful for the community.[19]

In a similar manner, Pope was attracted to the chatelaine of Holme Lacy House, Lady Frances Scudamore, who was left a widow at 31 years of age in 1716. Along with his friends the dramatist John Gay (1685–1732) and Lords Bathurst (1684–1775) and Digby (c.1661–1752), both early promoters of the landscape garden, Pope tried to convince Lady Scudamore that she should transform the polished Renaissance gardens at Holme Lacy and embrace the wider countryside. Lady Scudamore was a willing participant and let her new friends cut walks through her plantations, give her canal a more natural form and begin tearing up her topiary and mowing paths through her water meadows. She died in 1729 but an elegy written by her daughter, the duchess of Beaufort, described her as an ideal type of rural lady, embracing the pastoral idyll and altering her estate to include garden elements. Holme Lacy became a model for the ferme ornée, or ornamented farm, that was prevalent in the county during the early eighteenth century.[20]

By the beginning of the century Herefordshire had gained a reputation not only for its legendary fertility and good farming but also, as John Barrell (1980) suggests, as the home of an idealised view of English society, with landowners and tenants living in productive harmony. This was reinforced by local pastoral poets such as John Philips, whose *Cyder* (1708) celebrated the Georgic in Herefordshire, continuing Beale's flirtation with orchards. Here

> Sheaves of Corn,
> Oft interlac'd occur, and both imbibe
> Fitting congenial Juice; so rich the Soil,
> So much does fructuous Moisture o'er-abound!
> Nor are the Hills unamiable, whose Tops
> To Heav'n aspire, affording Prospect sweet
> To Human Ken; nor at their Feet the Vales
> Descending gently, where the lowing Herd
> Chews verd'rous Pasture; nor the yellow Fields
> Gayly enterchanged, with rich Variety
> Pleasing, as when Emerald green, enchas'd
> In flamy Gold, from the bright Mass acquires
> A nobler hue, more delicate to Sight.[21]

Philips also supplied a list of seats and their occupants who contributed to the county's reputation as the ultimate green and pleasant land, including Kentchurch Court, belonging to the senior branch of the Scudamores; Brinsop Court, occupied at this date by the Dansey family; Eau Withington, a small estate in the Lower Lugg valley farmed by the family of William Brome, a minor Oxford poet; and Burlton, near Hereford, which belonged to the family of the celebrated antiquarian Browne Willis.[22]

## Rebranding Herefordshire

During the eighteenth century the *literati* of Herefordshire began to rebrand themselves and create an identity distinct from those of both the Midlands and Wales. They chose the term Siluria/Silurian: a classical description for the people of South Wales and the southern borderlands who stubbornly resisted the Roman invasion, embraced druidism and were famed for their agrarian skills. The *Oxford English Dictionary* finds the first revived use of the term in Philip's *Cyder*, where he refers to 'Silurian Cyder'.[23] John Dyer also extends its usage to describe the sheep of the county in *The Fleece* (1757).[24] The concept was given tangible support by the many hillforts, standing stones and 'tumps' or hills in the county, which were claimed as Silurian monuments. Despite the indignation of Welsh scholars, the term 'Old Siluria' became commonplace in eighteenth-century Herefordshire as a romantic description for the county.[25] In 1752 the gentlemen of Hereford founded a club called the Society of Tempers, with the practical ambition of managing the public walks laid out on Castle Green in the city and to 'promote amiability'. To limit the membership an elaborate initiation ceremony was developed, full of celtic mysticism. They discovered in Welsh antiquarian sources that the Castle Green had Arthurian associations, which added another intriguing layer to its long history. In 1839 the geologist Sir Roderick Murchison annexed the name for the limestone rocks found in the county, which underlay the Old Red Sandstone. In the late eighteenth century Old Siluria was a useful concept in polite society to give historical credence to the distinctiveness of the shire's topography and countryside; moreover, as the Silures were a warlike people, it implied active defence if the homeland was threatened.[26]

**Tourists and artists**
In the mid-eighteenth century tourists began to arrive in Herefordshire. Some came to travel down the Wye from Ross but others came to escape from the industrial landscapes beyond the Malvern Hills, to find something more truly pastoral. The Wye became fashionable only after 1782, when the Revd William Gilpin published his *Observations on the River Wye and Several Parts of South Wales*.[27] Gilpin dismissed the countryside bounding the Wye above Ross because he regarded the water meadows, orchards and hop gardens as tainting it with utility.[28] He also found Ross to be uninteresting because the river there was tame and the banks were too low. The town became worth viewing only from a distance, preferably when seen 'through a pleasing haze'. This sort of trickery was epitomised in the 'Claude glass', which tourists used to frame their favourite views and exclude the working countryside.[29]

One artist, Thomas Gainsborough (1727–1788), relished his periods of rustication in the heartland of the county. After several years as a successful portrait painter in Bath he exclaimed, 'I am sick of portraits and wish very much to take my viola gamba and walk off to some sweet village where I can paint landskips and enjoy the fag-end of my life in quietness and ease.'[30] One of his refuges was Foxley, overlooking the village of Mansel Lacy in central Herefordshire. This was the estate of Uvedale Tomkyns Price (1685–1764) and Robert Price (1717–1761), the grandfather and father of Uvedale Price (1747–1829), who both loved music and had both been painted by Gainsborough.[31] As Barrell has explained, Gainsborough was the first English artist to paint the English countryside as it was. In many paintings he combined the Georgic with the pastoral: a farm labourer or woodcutter, for example, represented the hard work necessary to maintain the Georgic countryside, and his wife or a milkmaid was portrayed as the conventional icon of pastoral beauty.[32] As a guest of the Prices Gainsborough painted *Beech Trees at Foxley* (*c*.1760), which shows two groups of pollarded trees over-arching a rutted track (Plate 1.2).[33]

It is the sort of scene the younger Price was to eulogise in his first *Essay on the Picturesque* (1794), where he railed against road improvers who destroyed the special character of country lanes.

Pollarding had aesthetic implications and was an issue on the Price estate. The production of hops was an intensive activity, requiring high soil fertility, and it also created a demand for hop-poles. The lucky farmer might have access to a controlled coppice wood, but an alternative was to pollard hedgerow trees, which would also produce a crop of suitable poles. Hedgerow trees usually belonged to the landowner, as was the case at Foxley. The Prices initially tolerated pollarding, but, as Gainsborough's painting shows, there was an aesthetic consideration here: old pollards undoubtedly had high landscape value but regular cropping negated this. In 1774 the land agent Nathaniel Kent (1737–1810) carried out a survey of the estate and suggested the planting of small coppices – especially of willows on wet ground – to supply the need for hop-poles, thus protecting hedgerow trees, which, of course, in the long run would have value as timber if allowed to grow as standards. Robert Price built a gothic tower on a high point called the Ragged Castle (*c*.1744), which seems to be visible in Gainsborough's *Beech Trees* and also turns up in several other unlocated country scenes by the artist.[34]

Other tourists also found their way to Herefordshire. The artist Thomas Hearne (1744–1817) was commissioned by Richard Payne Knight (1751–1824) in 1784 to paint a series of scenes in the Downton Gorge. He came to Hereford and visited Sellack, on the Wye between the city and Ross, and at Moccas Court in 1789 painted veteran oaks, two of which were reproduced as etchings by B.T. Pouncey in 1798 with an accompanying patriotic caption referring to the timber from whence 'springs the British Navy which gives our Island so honourable a distinction among surrounding nations'.[35] Herefordshire was a major source of naval timber during the Napoleonic Wars and was included in Nelson's tour to inspect naval timber in 1802. Like Thomas Gray (1716–1771), who made a tour of Herefordshire before his friend Gilpin, Hearne discovered that 'from its fountain head to its junction with the Severn' the Wye contained 'a succession of beauties' (Plate 1.3).[36] As the Wye above Hereford was well away from public roads the local artist James Wathen (1751–1828) often acted as a guide for fellow artists and those with journals to write, in 1802 taking the gentleman artist Richard Colte Hoare on a tour up the Wye ending at Kington.[37]

Later in the eighteenth century there was a growing interest in touring above Ross and John Price (1773–1801), a Leominster schoolmaster, published 'A short Account of the River Wye and the Natural and Artificial Beauties contiguous to its Banks from Brobery [sic] to Wilton' in his *Historical Account of Hereford* (1796). This included a sketch-map, probably produced by Wathen.[38] George Lipscomb (1773–1846) journeyed through Hereford in 1799, taking a cross-country route from Ledbury to Presteigne. He recorded the picturesque scenes and the country houses, but also described the everyday countryside. He noticed the 'well wooded country abounding with orchards' near Ledbury, while near Tarrington he found 'a pleasing display of populous and fertile country'. Taking a detour to Fownhope, he was impressed by the woodland, 'which rises with great majesty from the Wye, whose beautiful meanders and well cultivated banks are seen from it to much advantage'. Brown's critics picked up on the lack of inhabitants in his landscapes and this became a significant issue during the Napoleonic Wars when the Continental System, designed to starve the British into submission, increased the importance of a productive countryside.[39]

Other observers also flattered the Herefordshire countryside. John Clark, from the Board of Agriculture, who had a chance to compare Breconshire with Herefordshire in 1794, found the latter a veritable paradise, in contrast to its highland neighbour:

> The county of Hereford is equalled by few spots in the island of Great Britain for the production of every article that can contribute to the comfort, the happiness, and in some degree the luxury of society. Here verdure almost perpetually reigns … clothed in nature's fairest robes, and enriched by a profusion of her most chosen gifts … hence the ancients, with much propriety, complimented this favourable district as the GARDEN OF ENGLAND.[40]

**Landscape improvement in Georgian Herefordshire**
In early eighteenth-century Herefordshire there were few incentives to extend parkland as many estates, such as Stoke Edith, Brampton Bryan and Moccas Court, still enjoyed their detached deer parks. However, some modest changes can be detected in the vicinity of the principal house, where formal pleasure gardens had been created in the late seventeenth century. The changes at Hampton Court and Holme Lacy have already been noted, but at Shobdon Court terracing, recorded in a print of *c.*1700, was removed by Thomas Greening (1684–1757), a London nurseryman who was employed by George II at Windsor. The work was completed in the 1740s by Richard Bateman, nephew of Lord Bateman, the owner of Shobdon, who was a friend of Horace Walpole. Acting as steward at Shobdon, he created woodland walks that were enhanced by informal planting of cultivated plants such as lily-of-the-valley, white aconites, honeysuckle and roses. To this new landscape he added the Romanesque 'arches' removed from the parish church and a classical temple.[41]
At Stoke Edith, between Hereford and Ledbury, the elaborate formal gardens were swept away in 1766 by a local surveyor/schoolmaster, John Bach, who created sweeping shrubberies around the house but left the great avenue – the

Tarrington Walk – to be removed by Repton.[42] At Newport Almeley in 1767, another Foley property, near Kington, Bach also produced an improvement plan with a bold perspective of the house. A prospect painting of the early eighteenth century, before Bach arrived, shows a formal arrangement around the house with several avenues, enclosures and a sunken pond.[43] Avenues were regarded with great affection in Herefordshire and at Longworth, Eywood, Holme Lacy, Whitfield and Croft they survived until the nineteenth century or later. At Croft the extensive Renaissance garden slowly disappeared in the eighteenth century but the framework of formal parkland – with several avenues – remains.[44]

Some large country houses in Herefordshire showed little evidence of extensive gardening in the eighteenth century. At Aramstone in Kings Caple, beside the Wye, Francis Woodhouse built a house *c.*1730 but was satisfied with a 'variety of swelling ground … the meandering river Wye' and an 'extensive ride through his woods'.[45] At Haywood Lodge, just to the West of Hereford, a Queen Anne house with an estate of over 1500 acres enjoyed the vestiges of the royal forest of Haywood and its owners were content with a small area of pleasure ground set within an orchard, where stonework remains from a cold bath.[46] Similarly, at The Lodge, near Richard's Castle, the Salweys were happy with a water garden and a cold bath. Eventually, in the early nineteenth century, one or two fields around the house took on a park-like character, with scattered tree planting. Like Haywood Lodge, this house enjoyed the proximity of the Haye, a royal hunting enclosure within Bringewood Chase, originally attached to Ludlow Castle. It remains connected to The Lodge by a fine sweet chestnut avenue.[47] Something similar occurred at The Mynde, Much Dewchurch, in south Herefordshire. The early owners of the estate from the mid-fifteenth century – the Pyes – enjoyed the park and forest attached to Kilpeck Castle. However, in the early eighteenth century this was not available for the new owner, Henry Gorge, a Bristol businessman, who married Elizabeth Pye. As he had no parkland attached to his own home at Eye Manor, adjoining Berrington, he created, between 1701 and 1710, a new 300-acre park at The Mynde, which was rendered superfluous when he sold the estate to James, 1st duke of Chandos. The park at The Mynde was the only new paled or hedged park to be established in the county in the eighteenth century before the arrival of Brown.[48]

The transition to extensive landscaping in Herefordshire in the mid-eighteenth century was gradual and informal. New parks were rare and because wood-pasture was ubiquitous the pastimes of shooting and foxhunting could be accommodated without converting arable to pasture. Ancient formality around mansions was quietly removed as stonework crumbled. The south terraces of Croft Castle, which were subject to regular repair in the seventeenth and early eighteenth centuries, were replaced piecemeal when the Castle was bought by Richard Knight *c*.1760. Today the lower terrace, running east–west above a former canal, now naturalised into a duck pond, can be easily traced.⁴⁹ At Hampton Court, near Leominster, the terraces were still in a neglected state in the 1780s. It is very rare to find the process mapped. John Bach's plan for Stoke Edith shows 'shrubberies' with a serpentine profile on the site of architectural gardens. Only at Shobdon, where metropolitan connections were close, was the new fashion for the woodland flower garden embraced with gusto. Herefordshire landowners preferred the more compatible ferme ornée – albeit they probably would not have used the term – which accommodated their agrarian and Georgic aspirations.⁵⁰

Moccas Court, already referred to, became a show-place of the ferme ornée. In the mid-eighteenth century, when Moccas was in the hands of Velters Cornewall (*c*.1698–1768), it had been celebrated as a place where rustic pastimes could be enjoyed in fine rural scenery. Cornewall was the 'idol of all classes in Herefordshire' for his stand on the proposed Cider Tax in 1763. Cider provided a steady income for small farmers and when the tax was repealed the

Figure 1.3 Jacob George Strutt (1784–1867) published a sketch of *The Great Oak at Moccas Court* in *Sylva Britannica* (1826), associating this ancient tree with the long pedigree of the Cornewall family. Reproduced by permission of the Cadbury Research Library: Special Collections, the University of Birmingham

bells were rung in every parish church in the county. Cornewall's letters to his neighbours show that he played the role of an unpolished farmer, a parody of Fielding's Squire Western; but at Moccas there was understated sophistication.[51] He employed a poet, John Lockman (1698–1771), a pupil of Alexander Pope, to write eulogistic poems about the estate, praising its bucolic and traditional lifestyle, which was enjoyed by a long list of notable visitors, including Lord Lyttelton of Hagley in Worcestershire.[52] The beauty of the landscape lay in its fecundity, its dew-lapped pastures, orchards and golden cornfields, as well as in a number of exceptional natural attractions: the proximity of the Wye, striking red-sandstone cliffs – Brobury Scar – a plethora of ancient trees and ravishing views for those energetic enough to climb to the top of the deer park (Figure 1.3). On returning to the Court there was 'vinous cider' cooled with 'Vaga's ice' (taken from the Wye in winter) or tea with the 'amiable Miss Cornewall', to whom Lockman's 'Tea-Table Song for Ladies' was dedicated.[53]

In the mid-eighteenth century the Herefordshire gentry were a fairly static group. Only the Batemans of Shobdon and the Foleys of Stoke Edith, who arrived in the late seventeenth century, were relative newcomers and, with properties elsewhere in England, they were unusual. Nevertheless, they were well integrated by the mid-eighteenth century and marriage with their neighbours sealed the process.[54] Politically they were united in their opposition to foreign adventures and high taxation. Income from trade or government office was welcomed to augment the relatively poor return from agriculture. The Herefordshire men in the metropolis met regularly at the convivial meetings of the 'Herefordshire Society' to discuss matters such as the Cider Tax. Estates were modest in scale, with a high level of small tenanted farms. There was spare land and most landowners organised settlements for the poor who, with hard work, could get an income from hops or apples. The poor rate was relatively low. Estates rarely came onto the market and, thus, opportunities for large landscaping schemes were rare. The creation of the Berrington estate in the 1770s, which brought 'Capability' Brown into the shire, was exceptional.

**'Capability' Brown in the county: Eywood, Berrington Hall and Moccas**
Brown arrived at Eywood, near Kington, the estate of Edward Harley, 4th earl of Oxford, in August 1775 after a long and uncomfortable journey from Dyneor in Carmarthenshire. Eywood was a typical Herefordshire estate put down to wood and pasture, which sustained the earl's famous herd of cattle (Figure 1.4). His grounds were rather uninteresting when Bishop Pococke described them in 1756: 'a fine lawn with a beautiful piece of water and a great wood on a hill'. There was also a long avenue that survived until the early twentieth century. The earl paid Brown £10 and, on the basis of this small sum, most modern

Figure 1.4 Eywood in *c.*1900, seen from the south-west across the garden pond with the dense shrubberies planted by Edward Harley, fifth earl of Oxford, or more accurately by his wife, Jane Elizabeth née Scott, a passionate gardener. Reproduced by permission of Edward Harley

commentators have assumed that Brown worked at Eywood, albeit no further payments from the earl were ever recorded in Brown's bank account.[55]

It seems most likely that Brown's visit to Eywood was arranged for the benefit of Thomas Harley (1730–1804), Edward's younger brother, a London MP, mayor of the City, banker and government contractor, who was actively seeking a base in Herefordshire, his native shire. The Harleys' family home was Brampton Bryan, near Knighton, which they had held since the early fourteenth century. Thomas was fortunate in his search, finding three contiguous estates to the north of Leominster – the manor of Eye, Berrington Castle and Stockton Bury – which were all for sale. Berrington had belonged to the Cornewalls since the early fourteenth century, but had been virtually abandoned by the family for metropolitan life, while Eye had also become superfluous for the Gorge family. Stockton had been monastic land until the Reformation but after a century of crown ownership passed through several private hands. In terms of buildings, there was a modest house at Eye built *c.*1675, at Stockton a farmhouse and at Berrington a building of indeterminate age, with the original castle ruins hidden in the woods to the east. Thus, Harley had a rare opportunity in Herefordshire to create a new polite estate.[56]

Brown's career elsewhere in the Midlands was to a degree predicated upon enclosure and rapid agricultural change, which enabled landowners to reorganise their estates and make additions to their pleasure grounds. At Berrington Harley found some residual open-field arable attached to the manor of Eye but Taylor's county map of 1754 suggests that below the house at Berrington there was enclosed wood-pasture and at Stockton, to the southeast, there was extensive woodland.[57] Thus, Brown had a fairly blank canvas. Modern LIDAR survey and a dusting of wind-blown snow in the winter, which highlights the medieval ridge and furrow, show that the old field boundaries and ploughlands are still evident in places.[58] In 1780 Lapidge and Speyer, Brown's foremen, worked up a plan and £1600 (£250,000 today) passed in four instalments from Thomas Harley into Brown's bank account. The work was still progressing when Brown died in 1783.[59]

Brown's endeavours at Berrington are regarded by modern commentators as a master-class in landscape design where Brown, at the climax of his career, confidently integrated a new house into a new landscape.[60] It seems today to have all the Brownian ingredients: a large open park within full view of the mansion, which itself is raised up on a podium; well-spaced clumps and single trees; belts in all directions but thinned on the south and west to bring in distant views; a large lake with an island with associated shrubberies and shooting areas; and, finally, beyond the belts on the east and west, long rides or gallops. Apart from the triumphal arch that introduces visitors to the pleasure grounds within the ha-ha, there are no other garden buildings. Brown was confident that the house, designed by Henry Holland, with its impressive portico was all that was needed; nature, restrained by man, was left without competition.[61]

Berrington remained a one-off in Herefordshire and its newness struck Lord Torrington as he passed through the county in 1784. He found it 'gay, just finished and furnished in all modern elegance'. He did not comment on the new parkland. It was a startling contrast to Hampton Court, a few miles back towards Hereford, where the ancient mansion of the Coningsbys, still surrounded by its seventeenth-century formal gardens, seemed to be 'old, grand and gloomy'. Here, he was dismayed to find that its absentee owner, Lord Malden of Cassiobury Park, Hertfordshire, was felling all the 'noble timber' in the park. He feared for 'the dryads of the grove' and lamented that he could not 'suspend the axe'.[62] Within a decade, Repton was touting for work here.[63]

There was one other estate in Herefordshire where Brown nearly gained a foothold, at Moccas Court in the Wye valley, which was inherited in 1768 by Catherine Cornewall, the only daughter of Velters Cornewall. In 1771 'the amiable' Catherine married George Amyand (1749–1819), a London banker with plantations in the West Indies. Like Thomas Harley, George, who took the name Cornewall, was in search of a parliamentary seat, of which there was a surfeit in Herefordshire before the reform of parliament. Moreover, George was keen to make his mark as a man of fashion and in 1775 commissioned plans from Robert Adam for a mansion with a grand portico like Berrington. Two years later Brown produced a plan designed to flatter the new mansion with a new park. Brown's plan envisaged integrating the medieval deer park into a new Berrington-like landscape, embracing the house and eradicating all signs of agriculture. It seemed as if local distinctiveness was about to be scrapped in exchange for an essay in metropolitan smartness. But a variety of influences seemed to restrain Sir George's ambitions. Traditionally, this is credited to his natural frugality. Brown's bill for £100 was paid but nothing more was transferred to his bank account. Adam's grandiose scheme was also conveyed to the family archive and the house was built by Anthony Keck, a provincial architect, who used local labour and materials.[64]

**The 'mechanic improvers'**
Berrington remains the only Brown landscape in Herefordshire but in the last decades of the eighteenth century a number of gentry landscapes were redesigned or replanted by local nurserymen-cum-landscapers, some of whom were disciples and assistants of Brown. The earliest example was at Brockhampton near Bromyard, where a new house was built for Bartholomew Barnaby by the Shrewsbury architect Thomas Farnolls Pritchard. The site was on high ground surrounded by enclosed pasture and woodlands. Thomas Leggett, an associate of William Emes, drew up a stilted plan in 1769. He tried to create clumps out of hedgerow trees and proposed a serpentine lake for a valley to the east of the house. Later, a new plan of 1825 shows that his proposals had been ignored and the Barnabys had simply manipulated their wood-pasture to provide a foreground for the house but otherwise kept the hedgerows and some open arable for the convenience of their farming activities.[65]

Another West Midland landscaper, John Davenport of Wem in Shropshire, offered his services in 1783–4 to Edmund Lechmere Pateshall of Allensmore Court, who was half-heartedly trying to establish some new parkland. He was a difficult employer and complained about Davenport's bills for landscaping and planting. Eventually Pateshall paid 25 guineas, probably for trees from Davenport's nursery at Wem. In the correspondence relating to the dispute Davenport cites his good working relationship with Edward Pytts of Kyre Park, just over the county border in Worcestershire, near Tenbury Wells. Here it seems Davenport laid out an extensive water garden c.1780. There is a family tradition that 'Capability' Brown improved the grounds of Kyre Park, which is perhaps explained by Davenport supplying him with trees in 1772–84 at Beechwood in west Hertfordshire.[66] Another nurseryman who was present in at least two places in Herefordshire was Edward Wheeler, a scion of a family of gardeners who owned a nursery in Gloucester.[67] He was employed between

1794 and 1796 laying out the grounds of Ledbury Park, on the edge of Ledbury, for John Biddulph, a banker. Two years later he was at The Mynde, which had recently been inherited by Thomas Symons, who required new pleasure grounds to be laid out to the north of the house. He entrusted the work to Wheeler, who arrived with his team of labourers and built a new greenhouse, surrounded by 'new plantations' to be enjoyed from serpentine walks. The work at The Mynde was supervised by John Harvey, the land agent, who wrote a letter to his employer in September 1798 that revealed the extent to which even minor alterations to the setting of a country house in Herefordshire had become a matter of great sensitivity:

> I was yesterday at the Meend, Wheeler is laying out the Grounds for planting, and employs as many labourers as he can procure. I understand from him that this was his first undertaking in Herefordshire and I took the liberty of observing to him that in the county where Mr. Uvedale Price and Mr. Rd. Payne Knight (the first Gentlemen Professors) reside, he must be particularly correct in his Taste and Execution.[68]

The Mynde was one of the few estates that regularly changed hands in the eighteenth century and Thomas Symons, a new broom, was unaware of the picturesque milieu and landscape conventions that prevailed in Herefordshire and therefore needed some advice from his steward about correct taste, especially since he was employing a 'mechanic improver' from Gloucestershire.[69]

### The Picturesque: Uvedale Price and Richard Payne Knight

Brown and his followers came in for a deluge of criticisms from these two 'Gentlemen Professors', who collaborated to write a scathing attack upon the system promoted by the 'Omnipotent Magician'.[70] This was to be found within Knight's *The Landscape* (1794) and, printed later in the same year, Price's first *Essay on the Picturesque*. They believed that Brown had damaged the English countryside, eroding its local distinctiveness. Furthermore, they believed he had spawned a plague of 'mechanic improvers': his foremen, surveyors and nurserymen, who spread out across England and Wales, applying his system without taste and skill to sundry landscapes (Figure 1.5).[71]

A year before Price and Knight published their works they were both at Bowood in Wiltshire and criticised Brown's work there, much to the chagrin of Lord Lonsdale, a political ally. They both felt strongly about the countryside of their native shire and with Brown's death recognised how lightly Herefordshire had been impacted by his dead hand. However, the danger had not passed, for in 1789 Humphry Repton arrived at Ferney Hall, a few miles from Knight's home at Downton, and began drawing up plans to reconstruct the garden of Samuel Phipps, a London barrister who had recently purchased the estate.

Figure 1.5 Richard Payne Knight besmirching the memory of 'Capability' Brown with his workers, the 'mechanic improvers', falling back in disgust. The monument is based upon the memorial erected by the sixth earl of Coventry at Croome in 1797. The illustration comes from *A Sketch from the Landscape* (1794) written by Knight's neighbour Dr John Matthews. Reproduced by permission of Herefordshire Libraries

Within three years Repton was also engaged at Belmont, Stoke Edith, Garnons and Sufton. He advertised himself as Brown's successor and adopted the title 'Landscape Architect', which upset Price. Repton's appearance no doubt triggered the publication of *The Landscape* and this, in turn, forced Price into print, as Knight inferred in the introduction to *The Landscape* that his verses were merely an introduction to his neighbour's more substantial work.[72]

Knight and Price disagreed on many issues – both philosophical and personal – but their shared antipathy for Brown and his 'tasteless band of followers' created common ground. They both agreed that Brown's aesthetics were out of date and that he was simply following Edmund Burke in classifying landscape as either sublime or beautiful, the latter epitomised by the 'vapid and smooth' lawns that dominated his compositions. Even William Gilpin had recognised that there was a third category between the sublime and the beautiful, which he called 'picturesque beauty'. Price and Knight saw a conflict here and dropped 'beauty', adopting simply 'picturesque', albeit they had differing philosophical views on how picturesque qualities should be perceived. Knight followed a lesser known work on aesthetics by the philosopher David Hume, which suggested that taste was simply a subjective emotion or sentiment, while Price accepted the more conventional and contemporary view that aesthetic qualities such as 'picturesqueness' were reflected in the atomic structure of objects and how they were arranged.[73] This debate made very little difference to their campaign against Brown and his followers. For example, they especially hated the serpentine 'line of beauty', which Brown introduced for boundaries and drives, and felt that his exclusion of straight lines was perverse and contrived. On the other hand, they believed Brown had sacrificed stimulus to beauty and symmetry. Moreover, his compositions could be enjoyed only from a single viewpoint and there was no invitation to explore; in a literal sense, his parks lacked picture-making qualities.[74]

Both men were enthusiastic about decayed formality, which they admired in Italianate landscape paintings and experienced on tours abroad. Senescence and decay created picturesque opportunities and added to the *couleur locale*, which became an essential element of romantic perceptions. Price regretted that as a young man he had swept away the terraces and yew hedges that provided the setting for his house and embraced the modern fashion for open lawns. Knight also espoused earlier garden design and stopped William Emes from blowing up the terraces at Powis Castle. Similarly, he took a dislike to Repton when he saw that his plans for Ferney Hall included the eradication of terraces with their summerhouses.[75] Equally in need of protection were the avenues that accompanied these early gardens, which were reaching maturity. Price wrote a eulogy on avenues, probably with those at Croft Castle in mind. Brown appeared to have little interest in avenues – they created straight lines – or veteran trees, which were not beautiful because they were contrary to Brown's old-fashioned aesthetic canons and he did not appreciate the picturesque admiration for senility. According to Knight, where he found primeval forest he destroyed it and 'from their haunts the secret Dryads drove' replacing the forest with superficial belts and clumps.[76] In the new shelter belts planted by Brown there were no glades, no intimacy and no room for flights of fancy. The landscape had simply been 'dressed' to flatter its owner.[77]

Brown's treatment of trees raised the larger issue of art and nature. For the Picturesque writers the essence of good design was 'connexion', which often occurred naturally. Nothing in a Brownian landscape looked accidental or natural. An example was the treatment of Brown's lakes, which were designed to have clean edges – that 'line of beauty' again – reed-beds and semi-wild areas were forbidden, so picturesque opportunities were excluded. Both Price and Knight were hands-on gardeners and Knight can be seen in one of the Hearne watercolours of Downton, in a thicket with a 'hacker' in his hand. Price refers to his favourite activity in the park as taking a neglected copse and treating it as if he was Michelangelo sizing up a block of marble to cut pictures in it. The key to the success of this sort of intervention was to make it look natural, or 'clandestine', as Knight would have said.⁷⁸

Price and Knight agreed that not all countryside could be picturesque or even beautiful but often even the most dull scene could be enlivened by elements such as a wayside cottage, a rutted lane, a watermill or a decaying bridge. This detail was often left out by Brown. His latest work, such as Berrington, was a single composition without any additional props, seen from the steps of the all too dominant mansion:

> Well mix'd and blended in the scene, you shew
> The stately mansion rising to the view.
> But mix'd and blended, ever let it be
> A mere component part of what you see.
> For if in solitary pride it stand,
> 'Tis but a lump, encumbering the land,
> A load of inert matter, cold and dead,
> The excrescence of the lawns that round it spread.⁷⁹

Humble utility could be eminently picturesque; thus, Price recommended the paintings of seventeenth-century Dutch artists such as Hobbema as a model, where uncherished cottages emerged organically from rough and ready countryside in a manner that caught the eye of Gainsborough and Constable (Figure 1.6). Contrary to Brown and Repton, Knight believed that a 'fertile field' could be picturesque with the right setting and appropriate figures and props. The countryside at work was, of course, a Georgic obsession and such scenes became the stock-in-trade of romantic artists. Much of the criticism of Brown came from the assumption that he had not studied landscape art. There was no connoisseurship and he simply applied a learnt formula wherever he was engaged. This was monotonous and soon, they thought, the whole of England, including Herefordshire, would be one endless Brownian park.⁸⁰

## Saving Herefordshire

Price was the more gregarious figure and seems to have been rooted to his own clay more than Knight, who was regarded locally as something of an arrogant intellectual. Nevertheless, Knight was a great tree planter and much of *The Landscape* is devoted to exploring the virtues (and vices) of trees in the man-made landscape. He is also credited with creating 200 acres of new water meadows on the Teme above Downton. It was his younger brother, Thomas Andrew Knight, however, who was revered locally for his experiments in various branches of agriculture and horticulture at Elton Hall, on the Downton estate and at Wormesley Grange, near Foxley, where he and his brother were

Figure 1.6 Uvedale Price found inspiration for the Picturesque in the work of Dutch and Flemish artists. This painting by Hobbema has all the ingredients of the 'village picturesque', including the rough texture of the inhabited countryside, the varied impression of light and shade and the sense of humanity living in harmony with nature. *A Wooded Landscape with Travelers on a Path through a Hamlet*, Meindert Hobbema (1638–1709) and Abraham Storck (1644–1708), c.1665. J. Paul Getty Museum. Digital image courtesy of Getty's Open Content Programme

born.[81] Price was also a hands-on farmer who believed that average agricultural landscapes could be managed to achieve both profits and picturesque beauty.[82] On the other hand, Downton was rugged, forested and a hard act to follow in lowland England. Also, as the sub-title to *The Landscape: a Didactic Poem* suggests, Knight had a dogmatic agenda to pursue, which included a political commentary on his times. For many of his readers this was an offensive distraction, undermining support for his landscape aesthetics. Knight also published other philosophical texts, such as the *Progress of Civil Society* (1796) and the *Analytical Inquiry into the Principles of Taste* (1810), which helped to provide a philosophical basis for the ideas expressed in *The Landscape*. Price saw his essays gathered together in a three-volume set in 1810. They were republished subsequently, and 'Price on the Picturesque' appears in virtually every country house library in Britain. Moreover, he attracted disciples, including William Sawrey Gilpin, the Revd William Gilpin's nephew, and

John Claudius Loudon, who promoted the Picturesque as the national style of Victorian England. Both Gilpin and Loudon were active as landscape improvers in Herefordshire in the years after the Napoleonic Wars.[83]

Locally the Picturesque – Price used the definite article, whereas Knight only accepted 'picturesque' as an adjective – chalked up notable victories. George Cornewall was in a quandary at Moccas, wondering if he should spend £1000 or so and implement Brown's proposal of 1778. Good sense and frugality suggested not, but there was also some indirect pressure from Knight and Price. Both men kept a close eye on Repton, who was surely likely to introduce himself to Sir George as Brown's successor and reactivate the shelved proposals. In July 1792 Price wrote to his friend Lord Abercorn, informing him that 'Mr. Repton, a layer out of grounds, or as he styles himself, a Landscape Gardener … has been making plans of improvements for some Gentlemen in my neighbourhood at whose houses I saw him.'[84] A year later Repton was engaged to improve the views from the ground-floor windows of the house towards Brobury Scar by lowering a prominent bank on the edge of the pleasure grounds. But this seems to be the full extent of his involvement at Moccas.[85]

Knight was also well known at Moccas Court and revered by Cornewall's eight children. From a reference in George Cornewall's accounts it seems that Knight secured rare books for the Moccas library. He also appeared on social occasions, which are recorded in the diary of Elizabeth Greenly of Titley Court, who was a close friend of Fanny Cornewall. Knight appeared with the family at the Three Choirs Festival in 1813 and later in the year invited the family to view the Downton Gorge. Moreover, there survives at Eastnor Castle a brief memoir of Caroline Duff Cooper née Cornewall (d. 1872) which refers fondly to Knight's visits to Moccas, taking the girls for walks in the countryside, pointing out the 'beauties of nature, the effect of light and shade etc'. Clearly, with Knight so firmly ensconced at Moccas, Brown's plan was kept securely in the muniment room until it was sold *c.*1950. Moccas thus remained a ferme ornée with mixed farming still taking place today, just beyond the ha-ha.[86]

Price's influence was similarly very strong at Holme Lacy, which since 1771 was the country home of Charles Howard, 11th duke of Norfolk. Notwithstanding the efforts of Alexander Pope and his friends to dismantle the formal gardens, they survived as a curiosity until the dawn of the Picturesque era. The Revd Stebbing Shaw visited Holme Lacy in 1788 and noticed the old gardens on the south side of the house, 'all in King William's style of fortifications' (a battle garden like the one in the late seventeenth century at Windsor, commemorating the battle of Maastricht); it was 'surrounded by yew hedges cut in a variety of forms' (Figure 1.7). He felt the garden was so unusual it should be preserved, a view that may have been shared by Price. On a fragment of a plan of Holme Lacy of *c.*1770 a walk running through the

Figure 1.7 Holme Lacy, in the Wye valley below Hereford, belonged to a branch of the Scudamore family. Built in 1672 the house was fronted by an unusual 'battle garden' to commemorate the siege of Maastricht in the Netherlands. Reproduced by permission of Herefordshire Libraries

park is named 'Price's Walk' and was similarly named in 1868 when the local naturalists' club took the same walk. Price's connection with Holme Lacy is also recorded in 1798, when he joined the company attending the Three Choirs Festival, who took boats to Holme Lacy to attend a concert amid 'the wild scenery which adorns the river'. The following year Price returned to the house as a guest of the duke of Norfolk in the company of Benjamin West, president of the Royal Academy, who was on a sketching tour of the Wye valley. Price returned to Holme Lacy in 1815 with the artist Sir George Beaumont, with whom he shared his worries about the future of the veteran oaks in the park following the death of the 11th duke. Today the formal gardens and the park contain one of the largest collections of veteran trees in the West Midlands. Holme Lacy has a landscape that since the seventeenth century has been left to itself and not improved by the hand of fashion and taste.[87]

## Conclusion

The picturesque response to the threat of Brown and his imitators secured the future and the past of a large number of Herefordshire's parks and gardens. Evolution, rather than abrupt improvement, marks their historic character. There is no doubt that Berrington is a masterpiece and was much celebrated during

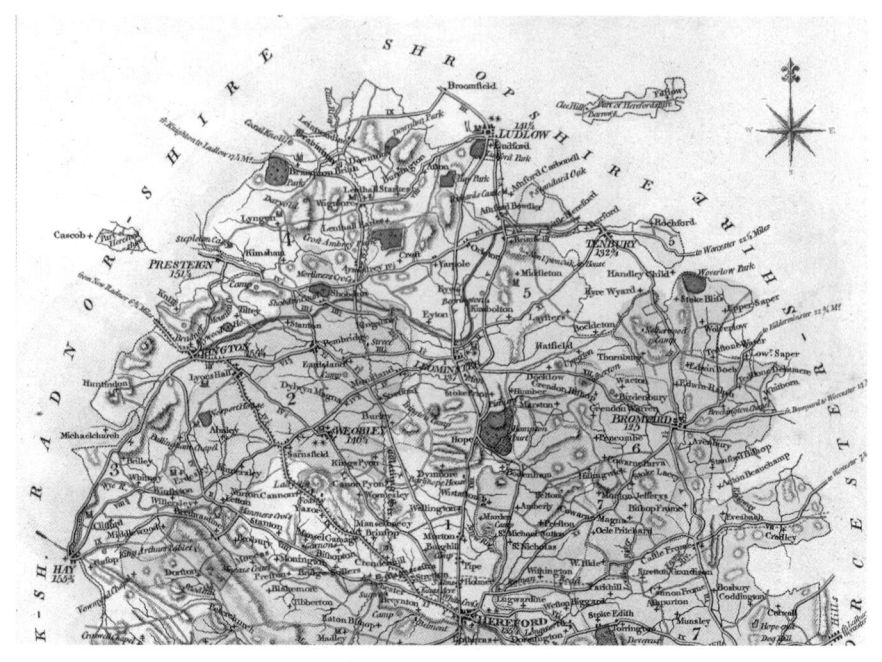

Figure 1.8 Detail of a map of Herefordshire from *The British Atlas of England and Wales* (1810), showing the variety of the county's parks and gardens. By permission of the Library of Birmingham

the tercentenary of Brown's birth in 2016, but the cautionary message of Price and Knight has left Herefordshire with a wide variety of characterful parks and gardens (Figure 1.8). The local colour predominates in places such as Moccas, Holme Lacy, Kentchurch, Croft and many more, and there has been no pressure to restore according to a prescribed style.[88] They might generally be described as 'Picturesque', but not because of an imposed style, but simply because that is how they have evolved through time – or, alternatively, as Knight would have said, through 'counterfeit neglect'.[89] Essentially, the art lies in disguising intervention so that it appears to be the result of time. Above all else, the line of beauty, clumps and belts have been kept at bay and the boundary between the productive countryside and parkland is difficult to identify, as the Picturesque is about the countryside in general, not just aristocratic pleasure grounds. Of course, one 'mechanic improver', Humphry Repton, broke through the *cordon sanitaire* established by Price and Knight in Herefordshire and was involved in varying degrees at Belmont, Stoke Edith, Garnons, Moccas, The Weir and Sufton Court. But Repton was no Brown, as Price recognised: 'tho a coxcomb he is very ingenious in his profession, and seems to me to have infinitely more resources and better principles than his predecessors'. Moreover, he recognised as his career progressed that picturesque gardening struck a chord with the romantically inclined generation enduring the French Wars. In his later Red Books Repton criticised Brown's system and at Stanage Park, near Knighton, five or six miles from Downton, he stated in the Red Book of 1803, without any obvious misgivings, that 'When I compare the picturesque scenery of Downton Vale with the meagre efforts of art which are attributable to the school of Brown, I cannot wonder at the enthusiastic abhorrence which the author of *The Landscape* expresses for modern gardening.' Repton had joined the enemy camp.[90]

## Notes

1  C. Stumpf-Condry and S.J. Skedd, 'Knight, Richard Payne (1751–1824)', *Oxford DNB* (Oxford, 2004); online edn <http://www.oxforddnb.com/view/article/15733>, accessed 20 October 2017; D. Whitehead, 'Price, Sir Uvedale, first baronet (1747–1829)', *Oxford DNB* (Oxford, 2004); online edn <http://www.oxforddnb.com/view/article/22769>, accessed 5 December 2016.

2  R.P. Knight, *The landscape: a didactic poem in three books* (London, 1794); U. Price, *Essay on the Picturesque as compared with the Sublime and the Beautiful* (London, 1794).

3  K. Ray, *The archaeology of Herefordshire* (Logaston, 2015), pp. 266–76.

4  J. Brewer, *The pleasures of the imagination* (New York, 1993), pp. 625–35, 655–8.

5  D. Whitehead, 'Some Picturesque influences upon the study of natural history in nineteenth-century Herefordshire', *TWNFC*, 57 (2009), pp. 21–3.

6  W. Camden, *Britannia, or, a chorographical description of Great Britain and Ireland*, tr. E. Gibson, 2 vols (1586, London, 1722), vol. i, p. 685.

7  J. Thirsk, 'The farming regions of England', in Thirsk (ed.), *The agrarian history of England and Wales*, pp. 100–109.

8  H. Cook and T. Williamson, *Water meadows: history, ecology and conservation* (Macclesfield, 2007), pp. 3–4, 28–30; J. Thirsk, 'Seventeenth-century agriculture and social change', in Thirsk (ed.), *Land, church*, pp. 153–8.

9  J. Cornforth, 'Hampton Court, Herefordshire – II', *Country Life*, 153 (1 March 1973), pp. 519–20; J. Harris, *The artist and the country house* (London, 1979), pls XV, XVIa, XVIb.

10  D. Whitehead, 'Some connected thoughts on the parks and gardens of Herefordshire', *TWNFC*, 48 (1999), pp. 214–15, pl. XXXI.

11  D. Whitehead, *A survey of the historic parks and gardens in Herefordshire* (Hereford & Worcester, 2001), pp. 40–41, 112; also Moor Court on the Arrow, pp. 276–7 and Harewood, near Ross, below the site of the mansion, recently excavated for the Duchy of Cornwall.

12  Ashmead Price, *The Moccas Court parkland plan for Historic England* (July 2013), pp. 41–2, map 17.

13  P. Woodland, 'Beale, John (*bap.* 1608, *d.* 1683)', *Oxford DNB* (Oxford, 2004); online edn <http://www.oxforddnb.com/view/article/1802>, accessed 5 December 2016; M. Stubbs, 'John Beale, philosophical gardener of Herefordshire', *Annals of Science*, 39/5 (1982), pp. 483–9.

14  P. Goodchild, '"No phantasticall utopia but a real place": John Evelyn, John Beale and Backbury Hill, Herefordshire', *Garden History*, 19 (1991), pp. 105–27.

15  D. Chambers, '"Wild pastoral encounter": John Evelyn, John Beale and the regeneration of the pastoral in the mid-seventeenth century', in M. Leslie and T. Raylor (eds), *Culture and cultivation in early modern England*, pp. 173–94.

16  J. Beale, *Herefordshire orchards: a pattern for all England* (London, 1657), p. 7.

17  D. Whitehead, 'Kyrle, John (1637–1724)', *Oxford DNB* (Oxford, 2004); online edn <http://www.oxforddnb.com/view/article/15831>, accessed 26 January 2017.

18  A. Pope, *Of the use of riches: an epistle to the Right Honorable Allan Lord Bathurst* (London, 1732).

19  D. Whitehead, 'Sense and sensibility: landscaping in Georgian Herefordshire', in Daniels and Watkins, *The Picturesque landscape*, pp. 18–19.
20  P. Martin, *The gardening world of Alexander Pope* (Hamden, CT, 1984), pp. 314–15; Whitehead, 'Sense and sensibility', p. 18.
21  J. Philips, *Cyder. A poem in two books* (London, 1708), pp. 34–5.
22  J. Barrell, *The dark side of the landscape: the rural poor in English painting* (Cambridge, 1980), pp. 95–6.
23  Philips, *Cyder*, p. 89.
24  J. Dyer, *The fleece. A poem in four books* (London, 1757), p. 30.
25  S. Daniels, S. Seymour and C. Watkins, 'Border country: the politics of the Picturesque in the Middle Wye Valley', in Rosenthal *et al.* (eds), *Prospects for the nation*, pp. 158–9.
26  D. Whitehead, *The castle green at Hereford* (Logaston, 2007), pp. 60–61.
27  W. Gilpin, *Observations on the river Wye and several parts of south Wales* (London, 1782).
28  Gilpin, *Observations*, pp. 6–16.
29  *Ibid.* p. 16; for the Claude glass, which 'fixed' the scene and reduced it to the size of a small picture, see M. Andrews, *The Search for the Picturesque* (Aldershot, 1989), pp. 67–83.
30  Quoted in I. Worman, *Thomas Gainsborough* (Lavenham, 1976), p. 70.
31  S. Sloman, *Gainsborough in Bath* (New Haven and London, 2002), pp. 145–60, which also provides a useful family tree of the Prices. See also Whitehead, 'Price, Sir Uvedale, first baronet (1747–1829)', which also includes notice of 'Robert Price (1685–1764)'.
32  Barrell, *Dark side of the landscape*, pp. 35–88.
33  Sloman, *Gainsborough*, pl. 125.
34  C. Watkins and B. Cowell, *Uvedale Price (1747–1829): decoding the Picturesque* (Woodbridge, 2012), pp. 11, 18, 45, 52–3.
35  Quoted in D. Morris, *Thomas Hearne and his landscape* (London, 1989), p. 98; see also pp. 90–102, 106–17; Whitehead, 'Some Picturesque influences', pp. 37, 44–6.
36  Quoted in R. Mack, *Thomas Gray: a life* (New Haven and London, 2000), p. 659.
37  J. Mitchell, *The Wye tour and its artists* (Logaston, 2010), pp. 27–30; M.W. Thompson (ed.), *The journeys of Sir Richard Colt Hoare* (Gloucester, 1983), pp. 199–200; D. Whitehead, 'Wathen, James (*bap.* 1752, *d.* 1828)', *Oxford DNB* (Oxford, 2004); online edn <http://www.oxforddnb.com/view/article/28821>, accessed 5 December 2016.
38  G. le G. Norgate, 'Price, John (1773–1801)', rev. Robin Whittaker, *Oxford DNB* (Oxford, 2004); online edn <http://www.oxforddnb.com/view/article/22756>, accessed 5 December 2016; J. Price, *A historical account of Hereford* (Hereford, 1796), pp. 176–212.
39  G. Lipscomb, *Journey into south Wales* (London, 1802), pp. 62–103.
40  J. Clark, *General view of the agriculture of the county of Hereford* (London, 1794), p. 28.
41  Whitehead, *Survey*, pp. 334–6.
42  D. Whitehead, 'The purchase and building of Stoke Edith Park', *TWNFC*, 43 (1980), pp. 186–7.
43  D. Whitehead, *Survey*, pp. 291–2.
44  Avenues are depicted on Isaac Taylor's 'New Map of the County of Hereford', 2nd edition (1786); see B. Smith, *Herefordshire maps, 1577–1800* (Logaston, 2004), pp. 80–82, pls 19–25.
45  Whitehead, *Survey*, p. 6.
46  D. Whitehead, 'The historical context for the relict water-garden at Haywood Lodge', for Anthony Priddle Architects in connection with the Hereford Western Relief Road (May 2016).
47  Whitehead, 'Sense and sensibility', p. 22.
48  *Ibid.*, p. 23.
49  Ray, *Archaeology of Herefordshire*, pp. 337–41.
50  C. Bruyn Andrews, *The Torrington diaries* III (New York and London, 1936), pp. 128–9; Whitehead, 'Purchase and building', pp. 186–7; Whitehead, *Survey*, pp. 334–6.

51  Ashmead Price, *Moccas Court*, pp. 11–15; C. Reade, *The house of Cornewall* (Hereford, 1908), pp. 107–10; Herefordshire Archive Service (HAS): A81/IV/379 Correspondence of William Brydges of Tyberton Court.

52  J. Sambrook, 'Lockman, John (1698–1771)', *Oxford DNB* (Oxford, 2004); online edn <http://www.oxforddnb.com/view/article/16912>, accessed 5 December 2016.

53  HAS: AF57/5A/25, The manuscript poems of John Lockman written at Moccas Court.

54  L. Stone, *Broken lives* (Oxford, 1993), pp. 117–38; D. Whitehead, 'John Nash & Humphry Repton: an encounter in Herefordshire in 1785–98', *TWNFC*, 47 (1992), p. 218; Croft Castle was lost to the Croft family in 1760: O. Croft, *The house of Croft* (Hereford, 1949), pp. 105–6.

55  D. Stroud, *Capability Brown* (London, 1975), pp. 180–81, 189; Whitehead, *Survey*, pp. 156–8.

56  C. Robinson, *Mansions and manors of Herefordshire* (London, 1872), pp. 116, 118–19; J. Price, *Historical and topographical account of Leominster* (Ludlow, 1795), pp. 154–5.

57  For Taylor's plan see Smith, *Herefordshire maps*, pl. 25. There is also a medieval survey of Stockton in Price, *Leominster*, pp. 155–7, which notices 345 acres of woodland, sufficient to employ a 'forester'.

58  LIDAR = Light Detection and Ranging, in which land surfaces are examined by electronic remote sensing conducted from aircraft.

59  Brown's fees (and their modern equivalents) are discussed by Sarah Rutherford, *Capability Brown and his landscape gardens* (London, 2016), pp. 77–85.

60  Rutherford, *Capability Brown*, devotes much of her book to Berrington and J. Brown, *The omnipotent magician* (London, 2011) finds the setting of the house 'the perfect stage for the view … typically Brownian', p. 248.

61  T. Mowl and J. Bradney, *Historic gardens of Herefordshire* (Bristol, 2012), pp. 91–6, regard Berrington as 'minimalist' and 'effortlessly beautiful' where the mansion serves as 'a giant garden building overlooking a Claudian landscape'.

62  Bruyn Andrews, *Torrington diaries* I, p. 129. Torrington refers to the new house as 'Berrington Castle'.

63  For Repton at Hampton Court see Whitehead, *Survey*, pp. 189–90.

64  Stroud, *Capability Brown*, pp. 233–4, pl. 58; Rutherford, *Capability Brown*, p. 77 calculates that £100 would today be between £10,000 and £12,000; this was the standard fee for a visit by Brown and a survey. The map of the survey published in Stroud has now disappeared.

65  Whitehead, *Survey*, pp. 63–4; J. Ionides, *Thomas Farnolls Pritchard* (Ludlow, 1991), pp. 98–101; M. Webb, *Brockhampton park survey for the National Trust* (London, 1989), passim.

66  Discussed more fully in Hereford and Worcester Gardens Trust, *Newsletter*, 46 (Winter 2015/16), pp. 14–15; the Allensmore letters are found in HAS A95/3/21, 36, 37, 512–20; for the connection with Brown at Beechwood, Hertfordshire Gardens Trust, *The parks and gardens of west Hertfordshire* (Letchworth, 2000), p. 41.

67  J. Broadway, 'The Wheelers of Gloucester: a provincial family of Georgian nurserymen', *Garden History*, 44/1 (2016), pp. 105–14, where it is difficult to place Edward in a complex family tree.

68  National Library of Wales, Mynde Park Deeds and Documents, 2473.

69  Whitehead, 'Sense and sensibility', pp. 23–4.

70  Brown, *Omnipotent magician*, p. 1 takes her title from William Cowper's *The Task* (London, 1785).

71  Both Price and Knight have recently received a good deal of scholarly attention. Among the most valuable are Watkins and Cowell, *Uvedale Price*; C. Watkins and B. Cowell, *The letters of Uvedale Price*, Walpole Society, 68 (Leeds, 2006); A. Ballantyne, *Architecture, landscape and liberty: Richard Payne Knight and the Picturesque* (Cambridge, 1997); M. Symes, *The Picturesque and the later Georgian Garden* (Bristol, 2012) and B. Harley, 'Functional Picturesque: Richard Payne Knight and Uvedale Price in Herefordshire', *The Georgian Group Journal*, XXIV (2016), pp. 135–58.

72  Watkins and Cowell, *Letters*, p. 29; Whitehead, 'John Nash & Humphry Repton', pp. 217–22; S. Daniels, *Humphry Repton: landscape gardening and the geography of Georgian England* (New Haven and London, 1999), pp. 103–47.

73. The philosophical differences between Price and Knight are discussed in Ballantyne, *Architecture, landscape*, pp.143–58 and briefly in Watkins and Cowell, *Price*, p. 72.
74. Ballantyne, *Architecture, landscape*, pp. 150, 203–5; Knight, *The landscape*, i, lines 140–144, 280–286; U. Price, *Essays on the Picturesque*, 3 vols, (London, 1810), vol. i, pp. 14, 345.
75. Price, *Essays*, ii, pp. 118–26; iii, 86–92; Daniels, *Repton*, pp. 109–10.
76. Price, *Essays*, i, p. 244 – for clumps; Knight, *The landscape*, i, line 304 – dryads.
77. Price, *Essays*, i, pp. 248–50, 292; Knight, *The landscape*, ii, lines 29–40, 51–54; iii, lines 19–12.
78. S. Daniels and C. Watkins, 'A well-connected landscape: Uvedale Price at Foxley', in Daniels and Watkins, *The Picturesque landscape*, pp. 40–44; Price, *Essays*, 3, pp. 45–50; Hearne watercolours, private collection, 'The view Upstream'; Watkins and Cowell, *Letters*, p. 274.
79. Knight, *The landscape*, i, lines 217–228.
80. Watkins and Cowell, *Price*, p. 73; Ballantyne, *Architecture, landscape*, pp. 202, 211; Knight, *The landscape*, i, lines 237–217; ii, lines 200–210, p. 43 note.
81. Knight, *The landscape*, iii; J. Duncumb, *A general view of the agriculture of the county of Hereford* (London, 1802), p. 115; J. Browne, 'Knight, Thomas Andrew (1759–1838)', *Oxford DNB* (Oxford, 2004); online edn <http://www.oxforddnb.com/view/article/15737>, accessed 5 December 2016.
82. Explored in S. Daniels and C. Watkins, 'Picturesque landscaping and estate management', *Rural History*, 3 (1992), pp. 141–69; Ballantyne, *Architecture, landscape*, p. 191.
83. S. Piebenga, 'William Sawrey Gilpin (1762–1843): Picturesque improver', *Garden History*, 22 (1994), pp. 175–6; S. Piebenga, 'Gilpin, William Sawrey (1761/2–1843)', *Oxford DNB* (Oxford, 2004); online edn <http://www.oxforddnb.com/view/article/10763>, accessed 5 December 2016; M.L. Simo, *Loudon and the landscape* (New Haven and London, 1988), pp. 4–5.
84. Watkins and Cowell, *Letters*, p. 79.
85. Mowl and Bradney, *Herefordshire*, pp. 109–11.
86. Eastnor Castle Muniments, copy of a letter written by Caroline Duff Cooper; Titley Court Archives, The Diary of Elizabeth Greenly, Titley Court Archives, Herefordshire.
87. D. Whitehead, 'Holme Lacy: history of its architecture and garden', in Lowe (ed.), *Essays in Honour of Jim and Muriel Tonkin*, pp. 85–6; D. Whitehead, 'Veterans in the arboretum: planting exotics at Holme Lacy, Herefordshire, in the late nineteenth century', *Garden History*, 32/supp. 2 (2007), pp. 102–3.
88. Croft belonged to Richard Knight, Richard Payne Knight's uncle, and Kentchurch Court, the home of the Scudamores, was replanted in the early nineteenth century after massive timber sales for the Navy by Price's gardener James Cranston, who came highly recommended as a Picturesque landscaper by Price himself. Today the deer park at Kentchurch is the epitome of everything Price recommended. Watkins and Cowell, *Price*, pp. 159–60; D. Whitehead, *Kentchurch Court parkland plan* (Hereford, 2012), passim.
89. Knight, *The landscape*, i, line 6.
90. Watkins and Cowell, *Letters*, p. 79; Daniels, *Repton*, pp. 135–6.

## Bibliography
*Primary sources*

Eastnor Castle Muniments, copy of a letter written by Caroline Duff Cooper
Herefordshire Archive Services (HAS)
    A81/IV/379, Correspondence of William Brydges of Tyberton Court
    AF57/5A/25, The poems of John Lockman in Moccas Court, miscellaneous deposit
    A95/3/21–37, 512–20, Allensmore Court, Patteshall letters
National Library of Wales, Mynde Park Deeds and Documents, 2473
Titley Court Archives, The Diary of Elizabeth Greenly, Titley Court Archives, Herefordshire

## Printed primary sources

Beale, J., *Herefordshire orchards: a pattern for all England* (London, 1657).
Camden, W., *Britannia, or, a chorographical description of Great Britain and Ireland*, tr. E. Gibson, 2 vols (1586, London, 1722), vol. i.
Clark, J., *General view of the agriculture of the county of Hereford* (London, 1794).
Duncumb, J., *A general view of the agriculture of the county of Hereford* (London, 1802).
Dyer, J., *The fleece. A poem in four books* (London, 1757).
Gilpin, W., *Observations on the river Wye and several parts of south Wales* (London, 1782).
Knight, R.P., *The landscape: a didactic poem in three books* (London, 1794).
Lipscomb, G., *Journey into south Wales* (London, 1802).
Philips, J., *Cyder. A poem in two books* (London, 1708).
Pope, A., *Of the uses of riches: an epistle to the Right Honorable Allan Lord Bathurst* (London, 1732).
Price, J., *A historical account of Hereford* (Hereford, 1796).
Price, J., *Historical and topographical account of Leominster* (Ludlow, 1795).
Price, U., *Essays on the Picturesque*, 3 vols (London, 1810), vol. i.
Price, U., *Essay on the Picturesque as compared with the Sublime and the Beautiful* (London, 1794).
Robinson, C., *Mansions and manors of Herefordshire* (London, 1872).

## Secondary sources

Andrews, M., *The search for the Picturesque* (Aldershot, 1989).
Ashmead Price, *The Moccas Court parkland plan for Historic England* (July 2013).
Ballantyne, A., *Architecture, landscape and liberty: Richard Payne Knight and the Picturesque* (Cambridge, 1997).
Barrell, J., *The dark side of the landscape: the rural poor in English painting* (Cambridge, 1980).
Brewer, J., *The pleasures of the imagination* (New York, 1993).
Broadway, J., 'The Wheelers of Gloucester: a provincial family of Georgian nurserymen', *Garden History*, 44/1 (2016), pp. 105–14.
Brown, J., *The omnipotent magician* (London, 2011).
Browne, J., 'Knight, Thomas Andrew (1759–1838)', *Oxford Dictionary of National Biography* (*Oxford DNB*) (Oxford, 2004); online edn <http://www.oxforddnb.com/view/article/15737>, accessed 5 December 2016.
Bruyn Andrews, C. (ed.), *The Torrington diaries* III (New York and London, 1936).
Chambers, D., '"Wild pastoral encounter": John Evelyn, John Beale and the regeneration of the pastoral in the mid-seventeenth century', in Leslie and Raylor (eds), *Culture and cultivation in early modern England*, pp. 173–94.
Cook, H. and Williamson, T., *Water meadows: history, ecology and conservation* (Macclesfield, 2007).
Cornforth, J., 'Hampton Court, Herefordshire – II', *Country Life*, 153 (1 March 1973), pp. 518–20.
Croft, O., *The house of Croft* (Hereford, 1949).
Daniels, S., *Humphry Repton: landscape gardening and the geography of Georgian England* (New Haven and London, 1999).

Daniels, S. and Watkins, C., *The Picturesque landscape: visions of Georgian Herefordshire* (Nottingham, 1994).
Daniels, S. and Watkins, C., 'Picturesque landscaping and estate management', *Rural History*, 3/2 (1992), pp. 141–69.
Daniels, S. and Watkins, C., 'A well-connected landscape: Uvedale Price at Foxley', in Daniels and Watkins (eds), *The Picturesque landscape*, pp. 40–44.
Daniels, S., Seymour, S. and Watkins, C., 'Border country: the politics of the Picturesque in the Middle Wye Valley', in Rosenthal *et al.* (eds), *Prospects for the nation*, pp. 157–81.
Goodchild, P., '"No phantasticall utopia but a real place": John Evelyn, John Beale and Backbury Hill, Herefordshire', *Garden History*, 19/2 (1991), pp. 105–27.
Harley, B., 'Functional Picturesque: Richard Payne Knight and Uvedale Price in Herefordshire', *The Georgian Group Journal*, XXIV (2016), pp. 135–58.
Harris, J., *The artist and the country house* (London, 1979).
Hereford and Worcester Gardens Trust, *Newsletter*, 46 (Winter 2015/16).
Hertfordshire Gardens Trust, *The parks and gardens of west Hertfordshire* (Letchworth, 2000).
Ionides, J., *Thomas Farnolls Pritchard* (Ludlow, 1991).
Leslie, M. and Raylor, T. (eds), *Culture and cultivation in early modern England* (Leicester, 1992).
Lowe, R. (ed.), *Essays in honour of Jim and Muriel Tonkin* (Hereford, 2012).
Mack, R., *Thomas Gray: a life* (New Haven and London, 2000).
Martin, P., *The gardening world of Alexander Pope* (Hamden, CT, 1984).
Mitchell, J., *The Wye tour and its artists* (Logaston, 2010).
Morris, D., *Thomas Hearne and his landscape* (London, 1989).
Mowl, T. and Bradney, J., *Historic gardens of Herefordshire* (Bristol, 2012).
Norgate, G. le G., 'Price, John (1773–1801)', rev. Robin Whittaker, *Oxford DNB* (Oxford, 2004); online edn <http://www.oxforddnb.com/view/article/22756>, accessed 5 December 2016.
Piebenga, S., 'Gilpin, William Sawrey (1761/2–1843)', *Oxford DNB* (Oxford, 2004); online edn <http://www.oxforddnb.com/view/article/10763>, accessed 5 December 2016.
Piebenga, S., 'William Sawrey Gilpin (1762–1843): Picturesque improver', *Garden History*, 22 (1994), pp. 175–96.
Ray, K., *The archaeology of Herefordshire* (Logaston, 2015).
Reade, C., *The house of Cornewall* (Hereford, 1908).
Rosenthal, M., Payne, C. and Wilcox, S. (eds), *Prospects for the nation*, Studies in British Art 4 (New Haven and London, 1997).
Rutherford, S., *Capability Brown and his landscape gardens* (London, 2016).
Sambrook, J., 'Lockman, John (1698–1771)', *Oxford DNB* (Oxford, 2004); online edn <http://www.oxforddnb.com/view/article/16912>, accessed 5 December 2016.
Simo, M.L., *Loudon and the landscape* (New Haven and London, 1988).
Sloman, S., *Gainsborough in Bath* (New Haven and London, 2002).
Smith, B., *Herefordshire maps, 1577–1800* (Logaston, 2004).
Stone, L., *Broken lives* (Oxford, 1993).
Stroud, D., *Capability Brown* (London, 1975).
Stubbs, M., 'John Beale, philosophical gardener of Herefordshire', *Annals of Science*, 39/5 (1982), pp. 463–89.

Stumpf-Condry, C. and Skedd, S.J., 'Knight, Richard Payne (1751–1824)', *Oxford DNB* (Oxford, 2004); online edn <http://www.oxforddnb.com/view/article/15733>, accessed 20 October 2017.

Symes, M., *The Picturesque and the later Georgian garden* (Bristol, 2012).

Thirsk, J. (ed.), *The agrarian history of England and Wales, IV 1500–1640* (Cambridge, 1967).

Thirsk, J., 'The farming regions of England', in Thirsk (ed.), *The agrarian history of England and Wales*, pp. 2–112.

Thirsk, J. (ed.), *Land, church, and people* (Reading, 1970).

Thirsk, J., 'Seventeenth-century agriculture and social change', in Thirsk (ed.), *Land, church*, pp. 148–77.

Thompson, M.W. (ed.), *The journeys of Sir Richard Colt Hoare* (Gloucester, 1983).

Watkins, C. and Cowell, B., *The letters of Uvedale Price*, Walpole Society, 68 (Leeds, 2006).

Watkins, C. and Cowell, B., *Uvedale Price (1747–1829): decoding the Picturesque* (Woodbridge, 2012).

Webb, M., *Brockhampton park survey for the National Trust* (London, 1989).

Whitehead, D., *The castle green at Hereford* (Logaston, 2007).

Whitehead, D., 'The historical context for the relict water-garden at Haywood Lodge', for Anthony Priddle Architects in connection with the Hereford Western Relief Road (May 2016).

Whitehead, D., 'Holme Lacy: history of its architecture and garden', in Lowe (ed.), *Essays in honour of Jim and Muriel Tonkin*, pp. 69–92.

Whitehead, D., 'John Nash & Humphry Repton: an encounter in Herefordshire in 1785–98', *Transactions of the Woolhope Naturalists' Field Club* (*TWNFC*), 47 (1992), pp. 210–36.

Whitehead, D., *Kentchurch Court parkland plan* (Hereford, 2012).

Whitehead, D., 'Kyrle, John (1637–1724)', *Oxford DNB* (Oxford, 2004); online edn <http://www.oxforddnb.com/view/article/15831>, accessed 26 January 2017.

Whitehead, D., 'Price, Sir Uvedale, first baronet (1747–1829)', *Oxford DNB* (Oxford, 2004); online edn <http://www.oxforddnb.com/view/article/22769>, accessed 5 December 2016.

Whitehead, D., 'The purchase and building of Stoke Edith Park', *TWNFC*, 43 (1980), pp. 181–202.

Whitehead, D., 'Sense and sensibility: landscaping in Georgian Herefordshire', in Daniels and Watkins, *The Picturesque landscape*, pp. 16–27.

Whitehead, D., 'Some connected thoughts on the parks and gardens of Herefordshire', *TWNFC*, 48 (1999), pp. 193–223.

Whitehead, D., 'Some Picturesque influences upon the study of natural history in nineteenth-century Herefordshire', *TWNFC*, 57 (2009), pp. 17–50.

Whitehead, D., *A survey of the historic parks and gardens in Herefordshire* (Hereford & Worcester, 2001).

Whitehead, D., 'Veterans in the arboretum: planting exotics at Holme Lacy, Herefordshire, in the late 19th century', *Garden History*, 32/supp. 2 (2007), pp. 96–112.

Whitehead, D., 'Wathen, James (bap. 1752, d. 1828)', *Oxford DNB* (Oxford, 2004); online edn <http://www.oxforddnb.com/view/article/28821>, accessed 5 December 2016.

Woodland, P., 'Beale, John (bap. 1608, d. 1683)', *Oxford DNB* (Oxford, 2004); online edn <http://www.oxforddnb.com/view/article/1802>, accessed 5 December 2016.

Worman, I., *Thomas Gainsborough* (Lavenham, 1976).

# 2

## Exploring a landscape garden: William Shenstone at The Leasowes

*John Hemingway*

Garden archaeology has contributed to the study of historic gardens for the last three decades and the results of its application in the restoration of gardens has led to a revised understanding of their evolution.[1] Archaeology, however, never tells the whole story, as all we are left with on the ground are sparse remains, but the subject's methodology and findings can equally support evidence from documentary material.[2] This study of William Shenstone's eighteenth-century landscape garden at The Leasowes, Halesowen, near Birmingham, applies a multi-disciplinary approach, utilising archaeological findings and his copious writings and watercolours, as well as additional contemporary texts and images (Figure 2.1).[3] William Shenstone (1714–1763) was a poet, but this chapter draws attention to his significance as a landscape designer.[4]

A diagrammatic representation of Shenstone's landscape was created to identify structures in his garden (Figure 2.2). The features shown include the circuit path that led visitors around his estate and the hydrological schemes, particularly the northern and southern drainage, the South Cascade and the High Cascade. Virgil's Obelisk was another object that he created, in this case to signpost the way into Virgil's Grove and elements within the Grove. The latter was a masterpiece of garden design that included the Dripping Fountain, which emulated the holy wells around Halesowen. Shenstone also placed memorial urns around his garden following the death of people whom he held in affection. The exact positions of most are unknown but the site of Maria Dolman's Urn has recently been discovered. Finally, the Ruinated Priory, an imaginary reconstruction of a medieval building and the most elaborate of his structures, has been partially excavated to reveal Shenstone's construction techniques.

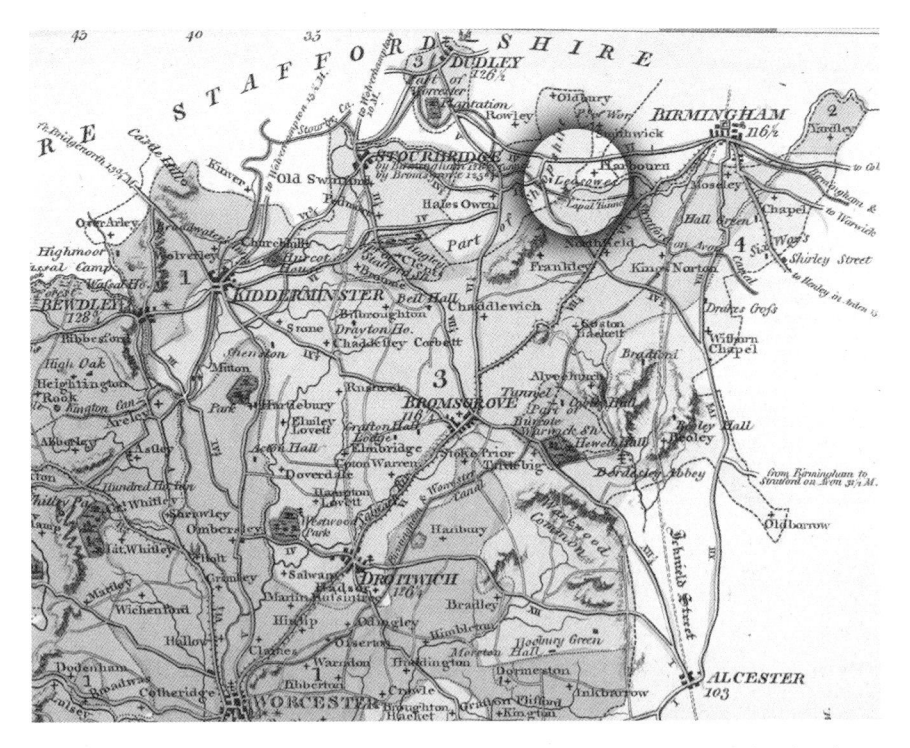

Figure 2.1 Detail of a map of Worcestershire from *The British Atlas of England and Wales* (1810), showing the location of The Leasowes and its wider environs, between Birmingham and Halesowen. Reproduced by permission of the Library of Birmingham

## Shenstone and The Leasowes

William Shenstone was born at The Leasowes farm in 1714 and died there in 1763 (Figure 2.3). He had a limited private income and therefore did not have to work for a living. Instead he devoted his time to writing letters, poetry and prose, painting watercolours and creating a landscape garden.[5] His farm lay on the east side of the Tame–Stour watershed and became a major visitor attraction in the eighteenth century. He called it a ferme ornée, an ornamented farm, implying that stock-rearing went on within his landscape garden. After he died, the garden underwent many changes and his structures began to disappear. Eventually the estate was turned into a public park by Halesowen District Council and the last structure to go was the Ruinated Priory and its cottage, which were demolished in 1955. Nothing other than the brooks and pools were left when Dudley Metropolitan Borough Council (DMBC) took over responsibility for the park, but in 1996 Heritage Lottery funding was secured to restore some of the features. As their positions were unknown it was part of my brief, as DMBC's Archaeological Officer, to search for any

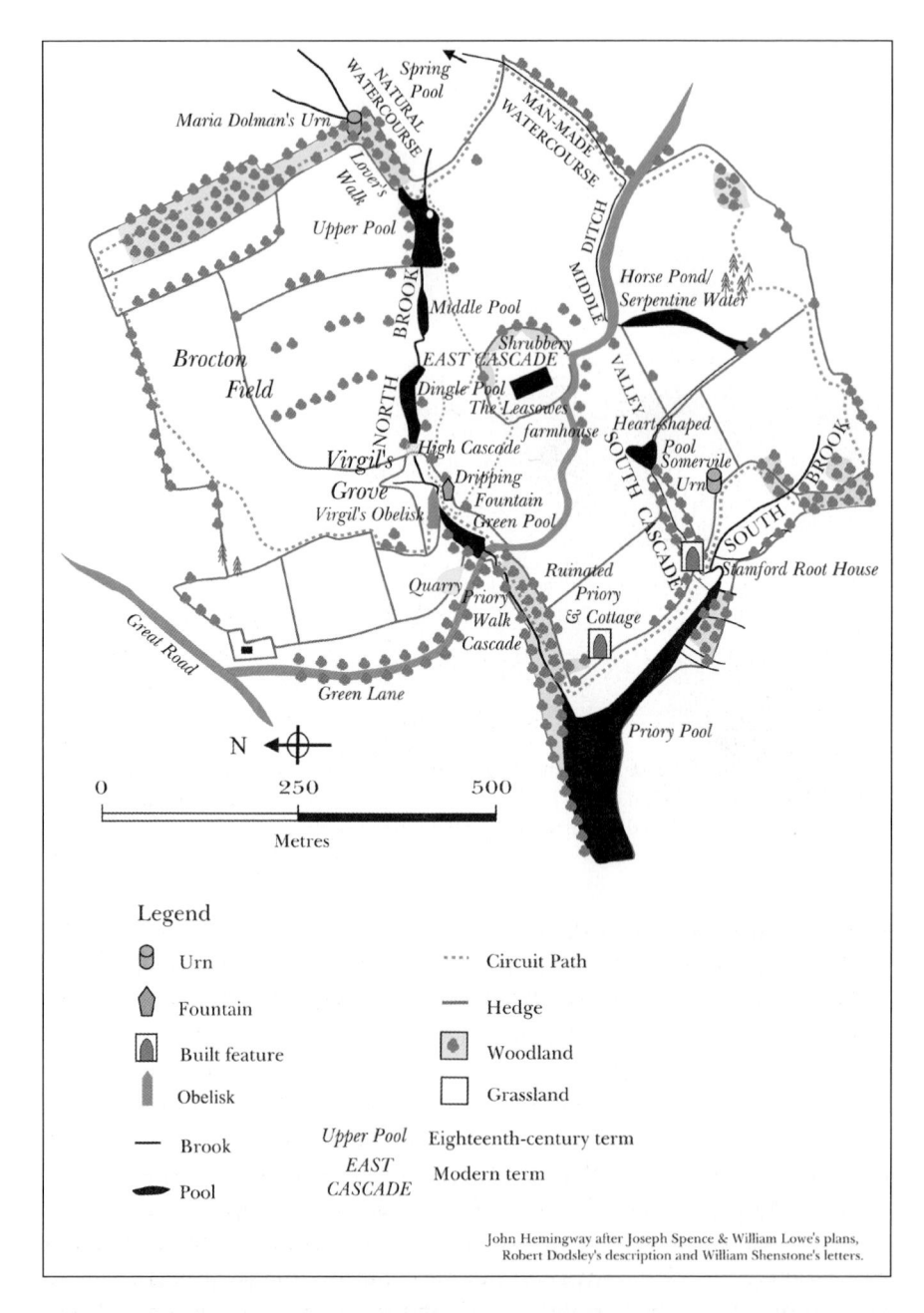

Figure 2.2 The main features of William Shenstone's landscape garden at The Leasowes.
© John Hemingway

Figure 2.3 William Shenstone, poet, essayist, correspondent and landscape gardener, memorialised in a classical style in Robert Dodsley's *Works in Verse and Prose of William Shenstone Esq.* (1768). © Private collection

surviving remains. Many of the features were associated with the watercourses, but only fragments were found. There was, however, enough material to begin archaeological investigations to uncover further evidence of Shenstone's work.

A geological survey in 1997 established that the underlying geology of the area consisted of Upper Carboniferous Westphalian sandstone and coal measures, with an area sub-section of Halesowen Sandstone.[6] Shenstone used this sandstone, obtained from a nearby quarry, to create structures. Stone plates were found beside the brooks during the watercourse survey, which were interpreted as materials used by Shenstone to construct his various cascades. The sandstone was easy to cut and dress, but was extremely porous and weathered quickly, which explains why many of the structures began to decay soon after he had created them.[7] Above the sandstone was a metre of boulder clays deposited by glacial activity.[8] Shenstone probably used these clays to make his cascades watertight. The shallow topsoil consisted of a thin loam over the clay and this restricted the planting outside the valleys. This is one of the reasons why he left the surrounding fields for livestock grazing.

## The Leasowes farmstead

Shenstone wanted his farmhouse to reflect his aspirations as a gentleman, so he made changes to the house and outbuildings to make it appear more elegant. However, the modifications probably affected the building's stability and it was demolished in 1775, after Shenstone's death. Shenstone made external alterations in an Italianate style to the farmhouse, implying that he wanted to see it as a classical structure, perhaps as a villa reminiscent of the Roman home of his favourite poet, Virgil.[9]

An isometric image of the house was created using surviving visual and textual evidence, including the inventory made on Shenstone's death.[10] The appraisers who created the inventory went from room to room and so it was a simple matter to trace their route around the house and then to use it to help to build the image. Shenstone commented in a letter of 1748 about changes he had made to his southern rooms:

> As you enter this last, the point of Clent Hills appears visto-fashion thro ye Door & one of ye windows. The same will be reflected in a Peer-glass at ye End of the former Room. This last room I purpose to cover wth Stucco-Paper, to place my Niche-chimney Piece from my Summer house at one end of it, over that Mr Pope's Busto, & on each side my Books. The windows open into my principal Prospect.[11]

The reference to a mirror to reflect the view demonstrates how important the external perspective – in this case the Clent Hills – was to Shenstone.

Evidence about the internal décor comes from an anecdote regarding Shenstone's wall covering published in *The Gentlemen's Magazine* in 1823. It told the story of John Baskerville, the Birmingham printer and friend of Shenstone, taking his acquaintance Dr William Small to The Leasowes. Several of the rooms were fitted out in the Gothic style and one was painted to imitate trellis work overhung with hazel trees. The décor prompted the following comment:

> Mr. Baskerville, who was intimate with Shenstone, one day took his friend Dr. S-ll to see the Leasowes. After admiring the tasteful disposition of the grounds, Mr. Shenstone conducted them into the house to take some refreshment, which was prepared in the room alluded to. 'How admirably this apartment is fitted up,' exclaimed Dr. S-ll. 'Those surely cannot be artificial (pointing to one of the walls): – they must be real hazel-nuts.' –'Wall-nuts, if you please,' replied Mr. B. drily. For once the sombre countenance of Shenstone disappeared, and, after various efforts to suppress a smile, he at length left the room in a complete laugh.[12]

Shenstone made watercolour paintings of his landscape garden (Plate 2.1). When the paintings of the late 1740s or early 1750s are compared with William

Lowes' 1759 plan of the estate there appears to have been a change to the area around the house. In a letter dated September 1760 Shenstone referred to the creation of a semi-circular boundary.[13] Why he chose this shape is unclear, because the rest of the boundaries on the farm are square or rectangular. He may have been copying the topography of his parish church in Halesowen: St John the Baptist's graveyard was round and many similar churchyards are thought to be of pre-Christian origin. Shenstone may have wanted to confer antiquity on the site of his farmhouse. The interior of the farmyard also took on this shape, with the shrubbery laid out in a curvilinear fashion. Situated towards the north and east, it acted as a shelter belt for the kitchen garden at the centre of the east side of the house. The position of the shrubbery was appropriate for a garden in England, where cold air tends to come from the north and east: it therefore protected the house and the kitchen garden. After Shenstone's farmhouse was demolished the subsequent owner, Edward Horne, built the present building, Leasowes House, in 1776–8 on the same site. This was subsequently occupied by Halesowen Golf Club, founded in 1906. In 2005 a planning application was granted to place a shed at the rear of the house. The build-up of soil was high, so the ground surface was reduced by approximately two metres, revealing a vertical section on its southern side. The layers showed a history of the site from the glacial boulder clays at the base through to the twentieth-century placing of topsoil.[14] The eighteenth-century level showed a comparatively deep layer of soil, which suggested that loam had been brought in to build up the surface. The undulating nature of the top of this layer suggested a semi-permanent area of mounded soil that in the twenty-first century might suggest the location of an asparagus bed. The surface of the layer was a dark colour, which indicates that weeds or grass had subsequently taken over the plot.

**Circuit path**
The circuit path that ran around the edge of the farm was one of the most important features of Shenstone's landscape garden. The circuit was designed to conduct visitors through the garden on a carefully considered route. In his study Ralph Harrington pointed out that although the path wandered around The Leasowes apparently aimlessly, it was in fact carefully controlled in order to present the scenes as Shenstone wanted them to be revealed.[15] The path followed the high and low points of the topography and thus increased the viewer's ability to see the maximum extent of the landscape, as well as leading visitors into enclosed glades and wooded walks. The idea of placing a path around his farm came slowly to Shenstone and it was not until 1754 that he wrote: 'the line of my path is now almost universally extended to the sides of my hedges'.[16] The path wound around the outside edge of his farm in what the author Philip Southcote called a 'garden belt'.[17]

Once the path extended to the farm's boundaries, Shenstone constructed features along its route. In Lover's Walk the path conducted the visitor on a metaphorical lifelong journey, from the 'young' bubbling brook through to the 'middle age' of calm waters in the Upper Pool, then along the 'old age' uphill climb to Maria Dolman's Urn: a sign that death followed life's journey. Map evidence demonstrates that the position of Shenstone's circuit walk and the pathway has survived in places as shallow depressions where it ran through the landscape.[18] Although many of Shenstone's paths have eroded, Christopher Currie excavated one near the remains of Virgil's Obelisk but found no sign of gravel metalling, raising a question about how Shenstone marked out the pathways.[19] In late spring and early summer the grass and other plants would have rapidly made the paths indistinguishable from their surroundings. Perhaps the lineal depressions in The Leasowes' landscape were the result of constantly cutting through the vegetation to make the course of the path clearer. Alternatively, the depressions could have been made by erosion caused by the many hundreds of visitors during the eighteenth and nineteenth centuries.

**Hydrological works**

The initial survey also revealed Shenstone's understanding of hydrology. The most important water feature was the Spring Pool, which lay towards the top of the hill outside the area of his farm. The Pool comprised a spring gushing out of a natural rock wall on the north side and falling into a basin approximately three metres square. A clay dam over a metre wide – typical of structures Shenstone had built elsewhere – was constructed to hold the water. Bricks lined the inside of the dam but as they were a larger size than was usual in the mid-eighteenth century they probably belonged to a later phase of construction. Evidence in Shenstone's letters suggests that a feature of this type and in this position was constructed before March 1751.[20] The Spring Pool was not on Shenstone's circuit path and was not intended to be seen by any of his visitors. The water from the reservoir originally flowed into two watercourses: a natural one that flowed west into the north brook and a man-made one that flowed south along the eastern boundary down to the Serpentine Water, then through the South Cascade to join up with the south brook (Plate 2.2).

Shenstone's operations on the rills and brooks in the landscape varied from the simple cleaning out of the watercourses and the laying of stones to the more complex work of constructing dams to make waterfalls and create cascades. In the north brook he cleared organic debris from rills between the reservoir and the Upper Pool and laid pebbles to keep the waters fresh. This created an aural as well as a visual experience. It seems probable that Shenstone appreciated the music of nature in his garden: representations of the calls of birds and beasts and the sounds of water occur regularly in his

Figure 2.4 The wooded landscape of Virgil's Grove at The Leasowes, from Robert Dodsley's *Works in Verse and Prose of William Shenstone Esq.* (1768). © Private collection

verse.[21] Robert Dodsley, in *The description of The Leasowes*, described the part of the brook that ran through Lover's Walk: 'Here the path begins gradually to ascend beneath a depth of shade, by the side of which is a bubbling rill, either forming little peninsulas, rolling over pebbles, or falling down small cascades, all under cover, and taught to murmur very agreeably.'[22] The stone and pebbles did not survive long after Shenstone's death: once they were washed away the brook dug deeper cuts, meandering from side to side and making new routes across the landscape.[23]

The Upper Pool existed in its present size in Shenstone's time as the dam was shown at this height in a watercolour he painted. He channelled the water of the Upper Pool via a waterfall that flowed over the southern end of the Pool and descended into the valley. Although Shenstone did not create the dam he added to it, as Currie's archaeological examination revealed. Pieces of unworked red sandstone rubble lay beside a concrete- stepped cascade, which is probably a modern feature installed by Halesowen District Council in the twentieth century. Currie suggested that the rubble was part of Shenstone's cascade. The pieces laid in the cascade area were intended to appear as a natural formation of rocks that the waters tumbled through in a way described in other parts of the estate by eighteenth-century visitors.[24] For example, in 1760 Thomas Hull described the 'water running over many rugged Stones & dividing into several little channels'.[25]

From the Upper Pool the brook entered a second water feature called the Middle Pool, where a small clay dam constructed by Shenstone lay at the west end.[26] The Pool did not have trees on either side in Shenstone's time so that the surface of the water acted like a mirror, reflecting the sky in the landscape.[27]

The brook then wound through the lower part of this section of the valley, forming the East Cascade. As the bedrock consisted of sheets of sandstone lying in broken layers, the waters formed a natural cascade down the slope, making a series of mini-waterfalls.[28] The winding brook then carried the water to the Dingle Pool that fed the High Cascade, a dominant part of Virgil's Grove (Figure 2.4). The dam that formed the west edge of the pool was constructed by Shenstone in about 1744. The waters of the brook flowed from the Grove into another pre-Shenstone feature, the Green Pool, and then down the Priory Walk Cascade into the Priory Pool.

Shenstone's ability to work in his landscape is best illustrated by the drainage scheme for the south brook. The watercourse leading south from the Spring Pool reservoir was not a natural component of the landscape, but was constructed to supply extra water for the features that lay below. It transported water through ditches from the reservoir in the north valley and then, via twists and turns, it entered the middle valley. The watercourse that fed the South Cascade entered the system above the Horse Pond. The Pond was a pre-Shenstone farming feature that collected the waters flowing from the top of the hill, which he extended and renamed the Serpentine Water.[29] It appeared to go under a false bridge on the north side and disappear into woodland on the south side to give the impression that it was part of a river. It was not seen close to: the circuit path was placed some way off, so as not to reveal this visual subterfuge. It drained into the Heart-shaped Pool, which Shenstone created as a reservoir above the South Cascade.

The South Cascade, noted by Robert Dodsley as a 'mini-Niagara', was another important feature in Shenstone's landscape design.[30] Archaeological excavation discovered the original bed of the Cascade, a ditch lined with stones that ran down the slope to the southern brook. The survey of the cascade area revealed that sandstone blocks were still embedded in the banks, while others had fallen into the present bed of the brook.[31] These blocks would have been part of Shenstone's construction work for both the original lining of the brook and the layers of stone plates that formed the cascades. One visitor, Sir John Parnell, noted that the 'criss cross dashing of the water' looked particularly striking.[32]

During archaeological excavation at The Leasowes a trench was dug in the area where the Stamford Root House was thought to be placed. Nothing survived of the structure, probably because it was built on the surface of the ground and exposed to the elements.[33] This root house was dedicated to the earl of Stamford, a neighbour of Shenstone's who lived at Enville Hall. Shenstone's root houses were places of shelter with moss seats on which visitors could rest. He created the houses out of the stumps and branches of trees, placed a crude stone archway at the front and grew climbing plants around the timber framework.[34]

## Structures in the landscape

Shenstone placed Virgil's Obelisk above Virgil's Grove to create an entrance feature. Documentary evidence shows that the Obelisk, sketched by David Parkes, the schoolmaster and antiquarian, was made of brick with a stucco covering (Figure 2.5).[35] It was inscribed with a dedication to the Roman poet Virgil; Shenstone placed extracts of Virgil's verse on 11 features in The Leasowes landscape, more than for any other poet.[36] The Obelisk does not survive above ground but Currie uncovered the brick plinth that formed its foundations.[37]

On the south side of the north brook dingle in Virgil's Grove, Shenstone erected one of his earliest features, The Dripping Fountain. This structure was built in stone around a spring that flowed through a rill into the brook that ran within the Grove. The stone work was possibly in the style of William Kent, as a similar feature can be seen at Rousham in Oxfordshire.[38] When the Dripping Fountain was excavated by Currie only a single stone from the arch survived, the rest having been washed away (Figure 2.6). Broken sherds of flower-pots with drainage holes in the side (not at the base, as in pots made later), were found close to the surface of the rill that flowed from the fountain. These pots were characteristic of gardenware made prior to 1760.[39]

GENIO P. VIRGILII MARONIS
LAPIS ISTE CVM LVCO
SACER ESTO.

Figure 2.5 Virgil's works were important to Shenstone and he erected an obelisk to the poet at the entrance to Virgil's Grove at The Leasowes. *Sketches in Shropshire* by David Parkes, reproduced with permission of Shropshire Archives, 6001/154

Figure 2.6 Excavation of the Dripping Fountain, one of the earliest features that Shenstone erected in his landscape, showing the sole surviving section of the stone arch, bottom right. © John Hemingway

The High Cascade was the main feature of Virgil's Grove, which Shenstone created to look like a natural waterfall flowing over the high dam. Currie's archaeological trench in the dam bank revealed that it had been constructed by piling local sandy clay on either side of a timber frame. To slow down the erosion Shenstone piled slabs onto the top and the downslope sides. So that the waterfall could be seen and heard from a distance, he intensified the flow over the dam with stones that disrupted the fall of the water. The circuit path ran over the top of the dam, giving his visitors two views: upstream, showing the open area of the pool, and downstream, showing the wooded landscape of Virgil's Grove. A tributary flowed from the north side of the main brook into the Grove just below the High Cascade and then returned in front of the waterfall.[40] His purpose was to surprise his visitors, who were suddenly confronted by the close proximity of the cascade. One visitor, Joseph Heely, described it as a 'white foaming sheet precipitately tumbling into a deep expanse'.[41]

Shenstone designed a number of urns that he placed in his grounds. The first was for his poetic mentor, William Somervile.[42] Others followed after the

Figure 2.7 Maria Dolman's urn at The Leasowes was a memorial to Shenstone's young cousin. *Sketches in Shropshire* by David Parkes, reproduced with permission of Shropshire Archives, 6001/154

deaths of people he was close to or admired: his brother Thomas, the poet James Thomson, a friend Anthony Whistler and, lastly, his cousin Maria Dolman. In a romantic gesture he placed her urn at the end of Lover's Walk (Figure 2.7). In 2012 I discovered the footings of this memorial when walking along the side of the brook after heavy rainfall had widened its channel. The stones were the same size as and laid in a similar manner to those in Virgil's Obelisk. As they were found at the end of Lover's Walk, it was concluded that this was the site where the urn had been placed.[43]

Shenstone was a competitive landscape gardener and constructed the Ruinated Priory in 1756 after Lord Lyttelton had built a ruined medieval castle at nearby Hagley Park (Plate 2.3). The carved ashlar stones for the windows came from the medieval remains of St Mary's Abbey, Halesowen, and were given to Shenstone by the Lyttleton family, who owned the site. Shenstone used an infill of stone rubble from his own farm within its construction. The Priory lay next to the Priory Pool, in imitation of the fish ponds that accompanied medieval abbeys.[44]

## Nature enhanced

A combination of archaeological and historical investigation has revealed the nature and extent of William Shenstone's work at The Leasowes. It shows that he did little to the structure of his hill farm other than to add features that sat easily within the topography and geology of the area. He applied his practical skills to creating cascades and constructing waterfalls using the local sandstone. He understood the erosive properties of water and how to keep it flowing to prevent silting. He had the ability to create an experience for his visitors by conducting them around an ever-changing landscape constructed to give them the opportunity to view the natural scene both within the estate and in the adjacent Stour valley. The structures he erected reflected his interests: Virgil's Obelisk to celebrate his favourite poet, the Dripping Fountain to signify the bounty of nature, the urns erected to his dead friends and the Ruinated Priory, which reflected his feelings about the medieval past. Although much investigative work has been conducted at The Leasowes, further research will help us to understand more fully how and why Shenstone created and shaped his landscape garden.

## Notes

1   C. Currie, *Garden archaeology: a handbook* (York, 2005), pp. 1–7.
2   Analysis has been undertaken using letters to and from William Shenstone; his paintings and drawings; writings by others, such as R. Dodsley, 'The description of The Leasowes', in W. Shenstone, *The works in verse and prose of William Shenstone Esq.*, 3 vols, 3rd edn (London, 1768), vol. ii; descriptions of the landscape garden by contemporary authors and various comments by students of Shenstone's work at The Leasowes.
3   P. Baines, 'Shenstone, William (1714–1763)', *Oxford Dictionary of National Biography* (*Oxford DNB*) (Oxford, 2004); online edn <http://www.oxforddnb.com/view/article/25321>, accessed 1 February 2017.
4   For a more detailed analysis see J. Hemingway, 'The origins, development and influence of William Shenstone's landscape garden at The Leasowes, Halesowen', PhD thesis (University of Birmingham, 2017).
5   W. Shenstone, 'Unconnected thoughts in gardening' in W. Shenstone, *The works in verse and prose of William Shenstone Esq.*, 3 vols, 3rd edn (London, 1768), vol. ii, pp. 125, 129, 139.
6   For Halesowen Sandstone see H. Kay, 'On the Halesowen Sandstone Series of the south Staffordshire coalfield, and the petrified wood found therein at the Witley Colliery, Halesowen (Worcestershire)', *Quarterly Journal of The Geological Society of London*, 69 (1913), pp. 432–54.
7   T. Palmer, *Geological report on stone samples recovered from various sites at the Leasowes, c. 1km east of Halesowen* (Aberystwyth, 1997), p. 6.
8   D. Maddy and S. Lewis, 'The Lower Severn valley', in Lewis and Richards (eds), *The Glaciations of Wales*, p. 76.
9   Hemingway, 'William Shenstone's landscape garden', p. 224.
10  The National Archives: C12/1892/22 S2485: Chancery Proceedings of The Leasowes Estate, 1765, Inventory. An isometric image is a two-dimensional representation of a three-dimensional object or structure.
11  William Shenstone to Lady Luxborough, 18 December 1748 in M. Williams (ed.), *The letters of William Shenstone* (Oxford, 1939), pp. 179–80.

12. *The Gentleman's Magazine*, August 1823, p. 105.
13. William Shenstone to Thomas Hull, 14 September 1760 in Williams, *Letters*, p. 588.
14. J. Hemingway, 'A watching brief during the construction of a building at the rear of Leasowes House' (DMBC, 2005).
15. R. Harrington, 'Nature dressed and redressed: William Shenstone, the Leasowes and the English garden in transition, c.1740–c.1763', MSt thesis (University of Oxford, 1994), p. 20.
16. William Shenstone to Sherrington Davenport, 1 July 1754 in M. Williams, *Letters*, p. 415.
17. D. Jacques, *Georgian gardens: the reign of nature* (London, 1990), p. 25; J. Martin, 'Southcote, Philip (1697/8–1758)', *Oxford DNB* (Oxford, 2004); online edn <http://www.oxforddnb.com/view/article/53221>, accessed 1 February 2017.
18. C. Currie, *Archaeological recording at The Leasowes, Halesowen, Dudley, West Midlands* (Eastleigh, 1998), pp. 11, 23–4.
19. William Shenstone to Lady Luxborough, 20 June 1750 in Williams, *Letters*, p. 280.
20. William Shenstone to Richard Jago, 28 March 1751 in Williams, *Letters*, p. 304.
21. Hemingway, 'William Shenstone's landscape garden', pp. 94–101.
22. Dodsley, 'Description of The Leasowes', p. 307.
23. H. Miller, *First impressions of England and its people* (London, 1865), p. 137.
24. Currie, *Archaeological recording*, pp. 9–10.
25. Beinecke Library, Yale University, New Haven, CT: Osborne c.20, 1 v., Hull, Thomas (c.1760) Shenstone's Walks, pp. 6, 7; Dodsley, 'Description of The Leasowes', p. 294.
26. Huntington Library, San Marino, CA: HM 303 12, Plan of The Leasowes Farm, 1758 drawn by Joseph Spence; William Shenstone to Christopher Wren, 9 September 1750 in Williams, *Letters*, p. 288.
27. Currie, *Archaeological recording*, p. 8.
28. Dodsley, 'Description of The Leasowes', p. 313; J. Hemingway, *A photographic survey of the Watercourses of Leasowes Park* (Dudley, 1994).
29. T. Williamson, *Polite landscapes: gardens and society in eighteenth-century England* (Stroud, 1995), p. 75.
30. W. Shenstone, *The works in verse and prose of William Shenstone Esq*, 3 vols, 3rd edn (London, 1768), vol ii, p. 294.
31. Currie, *Archaeological recording*, pp. 29–30.
32. The London School of Economics and Political Science, Coll. Misc. 38, Handwritten journal of Sir John Parnell entitled 'Journal of a tour thro' England and Wales', anno. 1769, Journal III, p. 103.
33. Currie, *Archaeological recording*, p. 19.
34. Hemingway, 'William Shenstone's landscape garden', pp. 196, 329–30.
35. L.H. Cust, 'Parkes, David (1763–1833)', rev. C.A. Creffield, *Oxford DNB* (Oxford, 2004); online edn <http://www.oxforddnb.com/view/article/21351>, accessed 1 February 2017.
36. Hemingway, 'William Shenstone's landscape garden', pp. 87–8, 238, 303–24.
37. Currie, *Archaeological recording*, p. 7.
38. Currie, *Garden archaeology*, p. 67; J. Harris, 'Kent, William (*bap.* 1686, *d.* 1748)', *Oxford DNB* (Oxford, 2004); online edn <http://www.oxforddnb.com/view/article/15424>, accessed 1 February 2017.
39. Currie, *Garden archaeology*, p. 110.
40. Hemingway, 'William Shenstone's landscape garden', pp. 178–96.
41. J. Heely, *A companion to the Leasowes, Hagley, and Enville* (Birmingham, 1799–1800), p. 31; E. Burke, *A philosphical enquiry into the origin of our ideas of the sublime and beautiful* (London, 1764), p. 224.
42. F. Burns, 'Somervile, William (1675–1742)', *Oxford DNB* (Oxford, 2004); online edn <http://www.oxforddnb.com/view/article/26026>, accessed 1 February 2017.

43   Hemingway, 'William Shenstone's landscape garden', pp. 249–51.
44   Ibid., pp. 261–6.

## Bibliography
*Primary sources*
Beinecke Library, Yale University, New Haven, CT
    Osborne c.20, 1 v., Hull, Thomas (*c*.1760) Shenstone's Walks
Huntingdon Library, San Marino, CH
    HM 303 12, Plan of The Leasowes Farm, 1758 drawn by Joseph Spence
The London School of Economics and Political Social Science
    Coll. Misc. 38, Handwritten journal of Sir John Parnell entitled 'Journal of a tour thro' England and Wales', anno. 1769, Journal III
The National Archives
    C12/1892/22 S2485: Chancery Proceedings of The Leasowes Estate, 1765; Inventory

*Printed primary sources*
Burke, E., *A philosophical enquiry into the origin of our ideas of the sublime and beautiful* (London, 1764).
Dodsley, R., 'The description of The Leasowes', in W. Shenstone, *The works in verse and prose of William Shenstone Esq.*, 3 vols, 3rd edn (London, 1768), vol ii.
*The Gentleman's Magazine*, August 1823.
Heely, J., *A companion to the Leasowes, Hagley, and Enville* (Birmingham, 1799–1800).
Jefferson, T., 'A tour to some of the gardens of England', in E.M. Betts (ed.), *Thomas Jefferson's garden book 1766–1824* (Philadelphia, 1981).
Shenstone, W., 'Unconnected thoughts in gardening', in W. Shenstone, *The works in verse and prose of William Shenstone Esq.*, 3 vols, 3rd edn (London, 1768), vol. ii.
Shenstone, W., *The works in verse and prose of William Shenstone Esq.*, 3 vols, 3rd edn (London, 1768), vol ii.
Williams, M. (ed.), *The letters of William Shenstone* (Oxford, 1939).

*Secondary sources*
Baines, P., 'Shenstone, William (1714–1763)', *Oxford Dictionary of National Biography* (*Oxford DNB*) (Oxford, 2004); online edn <http://www.oxforddnb.com/view/article/25321>, accessed 1 February 2017.
Burns, F., 'Somervile, William (1675–1742)', *Oxford DNB* (Oxford, 2004); online edn <http://www.oxforddnb.com/view/article/26026>, accessed 1 February 2017.
Currie, C., *Archaeological recording at The Leasowes, Halesowen, Dudley, West Midlands* (Eastleigh, 1998).
Currie, C., *Garden archaeology: a handbook* (York, 2005).
Cust, L.H., 'Parkes, David (1763–1833)', rev. C.A. Creffield, *Oxford DNB* (Oxford, 2004); online edn <http://www.oxforddnb.com/view/article/21351>, accessed 1 February 2017.
Harrington, R., 'Nature dressed and redressed: William Shenstone, the Leasowes and the English garden in transition, c.1740–c.1763', MSt thesis (University of Oxford, 1994).
Harris, J., 'Kent, William (*bap.* 1686, *d.* 1748)', *Oxford DNB* (Oxford, 2004); online edn <http://www.oxforddnb.com/view/article/15424>, accessed 1 February 2017.

Hemingway, J., 'The origins, development and influence of William Shenstone's landscape garden at The Leasowes, Halesowen', PhD thesis (University of Birmingham, 2017).

Hemingway, J., *A photographic survey of the watercourses of Leasowes Park* (Dudley, 1994).

Hemingway, J., 'A watching brief during the construction of a building at the rear of Leasowes House' (DMBC, 2005).

Jacques, D., *Georgian gardens: the reign of nature* (London, 1990).

Kay, H., 'On the Halesowen Sandstone Series of the south Staffordshire coalfield, and the petrified wood found therein at the Witley Colliery, Halesowen (Worcestershire)', *Quarterly Journal of The Geological Society of London*, 69 (1913), pp. 432–54.

Lewis, C. and Richards, A. (eds), *The glaciations of Wales and adjacent areas* (Logaston, 2005).

Maddy, D. and Lewis, S., 'The Lower Severn valley', in Lewis and Richards (eds), *The Glaciations of Wales*.

Martin, J., 'Southcote, Philip (1697/8–1758)', *Oxford DNB* (Oxford, 2004); online edn <http://www.oxforddnb.com/view/article/53221>, accessed 1 February 2017.

Miller, H., *First impressions of England and its people* (London, 1865).

Palmer, T., *Geological report on stone samples recovered from various sites at the Leasowes, c.1km east of Halesowen* (Aberystwyth, 1997).

Williamson, T., *Polite landscapes: gardens and society in eighteenth-century England* (Stroud, 1995).

# 3

## Coalbrookdale: more than an eighteenth-century industrial landscape

*Harriet Devlin*

In 1836 Charles Hulbert (1777–1857), a publisher and industrialist who lived in Shropshire, described the area from Coalport to Ironbridge along the river Severn as 'the most extraordinary district in the world'.[1] This label was also applicable to the small valley of Coalbrookdale, in the East Shropshire coalfield, where a number of elements converged to create an industrial landscape: access to minerals such as iron ore, coal, limestone, clay, natural bitumen and salt; transport via the river Severn; motive power from fast streams running down the steep valleys; plentiful supplies of wood for charcoal and, above all, the enterprise of a group of Quaker industrialists and entrepreneurs in the early eighteenth century (Figure 3.1).[2] The smelting of iron ore with coke rather than charcoal has been attributed to Abraham Darby I (1678–1717), founder of a dynasty of Quaker ironmasters.[3] In 1779 his grandson Abraham Darby III (1750–1789) manufactured and erected the Iron Bridge, which quickly became an iconic symbol of industrialising Britain (Figure 3.2).[4] Such was the fame of the Bridge that the whole area has become known as the Ironbridge Gorge. International recognition was formally achieved in 1986 when it was designated as a World Heritage Site by the International Council on Monuments and Sites UK (ICOMOS-UK). The UNESCO World Heritage list affirms:

> The Ironbridge Gorge provided the raw materials that revolutionised industrial processes and offers a powerful insight into the origins of the Industrial Revolution and also contains extensive evidence and remains of that period when the area was the focus of international attention from artists, engineers, and writers. The property contains substantial remains of mines, pit mounds, spoil heaps, foundries, factories, workshops, warehouses, iron masters' and workers' housing, public buildings, infrastructure, and transport systems, together with the traditional landscape and forests of the Severn Gorge.[5]

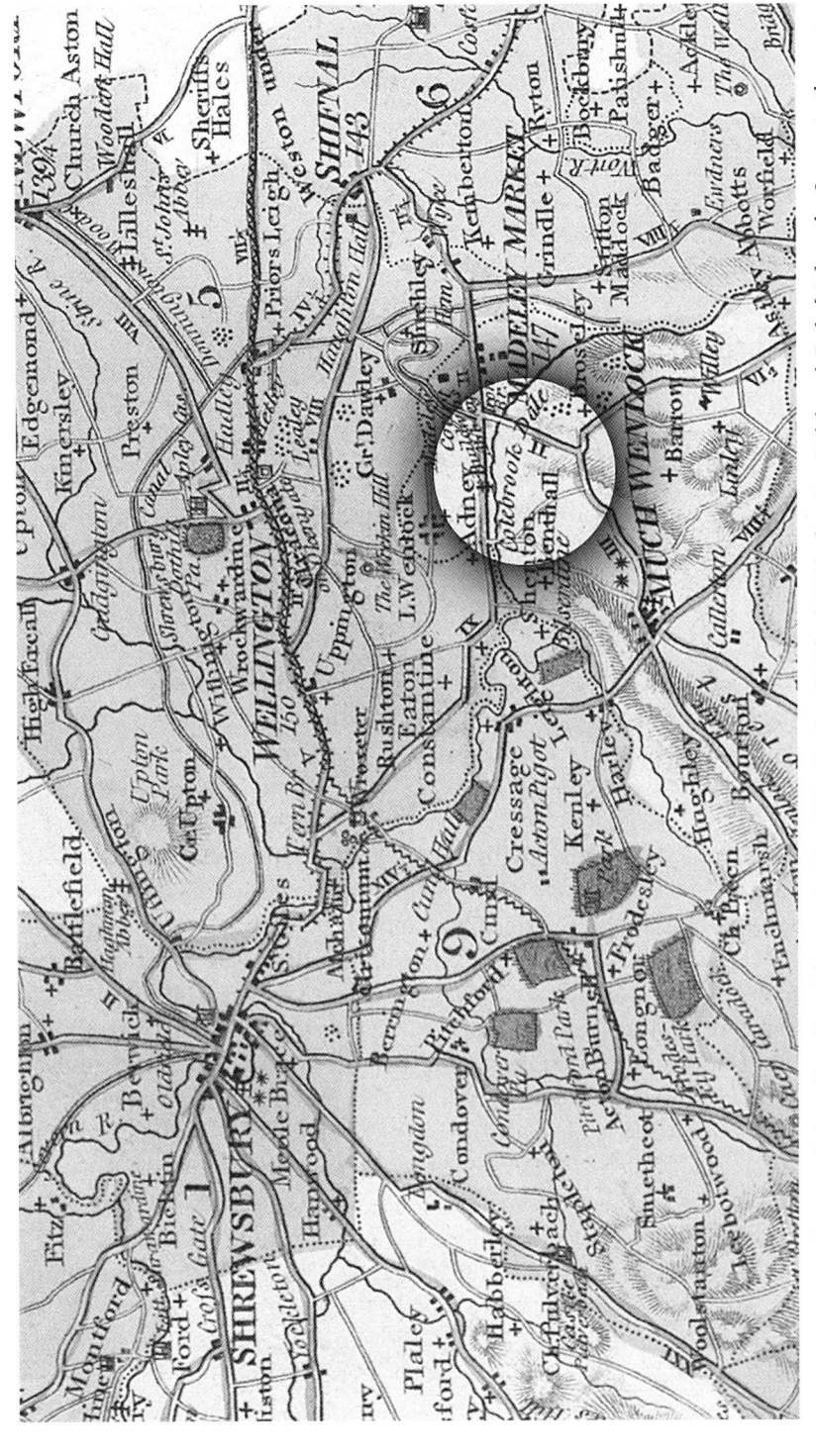

Figure 3.1 Detail of a map of Shropshire from *The British Atlas of England and Wales* (1810), showing Colebrook Dale [sic] on the Severn to the east of Shrewsbury. By permission of the Library of Birmingham

Figure 3.2 *Cast Iron Bridge near Colebrook-Dale* (1782), an early symbol of industrialising Britain. Yale Center for British Art, Paul Mellon Collection; digital image courtesy of Yale's Open Access Policy

Given the significance of the site, the question might be asked what the area has to do with designed landscapes. However, if some examples of twentieth-century housing are airbrushed from the picture, Coalbrookdale still retains features of an eighteenth-century picturesque landscape with the remains of heavy industrial processes and structures.[6] Studies of the importance of Coalbrookdale in the Industrial Revolution have concentrated on the manufacture of iron, but, using landscape studies, archaeological evidence and historical research, this chapter explores another dimension of the Quaker families at the heart of this area: their attitude to and engagement with contemporary ideas of gardening and the picturesque. Two features of the eighteenth-century landscape of Coalbrookdale are discussed. First, the chapter considers the private gardens of the Quaker ironmasters to evaluate their distinctiveness. Second, it explores the philanthropic activity of the ironmaster Richard Reynolds (1735–1816), son-in-law of Abraham Darby II, and the Coalbrookdale Company in providing the serpentine Workers' Walks, workers' housing and allotment gardens.[7] The Workers' Walks, later known as the Sabbath Walks, were created to provide an opportunity for leisure that did not conflict with religious expectations to keep the day free from boisterous activities. All are still visible in the twenty-first-century landscape.

Coalbrookdale, in the manor of Madeley, is a small valley running north–south approximately 31 miles north-west of Birmingham at the northern edge of the Ironbridge Gorge and on the east bank of the river Severn. The

Coalbrookdale or East Shropshire coalfield extends ten miles from north to south, and at a maximum four miles from east to west, and is not as deep or productive as the Staffordshire coalfields. Cast and wrought iron were made in the furnaces, forges and foundries, and the area was also renowned for ceramic production (ranging from brick and tiles to clay pipes and porcelain), tar extraction, chemicals and boat building. In the eighteenth century Coalbrookdale became a centre for industrial innovation and created such interest that it was visited and commented upon by numerous artists, writers and travellers.[8] The deep gorge of the river Severn was flanked by steep-sided valleys whose small streams, when dammed, provided the motive force for numerous waterwheels that powered the industries that sprang up along the watercourses. These valleys, particularly those on the eastern edge of Coalbrookdale, were cloaked in woodland, which was coppiced from the late Middle Ages to supply charcoal. The historic names of the coppices, such as Captain's Coppice and Dale Coppice, remain in use today. The charcoal was used to fuel furnaces and forges; early charcoal-burning platforms and tracks still exist in the landscape. Exploitation of the mineral resources is recorded from the Middle Ages, when the monks of Buildwas Abbey, nearly two miles upstream from Coalbrookdale, made iron in a bloomery (an early furnace which made small quantities of iron) in 'Caldebrooke'. In the sixteenth and seventeenth centuries the economy of the coalfield expanded greatly through the export of coal from the settlement of Broseley on the west bank of the river. In the 1660s it was claimed that over 100,000 tons of coal was sent down the Severn from the Gorge.[9]

## The Darby family private gardens

Abraham Darby I, who is inextricably linked with Coalbrookdale, was born at the Wren's Nest near Dudley in the Black Country. He was apprenticed in Birmingham to Jonathan Freeth, a fellow Quaker and a manufacturer of brass mills for grinding malt. Freeth encouraged Darby to become a highly active member of the Society of Friends, and he remained so all his life. In 1699 he moved to Bristol, where he set himself up as a malt mill maker. In 1708, with financial assistance from several Bristol Quaker industrialists, he acquired the charcoal-fired iron furnace established in the seventeenth century by the Brooke family at Coalbrookdale, close to supplies of low-sulphur coal. Darby is credited with producing marketable iron in a coke-fired furnace in 1709. He demonstrated the superiority of coke in terms of cost and efficiency by building much larger furnaces than were possible when using charcoal as a fuel. The quality of Darby's iron made it possible for him to manufacture thin castings using sand moulds, largely for making cooking pots and other hollow ware. From his arrival in Coalbrookdale in 1708 Abraham Darby I lived in a variety

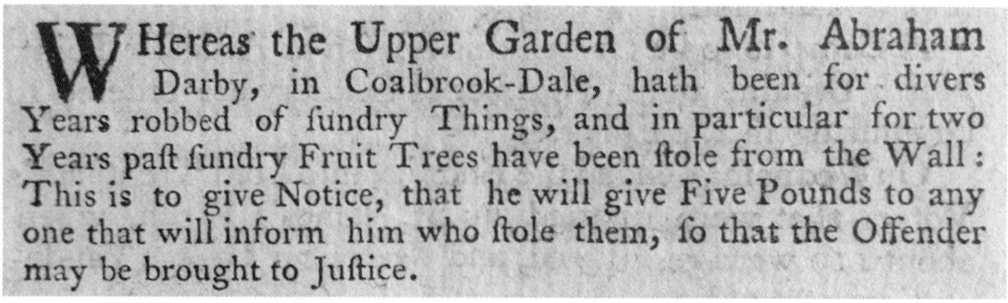

> Whereas the Upper Garden of Mr. Abraham Darby, in Coalbrook-Dale, hath been for divers Years robbed of sundry Things, and in particular for two Years past sundry Fruit Trees have been stole from the Wall: This is to give Notice, that he will give Five Pounds to any one that will inform him who stole them, so that the Offender may be brought to Justice.

Figure 3.3 In March 1750 Abraham Darby offered a reward for information regarding the theft of fruit trees from his garden. *Aris's Birmingham Gazette*, by permission of the Library of Birmingham

of houses, finally building a new house looking out over the Upper Furnace Pool and the Old Furnace. Dale House was completed just before Darby died in 1717.[10] His son Abraham Darby II (1711–1763) was only six on his father's death and the ironworks was therefore managed by Richard Ford, who married Abraham Darby I's eldest daughter Mary.[11] As the families grew, Richard Ford built Rosehill House in 1738; later, in 1750, Sunniside was built further up Coalbrookdale by Abraham Darby II.[12] By 1750, the garden at Sunniside was mature enough to contain fruit trees that were sufficiently enticing to be stolen (Figure 3.3).[13]

The earliest published views of Coalbrookdale are two 1758 engravings by Frances Vivares of drawings by Thomas Smith of Derby which are accompanied by an account of the dale written by George Perry, tutor to Richard Ford's children:

> The Beauty of the scene is in the meantime gratly increas'd by a near view of the Dale itself, Pillars of Flame and smoke rising to vast height, large Reservoirs of Water, and a number of Engines in motion, never fail to raise the admiration of strangers, who it must be confess'd these things join'd to the murmuring of Waterfalls, the noise of the Machines, and the roaring of the Furnaces, are apt to occasion a Kind of Horror in those who happen to arrive in a dark Night. UPON the whole, there are perhaps few places where rural prospects, and Scenes of hurry and Business are so happily united as in COALBROOKDALE.[14]

The engravings and Perry's account reveal the contrast between industrial activity and nature. *A View of the Upper Works at Coalbrook Dale* shows a number of important features (Plate 3.1). First, in the foreground, a magnificent cast-iron cylinder, ten feet long and weighing about six tons, is drawn along the road by a team of horses. The Quakers were astute businessmen and this engraving was widely distributed as an advertisement for their product. Cast-iron cylinders for pumping engines were first made at the Coalbrookdale works in 1722. By 1742 steam engines had replaced horse-drawn engines to drive the pumps in the Coalbrookdale works. The engraving also shows the Darby houses: Sunniside on the brow of the hill, Rosehill in the right foreground and Dale House beside, with a large walled garden rising up the hillside behind it. This garden is divided into four quadrants with a garden house on the rear wall. On the hill top there is a prominent tower, which looks hexagonal and is battlemented. Was the tower an eyecatcher in the landscape, was it a lookout tower or did it perhaps house a pumping engine to draw water supplies for the houses and cascades in the gardens below?

A second etching by Vivares, *The south west prospect of Coalbrook-Dale 1758*, shows an exaggerated view of an elongated walled garden, an avenue of trees leading up to the tower and, to the right, an enclosed garden in front of Sunniside house (Plate 3.2). Smoke rises from the furnaces and coke hearths in the left foreground; a train of heavily laden pack ponies wends its way down to the works. By the early nineteenth century Sunniside had gardens described by a visitor as being 'of great taste and ingenuity', with a 'hot house and green house with a good collection of plants native and exotic, also a bath and summerhouse'.[15] It is clear that the Darby family were engaged in developing their gardens as well as their businesses.

The connection between business enterprise and landscape development is linked to the connection between Coalbrookdale and the Goldney family. Arthur Raistrick argued that much of the innovation and enterprise in the industrialisation of Britain in the eighteenth century was undertaken by Quakers. This was largely because in this period, before banks were established, the Quakers, as a Society of Friends, were willing and able to lend money to one another.[16] The capital required to expand the Coalbrookdale works was derived from a number of prominent Bristol Quakers, particularly the Goldneys, who were majority shareholders in the works. Thomas Goldney III (1696–1768) was a merchant who sent fellow Quaker and Bristol-born Richard Reynolds to Coalbrookdale at the age of 21 in 1756. Reynolds became a partner in the Coalbrookdale Company and in 1757 married Abraham Darby II's daughter Hannah. Reynolds was a great innovator, casting the first iron wheels and axles for waggon ways in 1756 and iron rails in 1767. During his stewardship, Reynolds improved the profitability of the Coalbrookdale Company and amassed a considerable personal fortune. Goldney remained Reynolds' mentor throughout his life, and probably also influenced his ideas on landscape. The Goldneys' gardens at Clifton (now the site of halls of residence for the University of Bristol) were already laid out in the 1730s and included a magnificent shell grotto that took 27 years to complete. Thomas Goldney erected a rotunda in 1757 and created a canal in 1758–9.[17] In 1764 Goldney built a gothic tower to the south of the main house at Clifton to house a Newcomen steam engine, known as a 'fire engine'. The opening through which the beam of the steam engine would have passed can still be seen today on the north face of the tower. The steam engine, constructed using a boiler supplied by the Coalbrookdale works, was used to draw water from a 120-foot well-shaft directly in front of the tower and supplied both a fountain in the canal and the cascade in the grotto.[18] This tower bears a striking resemblance to the tower above Dale House in Coalbrookdale, depicted in the Vivares etching six years before Goldney built his tower.

A description of the gardens at Sunniside in 1780 is found in the journal of Samuel More (1726–1799), secretary of the Society of Arts from 1770 to 1799.[19] He qualified and practised as an apothecary in London and was an assistant experimental chemist to William Lewis, one of the most significant English chemists of the mid-eighteenth century. More was a friend of John Wilkinson, the Darby family's great rival, who had a major ironworks a few miles from Coalbrookdale at Willey. While visiting the furnaces at Willey, More also went to Coalbrookdale, a visit he described in his journal for 17 July 1790, like Perry in 1758 contrasting the presence of industry with the picturesque landscape:

> In the Afternoon I took Horse and visited Coalbrookdale having passed through this Land of Fire and Smoke we got to the Compting House and met Mr Sam Darby and after refreshing ourselves with him walked up to Sunniside the House of Dame Abiah Darby who may not improperly be called the Queen of the Dale, this House is built on the side of a very high and Steep Hill yet by winding paths and easy steps the approach to it rendered not difficult, And perhaps the Beauty of the Gardens and Variety of Objects that present themselves may not contribute a little to divert the Mind from the Fatigue which otherwise would be felt in rising this Hill, for the Ground being laid out with great Elegance and taste and ornamented with Grottoes formed of Moss Iron slags etc the Trees growing luxuriantly and Yeilding Fruit in Abundance and the Hills steep and rocky on the opposite side of the Dale, with Fish ponds and large Pools of Water; and Views of the Works intermixed, delight the Eye with their Grandeur at the Same Time that the Novelty of the Scene transports the Beholder with its Beauty for the Sudden Transition from Smoke and Fire to Verdure and Coolness is So amazing that a traveller almost beleives himself transported by Magick to Some other Climate.[20]

**The Picturesque and the Workers' or Sabbath Walks**
In the mid-eighteenth century many wealthy individuals travelled to Europe on the grand tour, but there was also an interest in visiting the new industrial sites in Britain. Several travellers wrote diaries or letters describing the sites they had seen. For example, on 17 June 1751 the Rev Richard Pococke commented on the nearby landscape 'that hill which is called Lincoln Hill … is most

remarkable for figured fossils … . Nothing can be imagined more romantick and beautiful than the views of the Severn when one is on these heights … .'[21] The visitors to Coalbrookdale in William Williams' painting 'Afternoon view of Coalbrookdale 1777' look down from Lincoln Hill onto the mighty pools and plumes of smoke rising from the furnaces in the Upper Works (Plate 3.3). Again, as with the Vivares engraving of 1758, this image was useful advertising for the Coalbrookdale Company and their products. Arthur Young (1741–1820), indefatigable traveller and social commentator, visited Coalbrookdale in June 1776 and remarked:

> These ironworks are in a very flourishing situation … . Colebrook Dale itself is a very romantic spot, it is a winding glen between two immense hills, which break into various forms, and all thickly covered with wood, forming the most beautiful sheets of hanging wood. Indeed too beautiful to be much in unison with that variety of horrors art has spread at the bottom: the noise of the forges, mills, etc. with all their vast machinery, the flames bursting from the furnaces with the burning of the coal and the smoak of the limekilns, are altogether sublime.[22]

Young, like other visitors, remarked on the contrast between the spectacular 'horrors' of industrialisation and the attractive wooded landscape adjacent.

The Iron Bridge, which was cast during 1777–9 and erected in 1779, became an additional magnet for industrial tourists. The *Shrewsbury Chronicle* of 20 January 1781 described how, since its opening, 'great numbers of carriages, besides horses and foot passengers have daily passed over the said bridge … '.[23] One visitor was the Lichfield poet Anna Seward (1742–1809).[24] In her poem 'Colebrook Dale', written in 1799, she described the industrialisation of Coalbrookdale in terms of the rape of the landscape, an explicit argument against the physical degradation caused by large-scale industrial processes:

> Scene of superfluous grace, and wasted bloom,
> O, violated Colebrook! in an hour,
> To beauty unpropitious and to song,
> The Genius of thy shades, by Plutus brib'd,
> Amid thy grassy lanes, thy woodwild glens,
> Thy knolls and bubbling wells, thy rocks, and streams,
> Slumbers! – while tribes fuliginous invade
> The soft, romantic, consecrated scenes;
> Haunt of the wood-nymph, who with airy step,
> In times long vanish'd, through thy pathless grove
> Rang'd; – while the pearly-wristed Naiads lean'd,
> Braiding their light locks o'er thy crystal flood,

Shadowy and smooth. What, though to vulgar eye
Invisible, yet oft the lucid gaze
Of the rapt Bard, in every dell and glade
Beheld them wander; – saw, from the clear wave
Emerging, all the watry sisters rise,
Weaving the aqueous lily, and the flag,
In wreaths fantastic, for the tresses bright
Of amber-hair'd Sabrina. – Now we view
Their fresh, their fragrant, and their silent reign
Usurpt by Cyclops; – hear, in mingled tones,
Shout their throng'd barge, their pond'rous engines clang
Through thy coy dales; while red the countless fires,
With umber'd flames, bicker on all thy hills,
Dark'ning the Summer's sun with columns large
Of thick, sulphureous smoke, which spread, like palls,
That screen the dead, upon the sylvan robe
Of thy aspiring rocks; pollute thy gales,
And stain thy glassy waters. – See, in troops,
The dusk artificers, with brazen throats,
Swarm on thy cliffs, and clamour in thy glens,
Steepy and wild, ill suited to such guests.[25]

Seward was the first writer to use 'pollute' in the modern sense of corruption by industry. In her verse the 'amber-hair'd' Sabrina (the river Severn) has been desecrated by the fires, smoke and noise of industry and Coalbrookdale's beauty debased.[26]

At the same time as Britain was industrialising and the countryside becoming scarred by extraction and manufacture, fashions in landscape design were changing. Formal gardens in the Italian style were rejected and attempts were made to create a 'natural' landscape in the gardens of the elite. In 1711 Joseph Addison (1672–1719) wrote a series of essays about landscape in *The Spectator*, including this description of the (fictitious) widow Leonora's Country Seat:

> which is situated in a kind of Wilderness … and looks like a little enchanted Palace. The Rocks about her are shaped into Artificial Grottoes covered with Woodbines and Jessamine. The Woods are cut into shady Walks, twisted into Bowers, and filled with Cages of Turtles. The Springs are made to run among Pebbles, and by that means taught to murmur very agreeably.[27]

Several examples of naturalistic, though still contrived, landscapes were created in the West Midlands. An influential example was William Shenstone's

The Leasowes, near Halesowen, an example of the ferme ornée or ornamented farm. In the 1740s Shenstone (1714–1763) created a garden of glades, streams decorated with white pebbles and seats adorned with lines from his poems.[28] At the same time, work started on the 'sublime' landscape owned by Sir Richard Hill (1733–1808) in north Shropshire at Hawkstone, with a hermit's cell, a moss-covered rustic seat, a grotto with 'Awful Precipice' and a medieval ruined castle containing a giant's well and lion's den, complete with stately stone lion.[29]

In order to fully appreciate these picturesque parks and gardens the visitor needed places from which to contemplate the rural scene, and a fashion for garden buildings for repose and reflection developed. In 1758 the architect James 'Athenian' Stuart designed the first Greek Revival garden building, the Temple of Theseus, for Lord Lyttleton at Hagley Hall in Worcestershire.[30] Another important local garden designer was William Emes (1729/30–1803), a pupil of Lancelot 'Capability' Brown, who carried out commissions throughout the West Midlands and Welsh borders.[31] In the 1780s Emes landscaped grounds at Badger Dingle, approximately eight miles east of Coalbrookdale, for Isaac Hawkins Brown, with serpentine walks and ornamental planting. A classical rotunda and bird house were designed by James Wyatt, the architect who remodelled Badger Hall.[32] Richard Reynolds was a frequent visitor to The Leasowes and Hawkstone, as well as to Hagley and Badger, and admired the gardens. They may have provided models for the features of the Coalbrookdale Workers' Walks.

These designed landscapes were all privately owned by the landed gentry and access was restricted to their guests. In the early eighteenth century, however, public walks began to appear in Shropshire. In Shrewsbury the Quarry Walks were laid out in 1719 at the mayor's expense on the town's common grazing land. In Low Town Bridgnorth a walk of elms, lime and chestnut was funded in 1739 by John Bell, a nurseryman, and in Ludlow the earl of Powis laid out walks around Ludlow Castle in 1772.[33] In the late 1780s a remarkable series of landscaped walks known as the Workers' Walks, with a temple, rustic cottage, rustic seats and an extraordinary cast-iron rotunda with a revolving seat, were created for public access and enjoyment in Coalbrookdale by Richard Reynolds. As a result of the construction of the Iron Bridge in 1778–9 and the acquisition of the Manor of Madeley, which included the freehold of the Coalbrookdale site and its mineral workings, Abraham Darby III ran up massive debts. Richard Reynolds loaned him money and as a consequence became Lord of the Manor of Madeley and owner of the freehold of the Coalbrookdale site in 1781.

In his new role Reynolds became increasingly involved in philanthropy and benevolence, constructing workers' housing and schools.[34] This charitable impulse also extended to the appreciation of the natural world. According to one account, 'His love for the beauties of nature amounted almost to a passion' and, when visiting London, he made visits on his way home to places of 'picturesque beauty such as Stowe, Hagley Park and the Leasowes'.[35] Reynolds also wrote a letter to John Maccappen on 23 July 1767, having visited The Leasowes; he wanted 'to cultivate a disposition to be pleased with the beauties of nature', noting that the mind devoted to the making of money can lose its appreciation of material creation.[36] Reynolds' granddaughter recalled in 1852:

> having made considerable purchases of land … he had great enjoyment in planting and improving these estates, and laying out walks through the woods. Those upon Lincoln Hill, which were of some extent, were made expressly for the workmen, and seats were put up at different points, where they commanded beautiful views; they were called 'The Workmen's walks', and were a source of much innocent enjoyment, especially on a Sunday, when the men, accompanied by their wives and children, were induced to spend the afternoon or evening there, instead of at the public house.[37]

The area that Richard Reynolds began to landscape was Lincoln Hill, which flanks the steep east side of Coalbrookdale and had been exploited for its coppice wood since the Middle Ages. Existing tracks and charcoal-burning platforms still bear witness to this fuel source for early iron production, and it was on this hill that Reynolds laid out his walks, levelling and widening the tracks, planting shrubs and sweet-smelling plants and building a number of structures. This part of Lincoln Hill and Dale Coppice was laid out formally as a beautiful woodland walk at a time when most of the rest of the gorge woodland had been coppiced for furnace fuel.

The Worker's Walks started in Coalbrookdale, close to the Upper Works, and the first structure to be reached was the Cottage in the Woods (Figure 3.4). This was built by Richard Reynolds for his daughter Hannah in 1784,[38] and its garden was provided with trees and plants, including false acacia, fly honeysuckle and laburnum. A visitor commented: 'This Cottage was built and fitted up in true cottage style some years ago by Hannah Mary Reynolds as a summer retreat until her marriage to William Rathbone.'[39]

As the visitor proceeded up the hill they came upon The Temple (Figure 3.5), described in 1801 as:

> a neat brick building with a seat running the whole length, the front supported by 4 pillars and the road bordered with a beautiful clump of laurels. The prospects from here are beautifully variegated with wood, water and fields … the confin'd sweeps of woods are truly noble, forming bold projections breaking forward in the highest style of beauty … the Dale is bordered on ev'ry side by hills and woods, whose uneven surface is clothed with neat plantations of firs and larches, the whole being enriched by different reservoirs and the river Severn.[40]

Figure 3.4 The cottage in the woods (photographed *c.*1870), built by Richard Reynolds on Lincoln Hill for his daughter Hannah in 1784. © The Ironbridge Gorge Museum Trust (1983–2853)

Figure 3.5 The Temple (photographed c.1870), built by Richard Reynolds on the Workers' Walks, Coalbrookdale. © The Ironbridge Gorge Museum Trust

Next came the Alcove, 'We arrive at the Alcove where we may sit and rest casting our eye over the meadows and woods below'.[41] Reynolds mentions the Alcove in a letter to his daughter in 1782:

> I have thought of thee often especially when I have been in your arbor if I so may call it – the laburnums and laycocks[lilacs] bloused pretty well – the honeysuckle and jasmine and roses flourish ... in that seat I have viewed three or four of as fine sunsets as I at any time have seen ... .[42]

Figure 3.6 Joseph Farington's *Pencil Sketch of Coalbrookdale* (1789), showing the steeply wooded Lincoln's Hill to the east of the Gorge where Richard Reynolds laid out the Workers' Walks. © The Ironbridge Gorge Museum Trust (CBD59.130.1)

Both the Cottage in the Woods and the Temple can just be made out in the top right-hand corner of the 1789 pencil sketch by Joseph Farrington (1747–1821) (Figure 3.6). Benches were thoughtfully provided for the weary traveller:

> We now mount a steep ascent passing by 2 seats erected for the purpose of resting, the prospect being confined … . The benches in general through the walks are composed of 2 stumps and a transverse board … . We arrive at a bench from which the near and distant views are exceeding fine, about 10 yards further stands another bench and at a distance of about 20 yards another.[43]

Finally, the walker arrived at the Rotunda, an unusual structure on the summit of Lincoln Hill which formed the main focus of the Walks. The Rotunda was supported on iron pillars and had a moveable seat:

> being the segment of a circle, fastened in the centre by a pin, and moves upon 3 wheels, running on a circular wooden ring and easily moved in any direction by the wind … perhaps this is the only spot in the world from which 2 Iron Bridges of such magnitude

can be seen, the one 100 and the other 130 feet span and both erected over the River Severn at a distance of about 2 miles from each other.[44]

The view provided a means of observing both the countryside and monuments to industry. One commentator on the Walks was the diarist and naturalist Katherine Plymley (1758–1829), who wrote in her diary for 4 June 1794:

> Got to the Iron Bridge in the late evening, walked through part of the walks planted by Mr Reynolds, and which he permits the public to enjoy, till we reached the Rotunda placed on Lincoln Hill, the pillars of it are of cast iron, from hence we had a fine view of the dale by night. The next morning after a delightful walk through other plantations of Mr Reynolds's we reached the Dale and look'd at the works, in the close walks it may be supposed that we are in a rural and retired spot, at convenient distances are placed seats which command views of a romantic country and discover how near we are to busy life; there is something in this contrast very pleasing … .[45]

Richard Warner, another visitor to the area, wrote on 27 July 1801:

> The great works at the Dale belong to a society called the Coalbrookdale Company … one of the chief proprietors Mr Reynolds is a landowner of this romantic spot; who, possessing as much liberality as taste, has preserved in a great measure its picturesque beauties and laid them open to the enjoyment of the public. This he has effected by conducting two walks in the most judicious manner over the brow of the vast amphitheatrical hill that rises above the vale of the Severn … . The first of these conducts to a plain Doric temple, through a thick shade occasionally opening and disclosing the rocky banks on the other side of the Dale … [W]e crossed the road to the second, which is led along a narrow ridge of an eminence agreeably planted with evergreens, which shut out the immense limestone pits to the left hand and interrupt the sight of a deep precipice to the right. This walk terminates with a rotunda, a most classical building, placed at a point of the promontory, whence a view of great extent, diversity and curious combination is unfolded … .[46]

Reynolds incorporated the topography of his industrial complex into the circuit of the woodland walks to provide glimpses of the fashionable tracts of water, the 'awful' new technology of the furnaces and, above all, views of the Iron Bridge. He also enhanced the varied flora of the woodlands by additional planting at key locations along the route. The robinia, false acacia, fly honeysuckle and cedar trees on Lincoln Hill are survivors of this planting. An account of Coalbrookdale in 1801 described his improvements: 'The environs have within a few years been highly improved by the present proprietor who permits free access not only to the neighbouring inhabitants, but to carry one whose curiosity invites them to this romantic spot.'[47] The cottage and the temple survived to be mapped by the tithe apportionment of 1847 and to be photographed, but were subsequently demolished. The site of the ornamental alcove, however, still survives in the woods. Richard Reynolds deserves to be remembered for creating what was perhaps the first publicly accessible designed landscape. The Sabbath Walks (or Workers' Walks) as well as much of the World Heritage Site are managed by the Severn Gorge Countryside Trust.

The Darbys and Reynolds also provided good housing and private allotment gardens within this landscaped setting. While several eighteenth-century industrialists built company housing, such as Sir Richard Arkwright for his workers at Cromford in Derbyshire in 1771 and Robert Owen, with his social experiments at New Lanark on the Falls of Clyde in 1786, the Coalbrookdale Company built housing considerably earlier. The first terrace of houses, Nailors Row at the lower end of Coalbrookdale, was built in 1733 and was followed by Tea Kettle Row in the 1740s. Following his purchase of Coalbrookdale in 1781 Richard Reynolds was responsible for the building of several additional terraces of high-quality housing: Carpenters Row in 1783 and Smokey Row, School House Row, Charity Row and Engine Row in the 1790s. George Perry commented as early as 1758:

> The face of the country shews the happy Effects of this flourishing Trade, the lower class of People who are very numerous here, are enabled to live comfortably; their cottages which almost cover some of the neighbouring Hills are throng'd with healthy children, who are soon able to find employment, and perhaps chearfulness and contentment are no more visible in any other place.[48]

The workers were encouraged to grow vegetables and fruit in their gardens, which were noted for their neatness and displays of flowers. Despite clearances in the 1980s for road improvements, Coalbrookdale still retains many of these cottages and their gardens.

Coalbrookdale was and is more than just an eighteenth-century industrial landscape. For the present-day visitor, the area is a testament to the landscape philanthropy of the local eighteenth-century Quaker ironmasters. Their commitment is displayed in their provision of both private and public green spaces: gardens, the Sabbath Walks and the rows of workers' cottages and allotments reveal their attempts to promote and preserve green spaces alongside industry.

## Notes

1   C. Sutton, 'Hulbert, Charles (1778–1857)', rev. A. McConnell, *Oxford Dictionary of National Biography* (*Oxford DNB*) (Oxford, 2004); online edn <http://www.oxforddnb.com/view/

article/14103>, accessed 21 September 2016; C. Hulbert, *The history and description of the county of Salop* (Providence Grove, near Shrewsbury, 1837), p. 348.
2   A. Raistrick, *Dynasty of iron founders. The Darbys and Coalbrookdale* (London, 1953).
3   Coke is derived from slowly burning coal to remove most impurities. It is suitable for smelting iron because of its high carbon content; N. Cox, 'Darby, Abraham (1678–1717)', *Oxford DNB* (Oxford, 2004); online edn <http://www.oxforddnb.com/view/article/7137>, accessed 21 September 2016.
4   B. Trinder, 'Darby, Abraham (1750–1789)', *Oxford DNB* (Oxford, 2004); online edn <http://www.oxforddnb.com/view/article/7139>, accessed 22 September 2016.
5   UNESCO, 'Ironbridge Gorge' <http://whc.unesco.org/en/list/371>, accessed 22 September 2016.
6   'Picturesque' refers to an aesthetic of landscape design that aims to create landscapes resembling a picture of a landscape in a painting.
7   B. Trinder, 'Reynolds, Richard (1735–1816)', *Oxford DNB* (Oxford, 2004); online edn <http://www.oxforddnb.com/view/article/23433>, accessed 21 September 2016.
8   For a selection of visitors' impressions see B. Trinder, *'The most extraordinary district in the world'. Ironbridge and Coalbrookdale* (London and Chichester, 1977; 3rd edn, Chichester, 2005).
9   For a history of the Coalbrookdale coalfield see B. Trinder, *The industrial archaeology of Shropshire* (Chichester, 1996), pp. 98–133.
10  R. Hayman and W. Horton, *Ironbridge: history & guide* (Stroud, 2003), p. 94. For Abraham Derby I, see Cox, 'Darby, Abraham (1678–1717)'.
11  B. Trinder, 'Darby, Abraham (1711–1763)', *Oxford DNB* (Oxford, 2004); online edn <http://www.oxforddnb.com/view/article/7138>, accessed 21 September 2016; Raistrick, *Dynasty*, pp. 47–64.
12  P. Stamper, *Historic parks & gardens of Shropshire* (Shropshire, 1996), p. 87.
13  *Aris's Birmingham Gazette*, 26 March 1750. Abraham Darby II offered £5 to 'anyone who will inform him who stole them, so that the offender may be brought to justice'.
14  G. Perry, A Description of Coalbrookdale … with perspective views thereof (n.d., *c*.1758), quoted in B. Trinder, *'The most extraordinary district'*, p. 31.
15  Stamper, *Historic parks & gardens*, p. 87.
16  Raistrick, *Dynasty*, pp. 26, 40, 81.
17  P. Stembridge, *The Goldney family: a Bristol merchant dynasty* (Bristol, 1998); K. Morgan, 'Goldney, Thomas (1696–1768)', *Oxford DNB* (Oxford, 2004); online edn <http://www.oxforddnb.com/view/article/56846>, accessed 23 September 2016; Trinder, 'Reynolds, Richard (1735–1816)'.
18  Stembridge, *Goldney family*, pp. 40–43.
19  D. Allan, 'More, Samuel (1726–1799)', *Oxford DNB* (Oxford , 2007); online edn <http://www.oxforddnb.com/view/article/38826>, accessed 21 September 2016.
20  Ironbridge Gorge Museum Library, *Transcription of Samuel More's Journal*, 1780, pp. 19–20 (original journal pp. 84–7). My thanks to Dr Roger Bruton for this reference. Original journal now at the British Library, Add MS 89126.
21  Richard Pococke quoted in Trinder, *'The most extraordinary district'*, p. 23.
22  G. Mingay, 'Young, Arthur (1741–1820)', *Oxford DNB* (Oxford, 2004); online edn <http://www.oxforddnb.com/view/article/30256>, accessed 21 September 2016; Trinder, *'The most extraordinary district'*, p. 44.
23  Raistrick, *Dynasty*, p. 197.
24  S. Bowerbank, 'Seward, Anna (1742–1809)', *Oxford DNB* (Oxford, 2004); online edn <http://www.oxforddnb.com/view/article/25135>, accessed 21 September 2016.
25  A. Seward, 'Colebrook Dale', in W. Scott (ed.), *The poetical works…in three volumes*, 3 vols (Edinburgh, 1810), vol. iii, pp. 314–17; fuliginous means sooty or smoky.
26  M. Dick, 'Discourses for the new industrial world: industrialisation and the education of the public in late eighteenth-century Britain', *History of Education*, 37/4 (2008), pp. 577–82.
27  J. Addison, *The Spectator*, 37, 12 July 1711.

28  See chapter by John Hemingway in this volume.
29  W. Sydney, 'Hill, Sir Richard, second baronet (1733–1808)', rev. S. Skedd, *Oxford DNB* (Oxford, 2004); online edn <http://www.oxforddnb.com/view/article/13290>, accessed 23 September 2016; Hawkstone Park, 'History' <http://www.hawkstoneparkfollies.co.uk/history/>, accessed 23 September 2016.
30  Historic England, 'Temple of Theseus' <https://historicengland.org.uk/listing/the-list/list-entry/1348599>, accessed 3 November 2017; for Hagley Park see chapter by Joe Hawkins in this volume.
31  K. Goodway, 'Emes, William (1729/30–1803)', rev. *Oxford DNB* (Oxford, 2004); online edn <http://www.oxforddnb.com/view/article/37398>, accessed 23 September 2016.
32  Stamper, *Historic parks & gardens*, p. 56.
33  Ibid., p. 71
34  The Ironbridge Institute, *Sabbath Walks draft conservation for consultation plan* (1999).
35  S. Smiles, *Industrial biography iron-workers and tool-makers* (Boston, 1864), pp. 126–7.
36  H. Rathbone, *Letters of Richard Reynolds with a memoir of his life* (Philadelphia, 1855), pp. 86–7.
37  Quoted in Stamper, *Historic parks & gardens*, p. 71.
38  The Ironbridge Institute, *Sabbath Walks*, p. 4.
39  Shropshire Record Office (SRO), 1987/64/6, Anon., *A description of Coalbrook Dale iron works and the environs* [*c.*1834–1850].
40  *Ibid.*
41  *Ibid.*
42  Rathbone, *Letters of Richard Reynolds*, pp. 86–7.
43  SRO, 1987/64/6, Anon., *A description of Coalbrook Dale*.
44  *Ibid.* The second iron bridge was Buildwas Bridge, which was cast at Coalbrookdale in 1796–7 after a disastrous flood in 1795 had destroyed all the bridges on the river Severn except the Iron Bridge.
45  J. Dahn, 'Plymley, Katherine (*bap.* 1758, *d.* 1829)', *Oxford DNB* (Oxford, 2005); online edn <http://www.oxforddnb.com/view/article/93057>, accessed 21 September 2016; SRO, 567, vol. 27; quotation from 'The Diary of Katherine Plymley', quoted in Trinder, *'The most extraordinary district'*, p. 64.
46  R. Warner,'The Great Works of the Dale', quoted in Trinder, *'The most extraordinary district'*, p. 64.
47  SRO, 1987/64/6, Anon., *A description of Coalbrook Dale*.
48  G. Perry, 'A Description of Coalbrookdale', quoted in Trinder, *'The most extraordinary district'*, p. 34.

## Bibliography
*Primary sources*
British Library
  Add MS 89126
Ironbridge Gorge Museum Library
  *Transcription of Samuel More's Journal*, 1780
Shropshire Record Office (SRO)
  1987/64/6, Anon., *A description of Coalbrooke Dale iron works and the environs* [*c.*1834–1850].

*Primary printed sources*
Addison, J., *The Spectator*, 37, 12 July 1711.
*Aris's Birmingham Gazette*, 26 March 1750.
Hulbert, C., *The history and description of the county of Salop* (Providence Grove, near Shrewsbury, 1837).

Rathbone, H., *Letters of Richard Reynolds with a memoir of his life* (Philadelphia, 1855).

Seward, A., 'Colebrook Dale', in W. Scott (ed.), *The poetical works ... in three volumes*, 3 vols (Edinburgh, 1810), Vol. iii.

## Secondary sources

Allan, D., 'More, Samuel (1726–1799)', *Oxford Dictionary of National Biography* (*Oxford DNB*) (Oxford, 2007); online edn <http://www.oxforddnb.com/view/article/38826>, accessed 21 September 2016.

Bowerbank, S., 'Seward, Anna (1742–1809)', *Oxford DNB* (Oxford, 2004); online edn <http://www.oxforddnb.com/view/article/25135>, accessed 21 September 2016.

Cox, N., 'Darby, Abraham (1678–1717)', *Oxford DNB* (Oxford, 2004); online edn <http://www.oxforddnb.com/view/article/7137>, accessed 21 September 2016.

Dahn, J., 'Plymley, Katherine (*bap.* 1758, *d.* 1829)', *Oxford DNB* (Oxford, 2005); online edn <http://www.oxforddnb.com/view/article/93057>, accessed 21 September 2016.

Dick, M., 'Discourses for the new industrial world: industrialisation and the education of the public in late eighteenth-century Britain', *History of Education*, 37/4 (2008).

Goodway, K., 'Emes, William (1729/30–1803)', rev. *Oxford DNB* (Oxford, 2004); online edn <http://www.oxforddnb.com/view/article/37398>, accessed 23 September 2016.

Hawkstone Park, 'History' <http://www.hawkstoneparkfollies.co.uk/history/>, accessed 23 September 2016.

Hayman, R. and Horton, W., *Ironbridge: history & guide* (Stroud, 2003).

Historic England, 'Temple of Theseus' <https://historicengland.org.uk/listing/the-list/list-entry/1348599>, accessed 3 November 2017.

The Ironbridge Institute, *Sabbath Walks draft conservation for consultation plan* (1999).

Mingay, G., 'Young, Arthur (1741–1820)', *Oxford DNB* (Oxford, 2004); online edn <http://www.oxforddnb.com/view/article/30256>, accessed 21 September 2016.

Morgan, K., 'Goldney, Thomas (1696–1768)', *Oxford DNB* (Oxford, 2004); online edn <http://www.oxforddnb.com/view/article/56846>, accessed 23 September 2016.

Raistrick, A., *Dynasty of iron founders. The Darbys and Coalbrookdale* (London, 1953).

Raistrick, A., *Quakers in science and industry*, 2nd edn (York, 1989).

Smiles, S., *Industrial biography iron-workers and tool makers* (Boston, 1864).

Stamper, P., *Historic parks & gardens of Shropshire* (Shropshire, 1996).

Stembridge, P., *The Goldney family: a Bristol merchant dynasty* (Bristol, 1998).

Sutton, C., 'Hulbert, Charles (1778–1857)', rev. A. McConnell, *Oxford DNB* (Oxford, 2004); online edn <http://www.oxforddnb.com/view/article/14103>, accessed 21 September 2016.

Sydney, W., 'Hill, Sir Richard, second baronet (1733–1808)', rev. S. Skedd, *Oxford DNB* (Oxford, 2004); online edn <http://www.oxforddnb.com/view/article/13290>, accessed 23 September 2016.

Trinder, B., 'Darby, Abraham (1711–1763)', *Oxford DNB* (Oxford, 2004); online edn <http://www.oxforddnb.com/view/article/7138>, accessed 21 September 2016.

Trinder, B., 'Darby, Abraham (1750–1789)', *Oxford DNB* (Oxford, 2004); online edn <http://www.oxforddnb.com/view/article/7139>, accessed 22 September 2016.

Trinder, B., *The industrial archaeology of Shropshire* (Chichester, 1996).

Trinder, B., *'The most extraordinary district in the world'. Ironbridge and Coalbrookdale* (London and Chichester, 1977).

Trinder, B., 'Reynolds, Richard (1735–1816)', *Oxford DNB* (Oxford, 2004); online edn <http://www.oxforddnb.com/view/article/23433>, accessed 21 September 2016.

UNESCO, 'Ironbridge Gorge' <http://whc.unesco.org/en/list/371>, accessed 22 September 2016.

# 4

## Duddeston's 'shady walks and arbours': the provincial pleasure garden in the eighteenth century

*Elaine Mitchell*

**Introduction**

In August 1749 Mary Delany (1700–1788) wrote to her sister:

> … and after dinner walked to Vauxhall, a good mile from hence. The garden is very neat and pretty, with a handsome bowling green and seats in several parts of the garden; in one of them we drank tea, eat [*sic*] bread and butter, and Rhenish and sugar.[1]

Mrs Delany's description of her visit to Birmingham's Vauxhall Gardens at Duddeston is notable not only for its favourable tone but also because it draws attention to the concept of the pleasure garden.[2] Vauxhall, like its better-known London peer, was part of the new urban infrastructure, described by Peter Borsay, of leisure and cultural experiences increasingly available in English towns following the Restoration.[3]

Pleasure gardens were public spaces but, unlike later public parks, they were commercial ventures offering amusements within a landscape setting, charging for admission and making a profit on refreshments and entertainments. From promenading, seeing and being seen, to music, ballooning and fireworks, proprietors working to a commercial agenda offered respite from the overcrowded town in their pleasure gardens.[4] Many developed around taverns or mineral springs, while others opened as new ventures to serve a new audience, such as the growing middle class.[5] Competition was fierce and many did not last long. Vauxhall Gardens in London, established on the south bank of the Thames from 1661, survived until 1859 and provided the model that many provincial gardens sought to emulate.[6] Its formula was such a success that the name 'Vauxhall' was adopted by pleasure gardens elsewhere in England, including Birmingham, as a shorthand to indicate that they were more than an inn or a tavern.[7]

Where London, the 'Vatican of pleasure', led, the provinces at varying speeds and to varying degrees followed.[8] Yet the provincial pleasure garden, and more so that in the manufacturing town, has almost entirely disappeared both on the ground and from the page. Perceived as synonymous with Georgian London, the pleasure garden is associated with metropolitan society and culture. The very name Vauxhall Gardens is weighted with a celebrity coloured by the leisure pursuits of the elite and the imagined pleasures that the shrubbery and a cloak of darkness might hide.

This chapter aims to illuminate the provincial pleasure garden with a series of insights that focus on the establishment of Birmingham's Vauxhall Gardens in the 1740s, highlight examples of its features and functions in the years between its Georgian birth and its Victorian demise and consider events surrounding its sudden closure in 1850. With the accent of Birmingham's historiography on its manufacturing and political past, it adds to our understanding of the town's social and cultural history.[9] In so doing it draws attention to the fruitful intersection where garden history and urban history meet. It shows that Birmingham's Vauxhall Gardens were an important aspect of the town's social and cultural capital, adopted to promote its attractions and, reflecting the nature of Birmingham's entrepreneurial character, a commercial enterprise that adapted to serve the changing nature of its audience.[10]

The study of gardens within an urban context is often overlooked in garden history, particularly in explorations of the eighteenth century, where the country landscapes of the elite remain the focus of attention.[11] There are notable exceptions, however, such as Peter Borsay's seminal work on the provincial experience of cultural revival, Jon Stobart, Andrew Hann and Victoria Morgan's exploration of consumption and public display and Jonathan Conlin's construction of the ideal, well-regulated city as reflected in communal space.[12]

While the study of metropolitan pleasure gardens received a fillip from the 2008 Vauxhall Revisited conference and ensuing publications, histories of provincial gardens remain thin on the ground.[13] The leisure towns of Brighton and Tunbridge Wells are exceptions, and other provincial towns find a mention, but substantive studies are lacking.[14] The pleasure gardens of the manufacturing towns are even less well explored. Open space designed for leisure purposes is more readily associated with towns such as Lichfield or Warwick, both identified to a large extent with polite social pursuits. While the concept of a polite town was as much to do with the people as the place, pleasure gardens and public walks were one indicator of a town's standing in the hierarchy of polite sociability.[15] There is opportunity, as highlighted by Stobart *et al.*, to investigate more fully the polite aspects of towns where rapid urban development between the late eighteenth and the early nineteenth centuries covered over what might have been considered a polite infrastructure.[16]

A variety of primary sources has been consulted to develop a history of Birmingham's Vauxhall. Evidence includes visual material, maps and surveys, where the most significant record is J. Pedley's painting of Vauxhall, captured on the eve of closure in 1850 (Plate 4.1).[17] Newspaper advertisements, town guides and directories attest to an appetite for the adoption of print culture as a polite promotional tool in a commercialising society.[18] Maps, directories and advertisements indicate how a town or business wished to represent itself, while the use of visitors' letters provides an outsider's view, and estate papers illustrate the lives and alliances of elite families.

**Polite identity**

Birmingham developed from a middle-sized market town in the sixteenth century to a populous and noted centre of metalworking by the mid-eighteenth century.[19] Even before tourists began arriving in numbers at the Soho manufactory during the 1760s, visitors from Robert Leland (1503–1552) onwards commented on Birmingham's nature as a manufacturing town, particularly noting its metal industries.[20] However, visitors also observed other features of the town, and their accounts and visual representations reveal aspects of Birmingham beyond its manufacturing identity (Figure 4.1).

In 1755 Resta Patching filled five days in Birmingham with visits to the leading manufactories as well as to Vauxhall and the landscape gardens at Hagley and The Leasowes.[21] If new streets, squares and buildings 'served as a tribute to the town and testament to the new discourses of civility', as suggested by Stobart *et al.*, visitors' accounts provide evidence that Birmingham was developing those attributes.[22] To Patching the newer, upper parts of the town around St Philip's, the 'very grand modern built church', appeared like 'another London, in miniature … like St James's' with 'new, regular streets, and a handsome square, all well built, and well inhabited'.[23]

While Mary Delany was not so taken with St Philips, 'so light and glaring 'tis *intolerable*', when she visited again in 1754 she acknowledged the 'riches and beauties of the place'.[24] In 1760 Samuel Derrick, soon to be Master of Ceremonies at both Bath and Tunbridge Wells, found the town 'spacious and well built … the inhabitants are rich, civil and industrious … they have balls, concerts, plays and assemblies'.[25] These accounts indicate something of the visible evidence of Birmingham's growing prosperity, reflected not only in its built environment but also in a range of cultural activities and amusements.

If we apply Stobart *et al.*'s formula that 'walks, promenades and pleasure gardens, theatres and assembly rooms, coffee houses and libraries' constitute evidence of polite sociability, Birmingham, which had several of these elements

Figure 4.1 'The Road to Vauxhall' was included in this detail from Samuel and Nathaniel Buck's *East Prospect of Birmingham in the County of Warwick* (1753). Its inclusion indicated that the town had an identity beyond its purely manufacturing image. By permission of The Library of Birmingham, 13996

in place, can perhaps be considered to have attained the status of a polite society.[26] But it has to be remembered that many of these additions to the town were the preserve of elite or middle-class patrons. In Birmingham, as in other towns, the rhythm of a different social life, one allied to markets and fairs, continued.[27]

As Birmingham's economy surged in the second half of the eighteenth century it became more prosperous and developed an affluent middle class that in turn drew professionals such as doctors to settle in the town.[28] While members of county society viewed Birmingham with mixed feelings, they overcame their reservations and began to visit in increasing numbers.[29] They were joined by tourists attracted to the town's manufactories, especially those that produced fashionable ornamental goods, such as Matthew Boulton's Soho.[30] John Money has argued that there was a direct correlation between the continuing prosperity of the town and the need to develop cultural assets that would appeal to the tastes of established society, whether residents or visitors.[31] Musical events, theatre, scientific lectures, clubs, societies, pleasure gardens and assemblies developed, providing a cultural infrastructure that would tempt visitors to stay longer, spend more money and add to the prosperity of the town.[32] It is within this growth of Birmingham as a manufacturing town but against the background of a wider cultural renaissance adopted for leisure purposes that the seeds of Vauxhall Gardens' emergence at Dudston Hall can be seen.

### The Making of Vauxhall Gardens

William Hutton, Birmingham's first historian, wrote of the town having 'a great variety of public gardens, suited to every class of people', but it was 'Duddeston, the ancient seat of the Holte family', that 'claims the pre-eminence'.[33] About a mile from the centre of Birmingham, the site of Dudston Hall functioned as a place of entertainment from the middle of the eighteenth century until its closure in 1850, offering gardens, concerts, dancing, firework displays, cockfighting and refreshments.[34]

The commercial context of the pleasure garden shaped the origins and evolution of Vauxhall. It is notable that the site at Duddeston displayed three of the same characteristics that contributed to the success of its London counterpart.[35] First, Dudston Hall was well positioned in relation to the town: it was within easy reach, yet offered a rural location. Second, Vauxhall developed around a mature site that offered a ready-made green and leafy retreat, having been the manorial seat of the Holte family until 1631, when Sir Thomas joined the country house building boom and moved to Aston Hall.[36] Finally, like London's Vauxhall, beyond the formal boundary of the gardens Dudston benefited from a borrowed landscape of surrounding small fields, many worked by artisans from Birmingham's growing metal industries.[37]

The gardens that this landscape enclosed were central to the venture. There is no known evidence of layout at the time the Holtes moved to Aston, but one could speculate about what might have remained that would lend itself to use as a commercial pleasure garden. A house of substance by the sixteenth century, Dudston Hall would have been matched, in keeping with the Holtes' status, by a garden of equal substance.[38] By 1631 its layout may have been one in the formal Renaissance style that ran from the knot gardens of the early Tudor palace through the alignment of house and garden in the Jacobean period, with associated water features and grottoes, and beyond to the elaborate parterres of the mid-seventeenth century.[39]

The building of Aston Hall began in 1618 and probably from this time Dudston would not have been given the attention necessary to maintain a garden in the latest fashion.[40] The essentially formal, geometric underpinning of a Renaissance-style garden may, therefore, have survived until the mid-eighteenth century. Nature would have outgrown its clipped Renaissance neatness and come to mirror the well-wooded landscape of London's Vauxhall Gardens, a landscape that added to its air of sylvan retreat. This older geometric style remained acceptable in pleasure gardens, as its compartmental layout

Figure 4.2 Vauxhall stands separate and distinct in this advertisement from Bisset's *Magnificent Guide* (1808). Its proprietor, J. Richards, promoted his business in a banner decorated with vines on the right of the image, perhaps suggesting that he sought to project Vauxhall at a remove from other hotels and inns. By permission of the Library of Birmingham, 17154

disposed itself well to their purpose, and this could be a further reason why the site at Dudston Hall lent itself to the business of a pleasure garden.[41] The exact date of the translation of the hall from private manor house to public pleasure garden is unclear, but it is unlikely to pre-date February 1738 – when the Dowager Lady Holte, who had been living at Dudston, died – or to be later than 1745.[42] Although the first advertisement for Dudston Hall as a place of entertainment appeared in *Aris's Birmingham Gazette* (*Aris's*) in June 1746, the account book of Walter Gough shows that a year earlier, in May 1745, he enjoyed a game of bowls 'at Dudston bowling green' and again in February 1746 he 'Pd Buttler of duddeston my forfeitures of the green'.[43]

If place was key to Dudston Hall's success, people and entrepreneurial skills were as necessary for the business of amusement as they were for the business of manufacturing. The proprietors of pleasure gardens have been noted as 'ambitious men of a relatively low social background', and the success or failure of the enterprise was entirely dependent on their entrepreneurial skills.[44] While much is known about Jonathan Tyers, the man who propelled London's Vauxhall to its position of pre-eminence by the mid-eighteenth century, little more than the names of the people behind the development of Birmingham's Vauxhall are known.[45]

The 'Buttler' paid by Walter Gough for bowling in 1746 may have been Andrew Butler, who was recorded in a Dudston Hall lease in 1755.[46] Butler announced in 1763 that Vauxhall was to be let and 'that he had a mind to retire', as he had 'no wife and family', who presumably might have carried on the business.[47] However, earlier newspaper advertisements also indicate how he had developed the business. In 1758 he advertised that, while 'The Garden for Publick Entertainment continues … Duddeston-Hall, commonly call'd Vauxhall' had been 'fitted up in a neat and commodious Manner for the reception of Travellers'.[48] This suggests that Butler was responding to the growth in trade and travellers that lay behind the increasing number of inns that offered accommodation during this period by doing the same at Duddeston.[49] By 1767 the proprietor of Vauxhall was Abraham Pemberton, who was still in possession some ten years later.[50] By 1791 Vauxhall had changed hands again; the master was now Mr Richards, who accommodated the Hutton family after their home was destroyed in the Priestley riots.[51] The Richards' stewardship lasted until at least 1808 (Figure 4.2).[52]

Birmingham's Vauxhall therefore presented a different pattern of ownership to London's, where, for almost a century from 1732, control remained in the hands of the Tyers family. However, although the proprietors changed, Vauxhall itself endured where other Birmingham pleasure gardens did not. Their fleeting nature and the entrepreneurial spirit of their proprietors is illustrated by Holte Bridgeman's Apollo Gardens at Aston: the gardens were open by 1747 for concerts and fireworks but by 1751 Bridgeman had returned to his business of house-painting.[53]

### The gardens and entertainments

In addition to location, there are three related areas fundamental to Vauxhall's success as a business venture: the garden space, the entertainments and activities it offered and the nature of the audience it attracted. As part of the commercial imperative these three themes are intimately connected. The Gardens' appeal and status were central to the number and type of visitors who might be persuaded to pay for admission, entertainments and refreshments.

Sampling a range of sources, it is possible to present a series of insights into the features and functions of Vauxhall in the second half of the eighteenth century and the early part of the nineteenth. Visual material such as Pedley's watercolour of the Gardens, maps and town guides combined with visitors' accounts reveal something of Vauxhall as a garden space. The regular record of events provided by newspaper advertisements illuminates the nature of activities at the Gardens. The type of audience Vauxhall attracted is more difficult to assess and is coloured by the nature of the evidence available. Visitors' accounts represent a small elite group and although town guides and histories offer one view on the changing nature of the audience at Vauxhall, especially from the turn of the eighteenth century, they are perhaps distorted by the lens of nostalgia.

Borsay has highlighted how the garden element of the pleasure garden has been overlooked in favour of entertainment. A scarcity of evidence is certainly a contributing factor in attempting to reconstruct Vauxhall as a garden space, especially in its early period.[54] Whilst a wealth of images is available for London's Vauxhall, the known visual record for Birmingham's Vauxhall is confined to Pedley's watercolour, a poor copy of this painting and a nostalgic drawing by E.H. New published in Dent's *Making of Birmingham*.[55] Although Vauxhall featured in town guides, directories and histories, these publications contained few illustrations of the attractions they promoted and, when they did, these usually celebrated the built environment rather than the natural.

To establish whether Pedley's painting provides a useful guide to the garden element of Vauxhall, rather than representing an idealised notion of a pleasure garden, its value as a source needs to be compared with other evidence. While little is known about the artist, the circumstances of the painting's execution are better documented: it was commissioned by the Victoria Building and Freehold Land Society, who bought the site of Vauxhall some months before the Gardens closed in September 1850.[56] The painting adopts the sixteenth- and seventeenth-century bird's eye view, where the elevated viewpoint gives the observer the advantage of encompassing the gardens at a glance and where the aim is to produce something instantly recognisable of a specific place.[57]

Buildings and structures in the picture compare well with evidence from newspapers and directories, supporting the depiction of the main garden area. The auctioneer's sales notice described the 'fifteen elegant, rustic, gothic, and other arbours' and 'the magnificent classic Grecian fountain', all of which can be identified in the painting.[58] The layout of the main garden is also mirrored in a directory published just a year before Vauxhall closed: 'the principal lawn … is now disposed into picturesque parterres, beautified by flowers and evergreens. These radiate from a centre division, in which a handsome fountain is erected … a sloping bank, adorned with vases and flowers, form a striking combination.'[59] If Pedley's watercolour offered a reasonably accurate account of Vauxhall on the eve of closure, is it possible to trace within it any echoes of the Gardens' Georgian beginnings? In contrast to the changing man-made elements, it is the enduring element of nature that can provide one path back to the mid-eighteenth century. Described in the Notice of Sale as 'timber', indicating that they were mature at the time, many of the Garden's encircling trees dated from an earlier period.[60] The main species were elm and horse chestnut, both significant plantings in formal gardens of the seventeenth century, where the elm was valued for providing shaded walks and alleys and the horse chestnut was planted for its ornamental qualities.[61]

The map evidence suggests a possible presence of walks along the boundaries, which would fulfil one of the primary features of a pleasure garden and also indicates a more wooded aspect than Pedley's mid-nineteenth-century view allows.[62] If this is the case, this change over time mirrors the evolution of London's Vauxhall, which saw a gradual felling of trees to accommodate the changing nature of entertainments, especially the annual commemoration of the Battle of Waterloo.[63]

Visitors' evidence goes some way to describing the gardens, but none of these accounts dwell on horticultural aspects. Mary Delany confined herself to describing the site as 'really pretty' on her second visit to Vauxhall in 1754.[64] Equally, however, her letters were not the descriptive accounts of a tourist such as Resta Patching, who, a year later, wrote a detailed account of his tour around the Midlands to his brother and sister in London. While he noted Vauxhall's 'several shady walks and arbours', he moved on to focus on the man-made features: 'statues, and a neat orchestra' – elements that contributed to the theatricality of the pleasure-garden experience.[65] This theatricality was projected through the garden design, in which the walks provided a stage on which to see and be seen and the arbours and supper boxes served as smaller theatres of display. The experience was reinforced by the nature of the amusements that Vauxhall provided, especially the musical entertainments and firework displays.

The Orchestra pavilion that Resta Patching noted would have been a central feature of the musical entertainments that were a staple of Vauxhall from at least May 1748 until the closing concert in 1850 (Figure 4.3).[66] In the late eighteenth century music, in all its variety, was one of the activities central to Birmingham's growing sense of cultural identity.[67] Vauxhall presented regular concerts during the summer months, between May and September (Figure 4.4). The Church provided much of the early infrastructure for musical events in Birmingham, and Vauxhall was no exception. Between 1758 and 1763 John Eversmann, organist at both St Martin's and St Philip's, took part in concerts at Vauxhall both as impresario and performer.[68]

If the concerts during this period were of a 'polite' nature, by 1800 a less genteel note can be detected. On 8 July 1800 the tone was very different: the programme was one of martial music performed by the Birmingham Loyal Association in full uniform, followed by a hardly less stirring firework display that included:

Figure 4.3 Detail from Pedley's *Vauxhall Gardens, Saltley, 1850*, showing the Orchestra pavilion. Photo © Birmingham Museums Trust

> A Battery of Maroons; Sky Rockets; The Lads & Lasses Dancing Round the May Pole; Bengola Lights; The Duke of York's Button & Feather; Flying Pigeons; A Sunwheel; The Admired Piece of a Chinese Temple, etc. The Whole to Conclude with a Representation of the IRRUPTION of MOUNT VESUVIUS.[69]

Patriotic and reassuring messages were conveyed through the performance in a way that reflected similar messages conveyed to audiences at the New Street Theatre in the 1780s.[70] At that time theatre performances were taking place against the background of the American Wars, but by 1800 the long war with

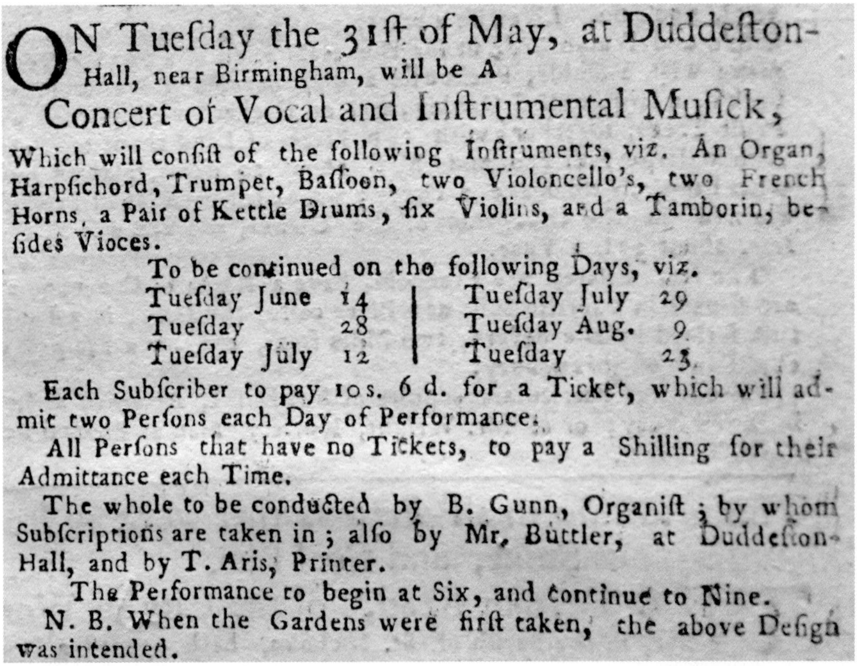

> ON Tuesday the 31st of May, at Duddeston-Hall, near Birmingham, will be A
> **Concert of Vocal and Instrumental Musick,**
> Which will consist of the following Instruments, viz. An Organ, Harpsichord, Trumpet, Bassoon, two Violoncello's, two French Horns, a Pair of Kettle Drums, six Violins, and a Tamborin, besides Vioces.
>
> To be continued on the following Days, viz.
>
> Tuesday June 14           Tuesday July 29
> Tuesday        28         Tuesday Aug. 9
> Tuesday July 12           Tuesday       23
>
> Each Subscriber to pay 10s. 6d. for a Ticket, which will admit two Persons each Day of Performance.
>
> All Persons that have no Tickets, to pay a Shilling for their Admittance each Time.
>
> The whole to be conducted by B. Gunn, Organist; by whom Subscriptions are taken in; also by Mr. Buttler, at Duddeston-Hall, and by T. Aris, Printer.
>
> The Performance to begin at Six, and continue to Nine.
>
> N. B. When the Gardens were first taken, the above Design was intended.

Figure 4.4 Concerts were a staple of the entertainments offered at Vauxhall. *Aris's Birmingham Gazette*, 2 May 1748. By permission of the Library of Birmingham

France depressed trade and, with it, the Birmingham economy. A series of bad harvests led to high bread prices followed by rioting in 1800; by September the military presence at the Gardens was 'to preserve order' rather than to entertain the crowds.[71]

**The visitors to Vauxhall**

The town's resident population with surplus income was still small by the 1780s and it would appear unlikely that they formed the bulk of Vauxhall's audience.[72] The elite of county society had their reservations about the growing town, as has been mentioned above, but they arrived in increasing numbers to enjoy its attractions and add to its prosperity.[73] Vauxhall advertised in *Aris's*, and therefore it is likely that the nature of the audience attracted to the Gardens was one that mirrored the paper's readership and circulation: one with the money to pay for a newspaper as well as the time to read it. The paper's circulation beyond Birmingham into its Warwickshire, Staffordshire and north Worcestershire hinterland also suggests that Vauxhall was one of the attractions that the increasing number of county visitors to Birmingham in the mid-eighteenth century came to enjoy.[74]

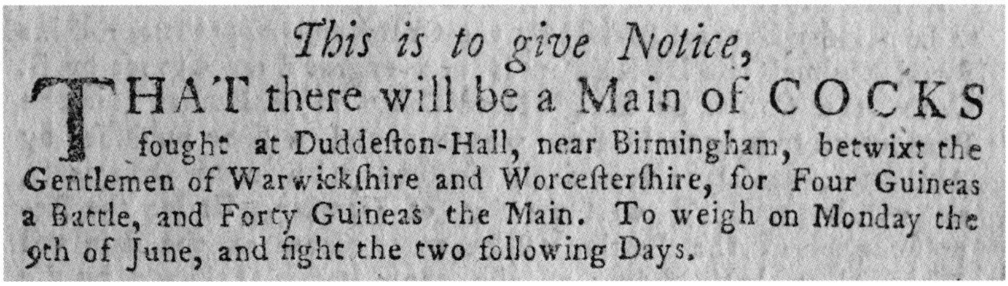

> *This is to give Notice,*
> THAT there will be a Main of COCKS fought at Duddeſton-Hall, near Birmingham, betwixt the Gentlemen of Warwickſhire and Worceſterſhire, for Four Guineas a Battle, and Forty Guineas the Main. To weigh on Monday the 9th of June, and fight the two following Days.

Figure 4.5 Vauxhall was a venue for cockfighting as well as 'polite' entertainments. *Aris's Birmingham Gazette*, 2 June 1746. By permission of the Library of Birmingham

But, just as there were changes in the nature of the entertainments at Vauxhall, so it is likely that there were changes in the nature of the audience. This should be qualified by noting that, like many leisure businesses, the Gardens catered for a different audience at different times in terms of both class and gender. For example, when Mary Delany visited in 1749 and drank tea and Rhenish, Vauxhall was also a venue for cockfighting, as it was when Patty Fothergill, daughter of Matthew Boulton's former business partner John Fothergill, visited for the fireworks in 1793.[75] Like the bowling that Walter Gough enjoyed, cockfighting was an acceptable pastime for Georgian men, although its appeal had waned in fashionable society by this time (Figure 4.5).[76]

After the turn of the century Birmingham's experience mirrored that of London's Vauxhall: nineteenth-century commentators bemoaned 'the decline of the Gardens from its prior grandeur and decorum', although, as Conlin suggests, these complaints may have been more about elevating the social status of those who made them than about reflecting reality.[77] Evidence from directories indicates that for a short time Birmingham's Vauxhall was also characterised by a changing audience. Pye noted that the Gardens were 'til of late years, resorted to by none but the genteeler sort of people' and complained about Vauxhall 'being turned into an alehouse … on which account the upper classes of the inhabitants have entirely absented themselves'.[78]

By 1839 any reference to class had disappeared and Vauxhall fits the pattern of 'not simply one of decline, rather of a broadening of their social base'.[79] As Birmingham's expanding industries drew in workers, this was the opportunity for Vauxhall, one of the remaining green spaces close to the town, to develop its audience. Eric Hopkins has noted that the cost of admission, at 1s 6d in the 1830s and dropping to 1s after 1842, did not preclude members of the respectable working class from visiting.[80] In terms of class and gender, the Gardens' audience certainly included women and, in the eighteenth century at least, it was a respectable place for elite and middle-class women to visit. At this stage it is not possible to demonstrate whether Birmingham's Vauxhall was the classless space so often highlighted in the histories of London pleasure gardens, although this notion is one that has been the subject of debate more recently.[81]

**'Adieu to Old Vauxhall!'**
The closure of Vauxhall was the result of several factors: the impact of urbanisation; social and cultural change; and commercial imperatives. Pedley's painting illustrates these themes. It depicts the Gardens as a space that has been abandoned; all the elements of its former life are still in place but the main ingredient, the audience, is absent. The gates are closed and the few people who do appear in the scene are excluded, placed in the street beyond the garden walls rather than in the green space within. It can be read as an image showing the remnants of an eighteenth-century past that had no place in the nineteenth-century present pressing in along the Gardens' eastern boundary. This mood is reflected in a nostalgic verse scribbled inside one of Vauxhall's alcoves in March 1850:

> … Old Vauxhall has had its day
> *Houses* are better far than trees,
> The pride and pleasure of the town
> It long hath been, it now must fall;
> *Improvement* wills it, so prepare
> To bid adieu to Old Vauxhall![82]

The gardens had fallen silent, but there are indications in the painting that the world beyond was all activity. The scene can be viewed as one that illustrates the improvement that the writer of the verse describes: trains come and go on

Figure 4.6 Detail from Pedley's *Vauxhall Gardens, Saltley, 1850*, showing the railway that helped to fuel urban industrial growth. Photo © Birmingham Museums Trust

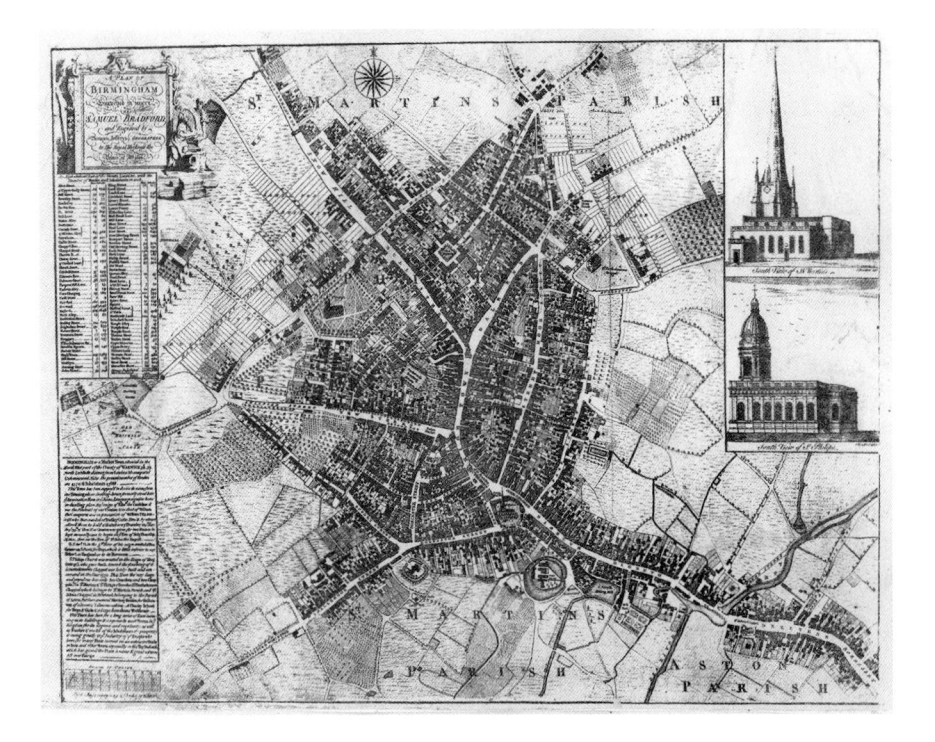

Figure 4.7 Bradford's *Plan of Birmingham Surveyed in 1750* showed a dense townscape where small gardens and open spaces within the urban centre still survived but were under pressure from population growth and the development of small workshops. By permission of the Library of Birmingham, 72830

the railway that fuelled urban industrial growth and opened up new leisure opportunities (Figure 4.6).[83] Pedley's view of Vauxhall illustrates the effects of urbanisation on the Gardens, his image alluding to ingredients in this process: the growth of suburban housing, the arrival of the railway and the development of industrial premises that accelerated Birmingham's growth. When Mary Delany paid her first visit to Vauxhall in the summer of 1749 she arrived in a town that was growing rapidly and saw its population triple to about 22,000 during the first half of the eighteenth century.[84] Bradford's map of 1750 showed open spaces and small gardens, but Birmingham was essentially a town of tightly packed streets starting to break its boundaries northwards and eastwards (Figure 4.7).[85] Vauxhall Gardens was just over a mile away to the east and Tomlinson's 1758 survey of the Duddeston and Nechells manors shows that its situation was still substantially rural.[86]

By 1795 this rural outlook had changed as Birmingham sustained a period of rapid growth and became the third most populous town in England.[87] As

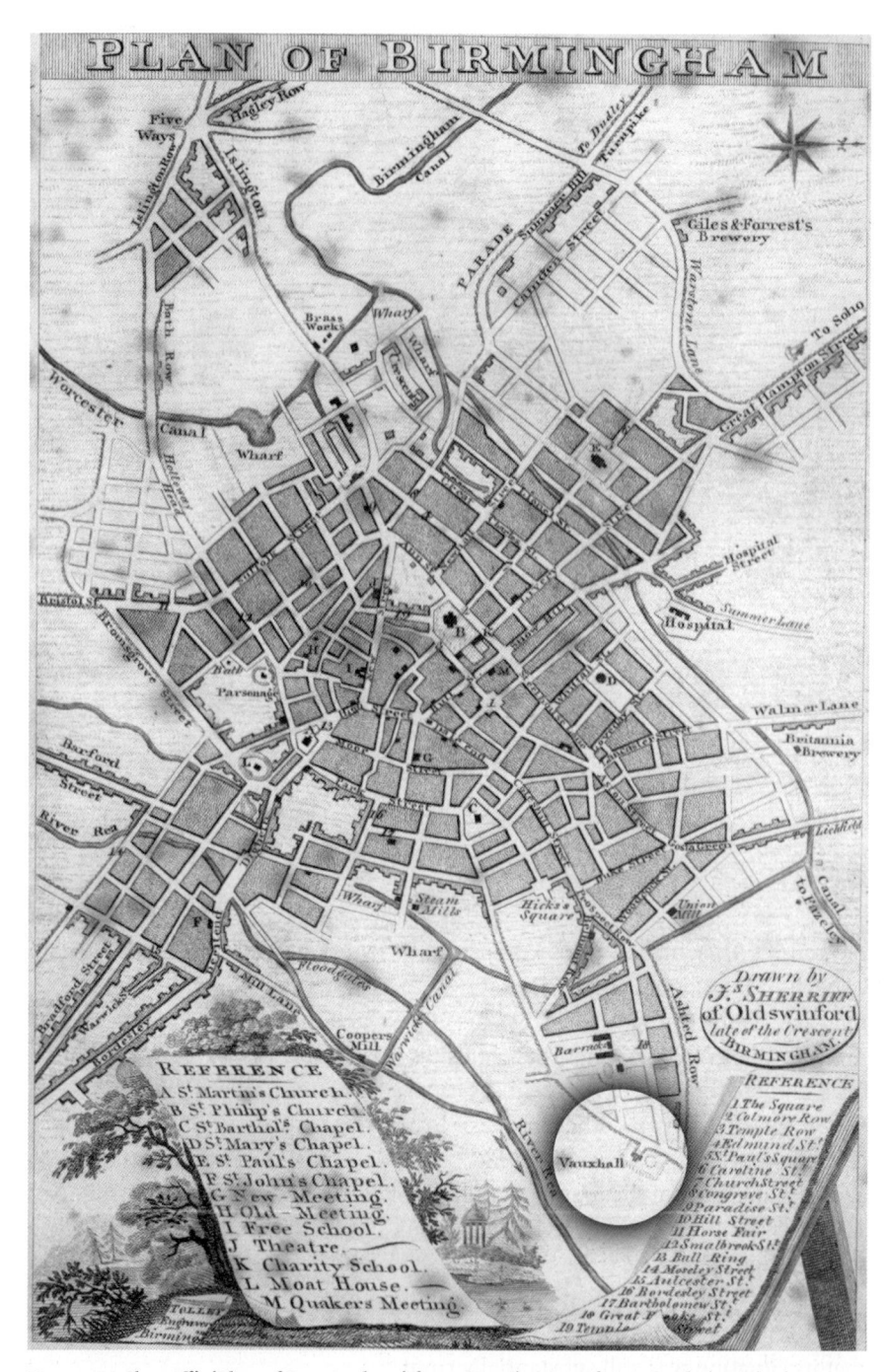

Figure 4.8 Sherriff's 'Plan of Birmingham' from Bisset's *Magnificent Guide* (1808), showing the Ashted Estate between Vauxhall and the encroaching town. By permission of the Library of Birmingham, 17154

Figure 4.9 *Birmingham from the North-East*, from William Hutton's *The History of Birmingham* (6th edn, 1836), presents the town's distant manufactories. Reproduced by permission of the Cadbury Research Library: Special Collections, the University of Birmingham

Sherriff's *Plan* indicates, eastward development continued, with the planned residential estate of Ashted being laid out opposite Vauxhall in the late 1780s (Figure 4.8).[88] Residential development was only one part of Birmingham's pattern of growth and Ashted did not remain as the intended elegant, middle-class suburb; industry quickly moved in from the 1790s, attracted by the proximity of the canals and access to cheap meadowland.[89] By 1850, when the Gardens closed, Birmingham was a town of nearly a quarter of a million people that had developed on all sides and where green space in the urban area had all but disappeared.[90] From the 1830s two railway lines skirted Vauxhall and the industrial development of the area continued throughout the 1840s until the Gardens lost their rural surroundings.[91]

Although urban development may be illustrated by maps, what such sources are unable to demonstrate are the effects on the atmosphere of burning coal, not only in the manufactories that Pedley depicted but also in the domestic hearths that he showed. The effect was the subject of contemporary comment: White's *Directory* celebrated the 'beautiful Manufactures of which Birmingham is the emporium', but also drew attention to the air that received 'an alloy from the vast congregated body of human beings, the smoke of numerous fires, and the effluvia arising from particular trades' (Figure 4.9).[92] The nineteenth century was not, as Ian Simmons described in a neat turn of phrase, 'a place of high nasal amenity'.[93]

Nevertheless, despite what was now an unpromising setting, Vauxhall continued its regular programme of music and fireworks throughout the 1840s. By 1847 it had been joined by competition close by at the Royal Victoria Gardens, or New Vauxhall as it came to be called.[94] It is difficult to assess what part the opening of New Vauxhall played in the closure of the old, although the latter seemed to be winning the war of attendance by undercutting admission prices and outdoing Old Vauxhall with their attractions.[95] New Vauxhall may have been more adept at offering the range of attractions that appealed to a broader social base and in meeting changes in demand.

Although the visible indicators of urbanisation encroached and contributed to the closure of Old Vauxhall, it is too simple to judge that pressure from the physical growth of the town alone was responsible. The results of urbanisation were expressed not only in bricks and mortar or iron and smoke but also in social and cultural change. In her examination of the issues that contributed to the closure of London's Vauxhall in 1859, Penelope Corfield identified not only changes to the surrounding landscape brought about by urban development but also changes linked to new patterns of working and the rise of new and competing forms of leisure activity.[96] One of those activities was the rise of domestic gardening associated with the new suburban villas that were so much a part of middle-class expression from the late eighteenth century.[97]

This 'cold wind of cultural change' may have contributed to the closure of many pleasure gardens.[98] Pedley's view of Vauxhall captured something of this cultural change applied to recreation. He presented a garden that had the look of a small Victorian public park: it displayed the features of axial symmetry and punctuating objects that were the favoured design ingredients of those, such as John Claudius Loudon, who were in the forefront of the public park movement.[99] Birmingham's first public park, Adderley, opened in 1856 six years after Vauxhall closed. The land was gifted to the town by Charles Adderley, landowner and MP for Staffordshire North, whose speech at the opening ceremony marked a clear break with the past.[100] The park that bore his name was

> not to be enjoyed in eating and drinking – not in Vauxhall amusements – not in tea garden style, but as a place of recreation for men employed in the active business of life, for the enjoyment of fresh air, and where they might enjoy the odds and ends of life in a rational manner.[101]

By the 1850s Vauxhall's entertainments of music, dancing, drinking and fireworks may not perhaps have constituted suitable recreations in a Victorian climate of social and moral improvement.[102]

However, Vauxhall's demise may not have been entirely due to the encroachment of the town, a declining audience or a failing business. Indeed, as the Gardens had been improved as recently as 1849, their closure so shortly afterwards is surprising.[103] In September 1850, advertising the closure of the Gardens, *Aris's* reminded its readers that if they were 'desirous of obtaining a county vote, that the opportunity which is offered on this estate will soon be lost, as nearly the whole of the shares are taken up: application should, therefore, be made forthwith'.[104] The Victoria Building and Freehold Land Society, which bought the Vauxhall site, was an example of a movement that began in Birmingham; these societies enabled people to buy new freehold properties and thereby qualify for a vote in parliamentary elections and to escape the chaos of the towns.[105] As the provision of individual garden plots for freeholders was an important part of the movement then perhaps the spirit, if not the traditions, of Vauxhall Gardens was retained.[106]

**Vauxhall's afterlife**
After Vauxhall closed in September 1850 the site was soon covered by residential streets. Echoing the history of Birmingham's earlier development, houses in their turn were soon converted to small factories and the area came to be dominated by gas works and railways in the later nineteenth century, followed by factories manufacturing cars and cycles in the twentieth.[107] A survival from the Gardens may have remained until at least the 1880s, as the 1887 Ordnance Survey map shows.[108] The Aston Union Offices occupied part of the site of Vauxhall Gardens and it is probable that the fountain shown at the rear of the building is the 'magnificent classic Grecian' one included in the Notice of Sale and illustrated in Pedley's painting.[109] Perhaps it was too magnificent to be moved. Today echoes of past use remain in the street names: Vauxhall Road, Vauxhall Grove and Ashted Walk. Standing on the site in the twenty-first century it is difficult now to conjure Duddeston's 'several shady walks and arbours'.

Historians have focused on the transformative nature that developments in manufacturing had on Birmingham in the mid-eighteenth century. But visitors did not simply characterise the town through its manufacturing landscape and built environment – they also noted and engaged with the town's green spaces. Vauxhall was one element in a polite infrastructure in the eighteenth century, an infrastructure not readily associated with the manufacturing towns of the period.

As Birmingham's manufacturing entrepreneurs developed the town's metalworking industries, entrepreneurs of a different type responded to the increasing number of travellers and visitors to the town by developing a range of services. Urbanisation contributed to the closure of the Gardens, but cultural and social change also hastened its end.

When Mary Delany wrote to her sister in 1749 she left a record that illustrates an aspect of Birmingham under-represented in the town's historiography – its eighteenth- and early nineteenth-century gardens. Vauxhall Gardens provides a framework within which to explore aspects of Birmingham beyond its manufacturing nature. It demonstrates how exploring green space in a manufacturing town illuminates both garden and urban history.

**Notes**

1. Lady Llanover (ed.), *The autobiography and correspondence of Mary Granville, Mrs Delany*, vol. ii (London, 1861), p. 509; for Mary Delany, artist and court favourite: B. Brandon Schnorrenberg, 'Delany, Mary (1700–1788)', *Oxford Dictionary of National Biography* (*Oxford DNB*), (Oxford, 2004); online edn <http://www.oxforddnb.com/view/article/7442>, accessed 8 October 2016 and M. Laird and A. Weisberg-Roberts, *Mrs Delany & her circle* (New Haven and London, 2009).
2. Duddeston is spelt in different ways. Unless quoting an original source, where text is used verbatim, Duddeston refers to the location, Dudston the manor house.
3. P. Borsay, *The English urban renaissance: culture and society in the English town, 1660–1770* (1989; Oxford, 2002).
4. For explorations of the pleasure garden see J. Conlin (ed.), *The pleasure garden, from Vauxhall to Coney Island* (Philadelphia, 2013).
5. P. Corfield, *Vauxhall and the invention of the urban pleasure gardens* (London, 2008), p. 5.
6. For a comprehensive, extensively illustrated history of London's Vauxhall see D. Coke and A. Borg, *Vauxhall Gardens: a history* (New Haven and London, 2011).
7. J. Conlin, *The pleasure garden*, pp. 1–2.
8. P. Clark and R.A. Houston, 'Culture and leisure 1700–1840', in Clark (ed.), *The Cambridge urban history of Britain*, p. 577.
9. For Birmingham see G.E. Cherry, *Birmingham: a study in geography, history and planning* (Chichester 1994); E. Hopkins, *The manufacturing town: Birmingham and the Industrial Revolution* (Stroud, 1998); P. Jones, *Industrial enlightenment: science, technology and culture in Birmingham and the West Midlands, 1760–1820* (Manchester, 2008). For a wider interpretation of the city's history see C. Chinn and M.M. Dick, *Birmingham: the workshop of the world* (Liverpool, 2016).
10. For the entrepreneurial nature of Birmingham see Jones, *Industrial enlightenment*, pp. 34–47.
11. For the élite see M. Symes and S. Haynes, *Enville, Hagley, The Leasowes: three great eighteenth century gardens* (Bristol, 2010); S. Bending (ed.), *A cultural history of gardens in the Age of Enlightenment* (London, 2015); D. Brown and T. Williamson, *Lancelot Brown and the capability men: landscape revolution in eighteenth-century England* (London, 2016). For exceptions see T. Longstaffe-Gowan, *The London town garden 1700–1840* (New Haven and London, 2001) and J. Uings, 'Gardens and gardening in a fast-changing urban environment: Manchester 1750–1850', PhD thesis (Manchester Metropolitan University, 2013).
12. Borsay, *The English urban renaissance*; J. Stobart, A. Hann and V. Morgan, *Spaces of consumption: leisure and shopping in the English town, c. 1680–1830* (Abingdon, 2007); J. Conlin, 'Vauxhall on

the boulevard: pleasure gardens in London and Paris, 1764–1784', *Urban History*, 35/1 (2008), pp. 24–47.
13    *Vauxhall revisited: pleasure gardens and their publics, 1660–1860* (Conference, Tate Britain, 2008); Conlin, *The pleasure garden*; Coke and Borg, *Vauxhall Gardens*.
14    S. Berry, 'Pleasure gardens in Georgian and Regency seaside resorts: Brighton, 1750–1840, *Garden History*, 28/2 (2000), pp. 222–30; K. Taylor, 'The oldest surviving pleasure garden in Britain: Cold Bath, near Tunbridge Wells in Kent', *Garden History*, 28/2 (2000), pp. 277–82; S.J. Downing, *The English pleasure garden 1660–1860* (Botley, 2009), pp. 39–45.
15    Stobart *et al.*, *Spaces*, p. 6.
16    *Ibid.*, p. 8.
17    Birmingham Museums Trust 1979V527, J. Pedley, *Vauxhall Gardens, Saltley, 1850*.
18    J. Stobart, 'Selling (through) politeness: advertising provincial shops in eighteenth-century England', *Cultural and Social History*, 5/3 (2008), pp. 309–28.
19    For the growth of Birmingham see R. Cust and A. Hughes, 'The Tudor and Stuart town' and M. Dick, 'The city of a thousand trades, 1700–1945', in Chinn and Dick, *Birmingham*, pp. 110–41.
20    For Soho: Jones, *Industrial enlightenment*, pp. 94–109; for John Leland: J.P. Carley, 'Leland, John (c.1503–1552)', *Oxford DNB* (Oxford, 2004); online edn http://www.oxforddnb.com/view/article/16416>, accessed 11 October 2016.
21    R. Patching, *Four topographical letters, written in July 1755 upon a journey thro Staffordshire, Northamptonshire, Leicestershire, Nottinghamshire, Derbyshire, Warwickshire, etc.* (Newcastle upon Tyne, 1757); for Hagley and The Leasowes see chapters in this volume by Joe Hawkins and John Hemingway.
22    Stobart *et al.*, *Spaces*, p. 6
23    Patching, *Four topographical letters*, p. 55.
24    Llanover, *Autobiography*, vol. iii (London, 1861), p. 274.
25    S. Derrick, *Letters written from Leverpoole, Chester, Corke, The Lake of Killarney, Dublin, Tunbridge-Wells, Bath*, vol. i (London, 1767), p. 4.
26    Stobart *et al.*, *Spaces*, p. 6.
27    *Ibid.*, p. 7.
28    Jones, *Industrial enlightenment*, pp. 44, 64.
29    J. Money, *Experience and identity: Birmingham and the West Midlands 1760–1800* (Manchester, 1977), p. 80.
30    Jones, *Industrial enlightenment*, pp. 43, 52.
31    Money, *Experience*, p. 81.
32    Jones, *Industrial enlightenment*, pp. 65–66; Money, *Experience*, p. 83.
33    W. Hutton, *An history of Birmingham to the end of the year 1780* (Birmingham, 1781), p. 130.
34    E. Mitchell, 'Duddeston's "Shady walks and arbours": Vauxhall Gardens, Birmingham c.1745–1850', BA dissertation (University of Birmingham, 2009).
35    Corfield, *Vauxhall*, pp. 7–9.
36    O. Fairclough, *The grand old mansion: the Holtes and their successors at Aston Hall 1618–1864* (Birmingham, 1984), pp. 57, 65.
37    Fairclough, *The grand old mansion*, p. 16.
38    A. Davidson, *A history of the Holtes of Aston, Baronets; with a description of the family mansion, Aston Hall, Warwickshire* (Cambridge, 1854), p. 15.
39    For this period see R. Strong, *The renaissance garden in England* (London, 1979).
40    Fairclough, *The grand old mansion*, p. 9.
41    A. Taigel and T. Williamson, *Parks and gardens* (London, 1993), p. 120.
42    Fairclough, *The grand old mansion*, p. 44.
43    *Aris's Birmingham Gazette* (*ABG*), 2 June 1746; Birmingham Archives and Heritage (BAH), MS

3145/247, *Journal and household and personal account book 1738–1752 of Walter Gough*, 9 May 1745; 22 February 1746.
44  Borsay, *Urban renaissance*, p. 213.
45  Coke and Borg, *Vauxhall Gardens*, pp. 33–84.
46  BAH, Holte Collection, MS 21/37, *Lease for a year*, 21 November 1755.
47  *ABG*, 23 May 1763.
48  *ABG*, 5 June 1758.
49  Hopkins, *The manufacturing town*, p. 13.
50  J. Sketchley, *Sketchley's Birmingham, Wolverhampton and Walsall directory* (Birmingham, 1767), p. 77; *ABG*, 14 July 1777.
51  W. Hutton (ed.), *The life of William Hutton, FASS* (London, 1816), p. 214.
52  J. Bisset, *Bisset's magnificent guide or grand copperplate directory for the town of Birmingham* (Birmingham, 1808), plate F.
53  *ABG*, 27 April 1747; 12 August 1751.
54  P. Borsay, 'The pleasure garden and urban culture', in Conlin, *The pleasure garden*, p. 51.
55  Birmingham Museums Trust, Cattell Collection, 1973 52692–1892, *Vauxhall Gardens c. 1850*; R.K. Dent, *The making of Birmingham: being a history of the rise and growth of the Midland metropolis* (Birmingham, 1894), p. 419.
56  Dent, *The making of Birmingham*, p. 418; *ABG* 30 September 1850.
57  L. Cabe Halpern, 'The uses of paintings in garden history', in Dixon Hunt (ed.), *Garden History*, pp. 188.
58  *ABG*, 16 September 1850.
59  F. White & Co., *Birmingham: history and general directory of the borough of Birmingham* (Sheffield, 1849), p. 55.
60  *ABG*, 16 September 1850; O. Rackham, *Trees and woodland in the British landscape* (London, 1976), p. 24.
61  S. Couch, 'The practice of avenue planting in the seventeenth and eighteenth centuries', *Garden History*, 20/2 (1992), pp. 181–2.
62  J. Tomlinson, 'Duddeston & Nechells Manors in the county of Warwick belonging to Sir Lister Holte Bart., surveyed 1758' from *Plans of Birmingham and vicinity, ancient and modern* (Birmingham 1884).
63  Corfield, *Vauxhall*, pp. 25, 37.
64  Llanover, *Autobiography*, vol. iii, p. 275.
65  Patching, *Four topographical letters*, p. 56; J. Dixon Hunt, 'Theaters, gardens, and garden theaters', in Dixon Hunt (ed.), *Gardens and the Picturesque*.
66  *ABG*, 2 May 1748; 2 September 1850.
67  Money, *Experience*, pp. 80–87.
68  *ABG*, 19 June 1758; 25 August 1760; 9 May 1763; Money, *Experience*, p. 83.
69  *ABG*, 7 July 1800.
70  Money, *Experience*, p. 92.
71  Hopkins, *The manufacturing town*, p. 72; *ABG* 1 September 1800.
72  Jones, *Industrial enlightenment*, p. 62.
73  Money, *Experience*, pp. 80, 81.
74  *Ibid.*, pp. 285, 80.
75  *ABG*, 29 May 1749; S. Mason, *The hardware man's daughter* (Chichester, 2005), p. 96.
76  Borsay, *The English urban renaissance*, p. 178.
77  C. Pye, *A description of modern Birmingham* (Birmingham, 1823), p. 55; J. Conlin, 'Vauxhall revisited: the afterlife of a London pleasure garden, 1770–1859', *Journal of British Studies*, 45 (October 2006), p. 720.

78  Pye, *A description*, p. 55.
79  Conlin, 'Vauxhall revisited', p. 720.
80  Hopkins, *The manufacturing town*, p. 169.
81  For this debate see Conlin, *The pleasure garden*, pp. 12–17 and H. Greig, '"All together and all distinct": public socialbility and social exclusivity in London's pleasure gardens, ca. 1740–1800', *Journal of British Studies*, 51/1 (2012), pp. 50–75.
82  *Birmingham Weekly Post, Impromptu, written by Edward Farmer in one of the Alcoves at Old Vauxhall, March 6, 1850* (1881).
83  L. Hollen-Lees, 'Urban networks', in Daunton (ed.), *The Cambridge urban history of Britain*, p. 64; D. Reid, 'Playing and praying', in Daunton, *The Cambridge urban history of Britain*, p. 746.
84  P.M. Jones, 'Industrial enlightenment in practice: visitors to the Soho manufactory, 1765–1820', *Midland History*, 33/1 (2008), p. 85.
85  S. Bradford, *A plan of Birmingham surveyed in 1750* (London, 1751).
86  Tomlinson, 'Duddeston & Nechells Manors'.
87  Jones, *Industrial enlightenment*, p. 34.
88  C. Pye, *Plan of Birmingham surveyed in the year 1795* (Birmingham, 1795).
89  E. Frostick and L. Harland, *Take heart: people, history & change in Birmingham's heartlands* (Birmingham, 1993), p. 25.
90  W.B. Stephens (ed.), *A history of the county of Warwick, vol. vii, the city of Birmingham* (London, 1964), p. 14; Cherry, *Birmingham*, p. 49.
91  Mclure, Macdonald & Macgregor, *Plan of Birmingham and its environs (with boundaries taken from the Reform Act* (London, c.1849).
92  White, *Birmingham*, Frontispiece; p. 2.
93  I.G. Simmons, *An environmental history of Great Britain* (Edinburgh, 2001), p. 151.
94  D. Reid, 'Labour, leisure and politics in Birmingham, ca. 1800–1875', PhD thesis (University of Birmingham, 1985), p. 337.
95  Reid, 'Labour, leisure', p. 337.
96  Corfield, *Vauxhall*, pp. 32, 24.
97  Conlin, 'Vauxhall revisited', p. 741.
98  Clark and Houston, 'Culture and leisure', p. 585.
99  H. Conway, *People's parks* (Cambridge, 1991), p. 78. For Loudon, who designed Birmingham's Botanical Gardens, see B. Elliott, 'Loudon, John Claudius (1783–1843)', *Oxford DNB* (Oxford, 2004); online edn <http://www.oxforddnb.com/view/article/17031>, accessed 21 September 2017.
100 J. de Montmorency, 'Adderley, Charles Bowyer, first Baron Norton (1814–1905)', rev. H.C.G. Matthew, *Oxford DNB* (Oxford, 2004); online edn <http://www.oxforddnb.com/view/article/30341>, accessed 21 September 2017.
101 Cited in Reid, 'Labour, leisure', p. 296.
102 Conway, *People's parks*, p. 34.
103 White, *Birmingham*, p. 55.
104 *ABG*, 9 September 1850.
105 M. Chase, 'Out of radicalism: the mid-Victorian freehold land movement', *The English Historical Review*, 106/419 (1991), pp. 320, 330.
106 *Ibid.*, pp. 330–31.
107 Frostick and Harland, *Take heart*, pp. 27, 41.
108 Ordnance Survey, *Birmingham, Sheet 146* (Southampton, 1887).
109 *ABG*, 16 September 1850.

## Bibliography

*Primary sources*

Birmingham Archives and Heritage (BAH)
    MS 21/37, *Lease for a Year*, 21 November 1755
    MS 3145/247, *Journal and household and personal account book 1738-1752 of Walter Gough*; Gough, Walter, *Account Book 1738-1752*

Birmingham Museums Trust
    Watercolour 1979V527, Pedley, J., *Vauxhall Gardens, Saltley*
    Cattell Collection, 197352692–1892, *Vauxhall Gardens c.1850*

*Printed primary sources*

Aris's Birmingham Gazette (*ABG*).
Birmingham Weekly Post, *Impromptu, written by Edward Farmer in one of the Alcoves at Old Vauxhall*, 6 March 1850 (1881).
Bisset, J., *Bisset's magnificent guide or grand copperplate directory for the town of Birmingham* (Birmingham, 1808).
Bradford, S., *A plan of Birmingham surveyed in 1750* (London, 1751).
Derrick, S., *Letters written from Leverpoole, Chester, Corke, The Lake of Killarney, Dublin, Tunbridge-Wells, Bath*, vol. i (London, 1767).
Hutton, C. (ed.), *The life of William Hutton, F.A.S.S.* (1816, reprinted Studley, 1998).
Hutton, W., *An history of Birmingham to the end of the year 1780* (Birmingham, 1781).
Llanover, Lady (ed.), *The autobiography and correspondence of Mary Granville, Mrs Delany*, vols ii and iii (London, 1861).
McLure, Macdonald and Macgregor, *Plan of Birmingham and its environs (with boundaries taken from the Reform Act)* (London, c.1849).
Ordnance Survey, *Birmingham, Sheet 146* (Southampton, 1887).
Patching, Resta, *Four topographical letters, written in July 1755 upon a journey thro Staffordshire, Northamptonshire, Leicestershire, Nottinghamshire, Derbyshire, Warwickshire, etc.* (Newcastle upon Tyne, 1757).
Pye, C., *A description of modern Birmingham* (Birmingham, 1823).
Pye, C., *Plan of Birmingham surveyed in the year 1795* (Birmingham, 1795).
Sketchley, J., *Sketchley's Birmingham, Wolverhampton and Walsall directory* (Birmingham, 1767).
Tomlinson, J., 'Duddeston & Nechells Manors in the county of Warwick belonging to Sir Lister Holte Bar., surveyed 1758' from *Plans of Birmingham and vicinity, ancient and modern* (Birmingham 1884).
White, F. and Co., *Birmingham: history and general directory of the borough of Birmingham* (Sheffield, 1849).

*Secondary sources*

Bending, S. (ed.), *A cultural history of gardens in the Age of Enlightenment* (London, 2015).
Berry, S., 'Pleasure gardens in Georgian and Regency seaside resorts: Brighton, 1750–1840', *Garden History*, 28/2 (2000), pp. 222–30.
Borsay, P., *The English urban renaissance: culture and society in the provincial town, 1660–1770* (1989; Oxford, 2002).

Borsay, P., 'The pleasure garden and urban culture', in Conlin (ed.), *The pleasure garden*, pp. 49–77.

Brown, D. and Williamson, T., *Lancelot Brown and the capability men: landscape revolution in eighteenth-century England* (London, 2016).

Cabe Halpern, L., 'The uses of paintings in garden history', in Dixon Hunt (ed.), *Garden history*, pp. 183–202.

Carley, J.P., 'Leland, John (*c.*1503–1552)', *Oxford Dictionary of National Biography* (*Oxford DNB*) (Oxford, 2004); online edn <http://www.oxforddnb.com/view/article/16416>, accessed 11 October 2016.

Chase, M., 'Out of radicalism: the mid-Victorian freehold land movement', *The English Historical Review*, 106/419 (April 1991), pp. 319–45.

Cherry, G.E., *Birmingham: a study in geography, history and planning* (Chichester, 1994).

Chinn, C. and Dick, M.M., *Birmingham: the workshop of the world* (Liverpool, 2016).

Clark, P. (ed.), *The Cambridge urban history of Britain, volume ii, 1540–1840* (Cambridge, 2000).

Clark, P. and Houston, R.A., 'Culture and leisure 1700–1840', in Clark (ed.), *The Cambridge urban history of Britain*, pp. 575–613.

Coke, D. and Borg, A., *Vauxhall Gardens: a history* (New Haven and London, 2011).

Conlin, J. (ed.), *The pleasure garden, from Vauxhall to Coney Island* (Philadelphia, 2013).

Conlin, J., 'Vauxhall on the boulevard: pleasure gardens in London and Paris, 1764–1784', *Urban History*, 35/1 (2008), pp. 24–47.

Conlin, J., 'Vauxhall revisited: the afterlife of a London pleasure garden, 1770–1859', *Journal of British Studies*, 45 (2006), pp. 718–43.

Conway, H., *People's parks* (Cambridge, 1991).

Corfield, P., *Vauxhall and the invention of the urban pleasure gardens* (London, 2008).

Couch, S., 'The practice of avenue planting in the seventeenth and eighteenth centuries', *Garden History*, 20/2 (1992), pp. 173–200.

Cust, R. and Hughes, A., 'The Tudor and Stuart town', in Chinn and Dick, *Birmingham*, pp. 110–33.

Daunton, M. (ed.), *The Cambridge urban history of Britain, vol. iii, 1840–1950* (Cambridge, 2000).

Davidson, A., *A history of the Holtes of Aston, Baronets; with a description of the family mansion, Aston Hall, Warwickshire* (Birmingham, 1854).

Dent, R., *The making of Birmingham: being a history of the rise and growth of the Midland metropolis* (Birmingham, 1894).

Dick, M.M., 'The city of a thousand trades, 1700–1945', in Chinn and Dick, *Birmingham*, pp. 125–58.

Dixon Hunt, J. (ed.), *Garden history: issues, approaches, methods. Revised texts of papers read at the symposium held in May 1989, Dumbarton Oaks Colloquium on the History of Landscape Architecture (13th: 1989)* (Washington DC, 1992).

Dixon Hunt, J. (ed.), *Gardens and the Picturesque: studies in the history of landscape architecture* (Cambridge, 1997).

Dixon Hunt, J. 'Theaters, gardens, and garden theaters' in Dixon Hunt (ed.), *Gardens and the Picturesque*, pp. 49–75.

Downing, S.J., *The English pleasure garden 1660–1860* (Botley, 2009).

Elliott, B., 'Loudon, John Claudius (1783–1843)', *Oxford DNB* (Oxford, 2004); online edn <http://www.oxforddnb.com/view/article/17031>, accessed 21 September 2017.

Fairclough, O., *The grand old mansion: the Holtes and their successors at Aston Hall 1618–1864* (Birmingham, 1984).

Frostick, E. and Harland, L., *Take heart: people, history & change in Birmingham's heartlands* (Birmingham, 1993).

Greig, H., '"All together and all distinct": public sociability and social exclusivity in London's pleasure gardens, ca. 1740–1800', *The Journal of British Studies*, 51/1 (2012), pp. 50–75.

Hollen-Lees, L., 'Urban networks', in Daunton (ed.), *The Cambridge urban history of Britain*, pp. 59–94.

Hopkins, E., *The manufacturing town: Birmingham and the Industrial Revolution* (Stroud, 1998).

Jones, P.M., 'Industrial enlightenment in practice: visitors to the Soho manufactory, 1765–1820', *Midland History*, 33/1 (2008), pp. 68–96.

Jones, P.M., *Industrial enlightenment – science, technology and culture in Birmingham and the West Midlands, 1760–1820* (Manchester, 2008).

Laird, M. and Weisberg-Roberts, A., *Mrs Delany & her circle* (New Haven and London, 2009).

Longstaffe-Gowan, T., *The London town garden, 1700–1840* (New Haven & London, 2001).

Mason, S., *The hardware man's daughter* (Chichester, 2005).

Mitchell, E., 'Duddeston's "Shady walks and arbours". Vauxhall Gardens, Birmingham c.1745–1850', BA dissertation (University of Birmingham, 2009).

Money, J., *Experience and identity: Birmingham and the West Midlands 1760–1800* (Manchester, 1977).

Montmorency, de J., 'Adderley, Charles Bowyer, first Baron Norton (1814–1905)', rev. H.C.G. Matthew, *Oxford DNB* (Oxford, 2004); online edn <http://www.oxforddnb.com/view/article/30341>, accessed 21 September 2017.

Rackham, O., *Trees and woodland in the British landscape* (London, 1976).

Reid, D., 'Labour, leisure and politics in Birmingham, ca 1800–1875', PhD thesis (University of Birmingham, 1985).

Reid, D., 'Playing and praying', in Daunton (ed.), *The Cambridge urban history of Britain*, pp. 745–807.

Schnorrenberg, B. Brandon, 'Delany, Mary (1700–1788)', *Oxford DNB* (Oxford, 2004); online edn <http://www.oxforddnb.com/view/article/7442>, accessed 8 October 2016.

Simmons, I.G., *An environmental history of Great Britain* (Edinburgh, 2001).

Stephens, W.B. (ed.), *A history of the county of Warwick, vol. vii, the city of Birmingham* (London, 1964).

Stobart, J., 'Selling (through) politeness: advertising provincial shops in eighteenth-century England', *Cultural and Social History*, 5/3 (2008), pp. 309–28.

Stobart, J., Hann, A. and Morgan, V., *Spaces of consumption, leisure and shopping in the English town, c. 1680–1830* (Abingdon, 2007).

Strong, R., *The renaissance garden in England* (London, 1979).

Symes, M. and Haynes, S., *Enville, Hagley, The Leasowes: three great eighteenth century gardens* (Bristol, 2010).

Taigel, A. and Williamson, T., *Parks and gardens* (London, 1993).

Taylor, K., 'The oldest surviving pleasure garden in Britain: Cold Bath, near Tunbridge Wells in Kent', *Garden History*, 28/2 (2000), pp. 277–82.

Uings, J., 'Gardens and gardening in a fast-changing urban environment: Manchester 1750–1850', PhD thesis (Manchester Metropolitan University, 2013).

*Vauxhall revisited: pleasure gardens and their publics, 1660–1860* (Conference, Tate Britain, 2008).

# 5

## Enterprising women: shaping the business of gardening in the Midlands, 1780–1830

*Dianne Barre*

Nurserymen played an important role in providing an ever increasing variety of plants for gardens and landscapes (Plate 5.1), but there has been no major publication on this topic since John Harvey's pioneering research, published in 1974.[1] The role of women (as businesswomen and horticulturists) in nurseries is little known, yet women would have had a significant input since many nurseries were family businesses. However, this is challenging to quantify. A start has been made in this study through a systematic search of newspaper advertisements online for a 50-year period focusing on businesswomen in Derbyshire, nearby Cheshire and the Birmingham area.[2] This revealed not only the names of firms, large and small, successful and unsuccessful, but also the names of women and proof that initials before a surname might not always be those of a man. This study starts with Mrs Spinks, a successful Derby businesswoman who used a rather special grotto in her garden to advertise and attract visitors to her shop.

**Frances Spinks**
By the early nineteenth century Derby was a centre for the manufacture of fluorspar ornaments for the home; eight such businesses were listed in 1829.[3] It was a competitive activity with proprietors, known as petrifactioners, dropping out at regular intervals. The range of products was eclectic, including vases, candelabra, inkstands, miniature versions of antique objects such as Cleopatra's Needle, the Warwick and Portland vases and, somewhat less tasteful but no doubt lucrative, models of dogs, horses, cows and sheep. Among these manufacturers were William (d. 1811) and Frances Spinks (1762–1819?), whose Spar Ornament Manufactory was in King Street, Derby, near the Methodist chapel (Figure 5.1). On Mr Spinks's death in 1811 Mrs Spinks, the only spar manufacturer in Derby to advertise in the *Derby Mercury*, took over

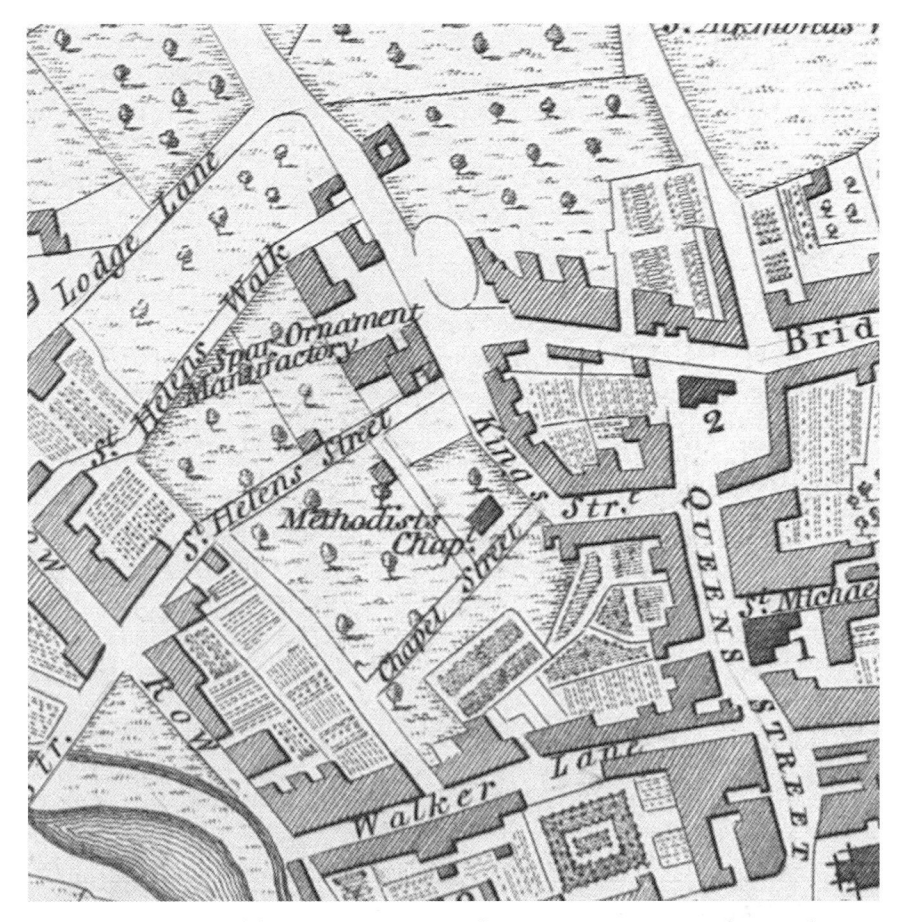

Figure 5.1 Francis Spinks' Spar Ornament Manufactory on King Street, Derby. Detail of map of Derby from *The British Atlas of England and Wales* (1810). Reproduced by permission of the Library of Birmingham

the business and had an inspired idea that she advertised in the newspaper. The advertisement asserted:

> F. Spinks, (widow of the late Wm. Spinks) … intends to continue the Manufacturing of Ornaments in Spar, etc. of every description … She takes the liberty too of soliciting the particular attention of the curious, to AN ELEGANT GROTTO which she now has open for public inspection. It was designed, and partly constructed, by her late Husband, and is just completed, agreeably to the Plan projected by him. The Building is of an octagonal form, with a pyramidal Roof, terminating in a glazed Dome; from whence the light is transmitted internally through polished circular Specimens of choice transparent Fluors, the various and beautiful hues of which are by this means shewn to

great advantage. It receives light also from four Gothic Windows of transparent Paintings on Glass, representing the Four Seasons. The internal decorations of the Walls consist of fine Specimens of the Crystallizations of Minerals, Stalactites, etc. collected at a very considerable expence from various parts of the Kingdom, but particularly Derbyshire. Also a great diversity of Corals, Shells, and other marine Productions, from many different parts of the World. And opposite the Entrance, is a curious Chimney-piece supported by Columns of Alabaster cut in diamonds.[4]

Grottos were expensive follies for a private pleasure garden or a landscape park, usually placed by water (Figure 5.2). This grotto, in a garden behind the manufactory, would have been an attraction and curiosity because most people would not have seen one *in situ*, other than those who had visited major parks such as Chatsworth, Stowe and Stourhead.[5] Mrs Spinks had clearly left no spar unturned to incorporate all the latest fashions and this gem was available to view at 1s, with children's tickets at 6d. With its 'combination of natural and artificial Beauties', this grotto/summer-house appeared to have been a success, and Mrs Spinks also stressed that 'the Virtuosi will find it an interesting Collection of rare and valuable Curiosities'.[6] Soon afterwards Mrs Spinks announced proudly that it 'has lately been enriched with several additional Curiosities' at no extra

Figure 5.2 Restored late nineteenth-century grotto in Derwent Gardens, Matlock Bath, Derbyshire. Courtesy Dianne Barre

cost to view.⁷ An apparently redoubtable lady now aged 50, at the same time as continuing to run her husband's business she publicly announced that she had no connection with a Mr T. Spinks's shop, 'lately opened in Queen Street'.⁸ Thomas Spinks was her brother-in-law and in the next issue of the newspaper he riposted, using practically identical words, to repudiate any connection with 'Mrs F. Spinks's Manufactory'.⁹ Frustratingly, the details of this family quarrel or business rivalry are not known.

Nothing then appeared until 21 April 1814, when 'Frances Spinks' (note the increased confidence, no longer just 'F. Spinks, widow') announced that she had embellished her shop with a new range of ornaments 'comprising great variety of natural and artificial Curiosities'.¹⁰ These included 'a choice selection of Busts, Statues etc. of distinguished Personages, as well as a copious variety of Chimney Ornaments, Devices, Artificial Fruit and other Ornaments of Spar, Marble and Gypsum of every description'.¹¹ She reiterated again that she had no connection whatever with Thomas Spinks. Then, on 13 July 1815, she announced a further attraction for visitors and customers besides the grotto, 'the beauty of which has been universally admired and approved'.¹² This new attraction was a decorated room in her premises that contained: 'Superb Paper Hangings *Of the finest French Manufacture*, on which are displayed in admirable style, *Correct Representations of the Principal Architectural Beauties* IN PARIS, With beautiful Scenery on the River Seine etc. for which no additional charge will be made.'¹³ Since the continent had been open for travellers and tourists only after the defeat of Napoleon in 1814, this was truly an inspirational piece of marketing for a small provincial town such as Derby. The wallpaper would have been the panoramic scene 'Les Monuments de Paris', after a design by Jean Broc, manufactured by Dufour and Leroy *c.*1812–14; in fact almost hot off the press and tremendously fashionable.¹⁴

The next notice in the *Mercury* is three years later, when on 13 August 1818 Frances Spinks decided to offer the grotto for sale as

> That most beautiful and universally admired Grotto, situate in a Garden, the property of WIDOW SPINKS, at the Spar manufactory, King Street, Derby.
> 
> This Grotto is composed of the most elegant, rare and valuable Spars, Fossils etc. obtained from different parts of the County of Derby, tastefully arranged, and the upper part forming a Dome is allowed by competent and experience Judges to be the finest specimen of its kind in Derbyshire.¹⁵

Some suitable aspirant to gentility must have acquired this masterpiece, to be admired by friends and visitors, for in the following year, 1819, Mrs Spinks, now advertising as a 'Dealer in Fossils', announced that 'she has just completed the erection of an ENTIRE NEW GROTTO which is now ready for exhibition in her Flower Garden'.¹⁶ This seems to have been a close copy of the original, but now its display in an appropriate setting was stressed.

> The Grotto is of an octagonal form, approached by a group of romantic rock work, and is enriched and ornamented by a choice and valuable collection of British and Exotic Minerals, including a complete variety of the produce of Derbyshire, comprising Fluors, Spars, Stalactites, Fossils etc. besides a curious collection of rare Shells, Corals, Sea Weeds, and other Marine productions. It receives light through rich transparent Paintings [windows].
>
> The whole forms an Exhibition which she trusts will not be deemed unworthy the notice of the curious and scientific Spectator and she respectfully solicits their attention to it.¹⁷

Sadly Mrs Spinks, then in her late fifties, vanishes from the advertisements. Shortly after, in September 1819, William Johnson, Boot and Shoe Maker, advertised from Mrs Spinks' shop in King Street and on 3 July 1822 the second grotto was for sale, advertised with its 'tasteful arrangement of numerous Shells, Corals, Spars, Fossils etc and of the most curious and beautiful kinds; the Roof terminating in a Dome of Stained Glass, through which the rays of the Sun are transmitted so as to produce the most pleasing effect.'¹⁸ The garden of 5,000 square yards was soon on the market as well, to be disposed of in lots for building.¹⁹

One would like to know more about the indomitable Frances Spinks, businesswoman, entrepreneur and lady of taste. And one would like to know from where the Spinks took their designs for their remarkable grottos. The original impetus might have come from the ready availability of the ornamental spar used in their manufactory – perhaps the use of unwanted or unsuitable pieces. On the other hand they would have needed to buy in the shells and other materials. In Derbyshire at that time the only recorded octagonal grotto was at Alfreton Hall, some 15 miles north of Derby, which was, according to a local historian in 1812, 'built of different mineral productions of all that diversity of form and colour exhibited by the mineral substances of the Peak. It is of an octagonal figure and painted within are several representations of scenes in Walton's "Angler"'.²⁰ This is the only known description of a building that may have been designed by the famous Derbyshire geologist and grotto builder White Watson.²¹ It has similarities to the description of Mrs Spinks' example. The only other example of a grotto advertised in a newspaper as open for public display at this period was at Cheltenham in July 1819, at Moore End Cottage on the Bath Road. This grotto, decorated by an un-named lady, was open to visitors for only a single day.²² Mrs Spinks may well have been a unique combination of businesswoman and grotto designer; more orthodox was the entrepreneurial nurserywoman, with a sound knowledge of the business and of plants.

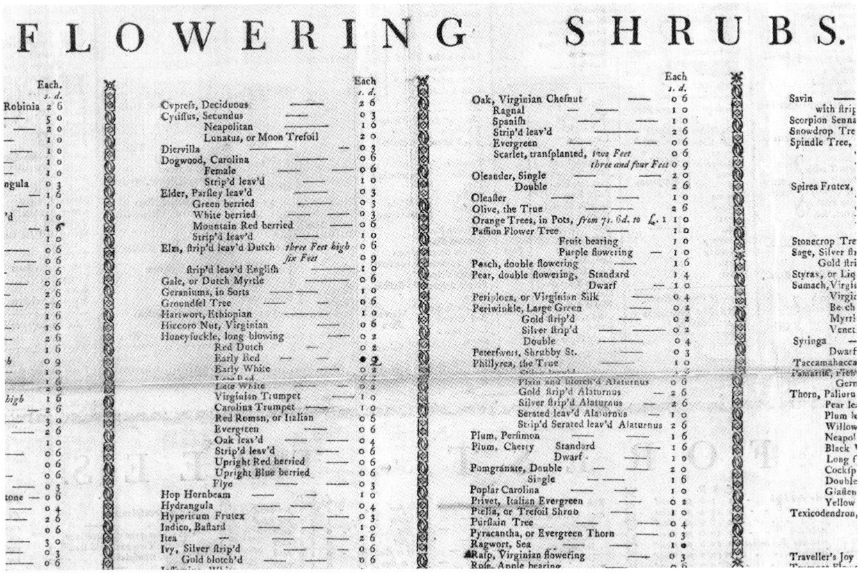

FLOWERING SHRUBS.

| | Each s. d. |
|---|---|
| Cypreſs, Deciduous | 2 6 |
| Cytiſus, Secundus | 0 3 |
| Neapolitan | 1 0 |
| Lunatus, or Moon Trefoil | 2 0 |
| Diervilla | 0 3 |
| Dogwood, Carolina | 0 6 |
| Female | 0 6 |
| Strip'd leav'd | 1 0 |
| Elder, Parſley leav'd | 0 3 |
| Green berried | 0 3 |
| White berried | 0 3 |
| Mountain Red berried | 0 6 |
| Strip'd leav'd | 1 0 |
| Elm, ſtrip'd leav'd Dutch *three Feet high* | 0 6 |
| *ſix Feet* | 0 9 |
| ſtrip'd leav'd Engliſh | 1 0 |
| Gale, or Dutch Myrtle | 0 6 |
| Geraniums, in Sorts | 1 0 |
| Groundſel Tree | 0 6 |
| Hartwort, Ethiopian | 1 0 |
| Hiccoro Nut, Virginian | 0 6 |
| Honeyſuckle, long blowing | 0 2 |
| Red Dutch | 0 2 |
| Early Red | 0 2 |
| Early White | 0 2 |
| Late Red | 0 2 |
| Late White | 0 2 |
| Virginian Trumpet | 1 0 |
| Carolina Trumpet | 1 0 |
| Red Roman, or Italian | 0 6 |
| Evergreen | 0 6 |
| Oak leav'd | 0 4 |
| Strip'd leav'd | 0 6 |
| Upright Red berried | 0 6 |
| Upright Blue berried | 0 6 |
| Flye | 0 3 |
| Hop Hornbeam | 1 0 |
| Hydrangula | 0 4 |
| Hypericum Frutex | 0 3 |
| Indico, Baſtard | 1 0 |
| Itea | 2 6 |
| Ivy, Silver ſtrip'd | 0 6 |
| Gold blotch'd | 0 6 |

| | Each s. d. |
|---|---|
| Oak, Virginian Cheſnut | 0 6 |
| Ragnal | 1 0 |
| Spaniſh | 1 0 |
| Strip'd leav'd | 2 6 |
| Evergreen | 0 6 |
| Scarlet, tranſplanted, *two Feet* | 0 6 |
| *three and four Feet* | 0 9 |
| Oleander, Single | 2 0 |
| Double | 2 6 |
| Oleaſter | 1 0 |
| Olive, the True | 2 6 |
| Orange Trees, in Pots, *from 7s. 6d. to* £. | 1 1 0 |
| Paſſion Flower Tree | 1 0 |
| Fruit bearing | 1 0 |
| Purple flowering | 1 0 |
| Peach, double flowering | 1 6 |
| Pear, double flowering, Standard | 1 4 |
| Dwarf | 1 0 |
| Periploca, or Virginian Silk | 0 4 |
| Periwinkle, Large Green | 0 2 |
| Gold ſtrip'd | 0 2 |
| Silver ſtrip'd | 0 2 |
| Double | 0 4 |
| Peterſwort, Shrubby St. | 0 3 |
| Phillyrea, the True | 1 0 |
| Plain and blotch'd Alaturnus | 0 6 |
| Gold ſtrip'd Alaturnus | 2 6 |
| Silver ſtrip'd Alaturnus | 2 6 |
| Serated leav'd Alaturnus | 1 0 |
| Strip'd Serated leav'd Alaturnus | 2 6 |
| Plum, Perſimon | 1 6 |
| Plum, Cherry Standard | 1 6 |
| Dwarf | 1 0 |
| Pomgranate, Double | 2 0 |
| Single | 1 6 |
| Poplar Carolina | 1 0 |
| Privet, Italian Evergreen | 0 2 |
| Ptelia, or Trefoil Shrub | 1 0 |
| Purſlain Tree | 0 4 |
| Pyracantha, or Evergreen Thorn | 0 3 |
| Ragwort, Sea | 1 0 |
| Raſp, Virginian flowering | 0 3 |

Figure 5.3 Flowering shrubs were a popular choice for the garden. Detail of Brunton and Forbes' *Catalogue of Seeds, Forest-Trees, Fruit-Trees and Flowering Shrubs* (17[76]). Reproduced by permission of the Library of Birmingham, MAP788682

## The nurserywomen

Running a nursery was a skilled and risky business with problems including inclement weather, plant disease, theft and competition, and not a few nurserymen were declared bankrupt. Since most could not afford to buy enough land, enforced moves occurred when leases expired, with consequent quick sale of stock. Financial acumen was needed as well as horticultural skills. Many were family businesses over several generations, with brothers and cousins and extended family with their own nurseries, often fairly locally, which makes identification a minefield, especially where there were common family Christian names. Women members of the family must have been involved at all levels of the business, but only rarely do their names appear. A common theme in newspaper advertisements is for a widow to announce that she intends to continue her husband's business, and glimpses are seen of young and old, of success and failure. Even with help to run the nursery, considerable horticultural knowledge was still necessary, besides the necessary business skills (Plate 5.2). The examples here show women in the nursery trade owning and running a family business as partners and widows. Since advertising was expensive (with a government tax of three shillings per advert), it is rare to find a continuous run of advertisements, but rather the occasional one to mark something special, and from this a tentative picture may be drawn.

An early example is Anne, wife of Charles Sandys (1725–1761). In 1758–9 at Lady-Grove, near Ashbourne, Derbyshire, Charles advertised as a nurseryman offering for sale a large variety of fir trees, evergreens and flowering shrubs (Figure 5.3). He advertised four times in the *Derby Mercury*, which was quite an outlay at 3s 6d for the initial advertisement and 3s each repeat.[23] Charles Sandys was clearly a well-known and respected nurseryman who supplied many of the flowering shrubs for Kedleston (where his brother was head gardener) in 1760.[24] No doubt he was the 'Mr Sands' who supplied cherry trees to Okeover, where the head gardener informed the owner, Leake Okeover, that from this nursery 'if you please you may be fitted with as good plants as [you] can have in the Nurseries near London'.[25] Charles Sandys married Anne Gell (1733–1796) in 1753 and after his death in 1761, left with at least three young children, Anne continued the business: 'She begs leave to assure those Gentlemen, or Ladies, who will do her the Honour to encourage her, they may depend upon her constant Endeavours to serve them in the best Manner, at the most reasonable rates'.[26] Anne Sandys was sufficiently established to supply flowering shrubs to Sir Robert Burdett of Foremarke Hall in 1762 and 1765.[27] However, by 1763 there must have been a temporary 'cash flow' problem, as all the stock was offered for sale and 'for the sake of present Money will be

Figure 5.4 The parkland trees and shrubs at Ashbourne Hall, Derbyshire were typical of the varieties that nurserywoman Anne Sandys supplied (1839 lithograph). Courtesy of Dianne Barre

sold very cheaply'.[28] Yet somehow Anne Sandys managed to bring round the business and went from strength to strength. In 1767 she was advertising for sale 'at her Nursery near Ashborne … A large Quantity of Forest Trees of various Sizes. Likewise all sorts of Fruit Trees, Ever-Greens, Flowering Shrubs, Greenhouse Plants, Seeds and Mats' (Figure 5.4).[29]

By 1773 Anne Sandys had the confidence to describe herself as 'Nursery and Seeds-woman' (an extremely rare example), offering a wide range of trees, shrubs and bulbs 'which are all included in my printed catalogue'.[30] She also offered 'every other Article in the nursery and Seed Business' and asserted that 'notwithstanding what has been insinuated, either through Mistake or Design, that I had left off Business, my Nursery never was in greater Perfection'.[31] In a clever selling point she drew attention to the fact that: 'The situation of my Nursery being in a cold Country [county], consequently the Plants are much hardier, and will flower better than those drawn out of warmer Nurseries.'[32] She was in a position to advertise on behalf of an experienced gardener who wanted a job, with particulars available from her or her assistant Daniel Haywood.[33]

Anne Sandys last advertised on 16 February 1786, when her prices were reduced, so she may have retired soon afterwards.[34] By then she was an established member of the town with her own pew 'in the organ loft of the parish church of Ashbourne for ever'.[35] She had run a successful nursery for 25 years and must have been a very acute businesswoman and knowledgeable plantswoman. Her son John may have continued the business, but information is problematic as other family members ran a separate nursery, also near Ashbourne.

We only know about Mary Ayres of Duffield, Derbyshire, gardener and nurserywoman, through a tantalising single notice in one edition of the *Derby Mercury* in 1835.[36] The background is that her husband Thomas Ayres (1775–1825), gardener to Lord Scarsdale at Kedleston, set up a nursery business at nearby Duffield, where he sold a wide variety of trees and shrubs.[37] His son Thomas (1804–1838) then took over, running the firm as a young man during his father's long illness.[38] Thomas junior seems to have been a very ambitious young man who in 1825 advertised not only as a nurseryman but also a 'Landscaper Gardener', who planned, designed and laid out:

> Parks, Lawns, Lakes, Pleasure Grounds, Parterres, Kitchen Gardens & & [besides designing] Hot-houses, Green-houses, Conservatories, and every other kind of Horticultural Buildings, and The Planting, and general Management of Woods and Plantations, by Contract or otherwise.[39]

In this family business, while Thomas junior concentrated on his landscape gardening practice, his brother John and Thomas (a relation) ran the nursery.[40]

Mary Ayres is never mentioned in advertisements or trades directories, but this was the usual state of affairs for a woman in business. However, as can happen with family relationships, quarrels arose. Thomas Ayres must have been a somewhat over-confident and pushy young man and a family quarrel seems to have erupted in 1835. His mother Mary, wife of Thomas Ayres senior, had been left the nursery business by her husband for her lifetime.[41] In 1835 'Mrs Mary Ayres, Gardener', inserted a public notice in the *Derby Mercury* that shows that she ran the business side of the nursery:

> All Persons, who are now, or hereafter may by indebted to MRS MARY AYRES, of Duffield, in the county of Derby, Gardener, are respectfully requested not to pay the accounts to her Son, Mr. THOMAS AYRES, of the same place, gardener, he not being authorized to receive them; nor in any way connected with her, in her business. The receipts of Mrs Ayres alone, or of such person as she shall authorize in writing, will only be a valid discharge.[42]

Intriguingly, a hasty recantation appeared in the next issue of the *Mercury*, where Thomas Ayres's solicitor inserted an announcement that Mrs Ayres had asked for the following notice to be printed: 'The Notice dated Duffield, that appeared in the Mercury of the 22nd instant, was inserted thro' *inadvertence and mistake*.'[43] The notice affirmed that 'The business of Landscape Gardener, Nursery and Seedsman, continue as heretofore under the "name and conduct of Mr. THOS. AYRES".[44] Goodness knows what lay behind this rather bitter exchange. Thomas Ayres junior died in 1838 and his brother John sold the remaining stock and left the business in 1841, when the Ayres vanish from print.[45]

William Hodgkinson was a prosperous gardener and nurseryman in Derby by at least the 1740s, and on his death in 1763 his nephew and partner Joseph Yates (1735–1786) took over and enlarged the business to become gardener, seedsman and nurseryman.[46] Then, on Yates' death in 1786, his sister Lydia and nephew Joseph Wilson took over the business. The notice in the *Derby Mercury* of 30 November 1786 shows the importance of Lydia Yates in the business:

> LYDIA YATES, (sister of the late Mr JOSEPH YATES, Nurseryman and Seedsman in Derby deceased) and JOSEPH WILSON, (his Nephew) beg to return Thanks for all Favors conferred on the said Mr. Yates, and to solicit a Continuance, as the Business, in all its Branches, will be carried on by them, as usual.
>
> N.B. All Persons indebted to the late Mr. Yates, are desired to pay their respective Debts to his Sister above-mentioned, being the sole Executrix of her late Brother's Will. And all Persons who have any Demands upon his estate and effects, are desired to send an Account of the same to the said LYDIA YATES.[47]

Figure 5.5 Pineapples were difficult and expensive to grow, requiring a skilled nurseryman. *Pineapple (Ananas comosus) with metamorphosis of bamboo page (Philaethria dido) and twice-stabbed lady bird beetle (Chilocorus cacti)* by Maria Sibylla Merian (1647–1717). GRI Digital Collections courtesy of Getty's Open Content Programme

After this announcement, however, she did not appear again. Joseph Wilson (or one of his sons) must have been a skilled nurseryman, advertising 500 'pine apple plants' for sale on 31 August 1825 (Figure 5.5).[48] These were difficult and very expensive to grow, so this advertisement was also a statement of professional skill. Their nursery was also laid out to appear as attractive as possible and included a huge ornamental weeping ash, which was purchased by the duke of Devonshire following Joseph Wilson's death in 1830.[49] This was moved to Chatsworth to the admiration of all and was no doubt a very good advertisement for the nursery.[50] Wilson or his son, another Joseph, gained a reputation for not only selling but also for setting out shrubs and plants in the landscape.[51]

After Joseph Wilson's death his wife Mary and sons continued the nursery business as 'Joseph, Joshua and Thomas Wilson', usually just referred to as 'Messrs Wilson'. Joseph Wilson junior died in 1832 at the age of 41.[52] In August 1838 Mary Wilson senior sold the business to her son William (1790–1841), his wife Mary and a William Sadler, who became 'Messrs Wilson and Sadler'.[53] This prompted Joshua Wilson to branch out on his own with ambitious aspirations as 'Landscape and Ornamental Gardener', announcing on 29 August 1838 that:

> Joshua Wilson Nursery and Seeds-man, and Landscape Gardener, Green Lane, Derby' thanked past customers 'for the extensive and liberal patronage with which his Mother, Brothers and Sisters, and himself, have been honoured during the superintendence of the old-established concern, since the decease of his father.[54]

When William Wilson died in 1841 his widow Mary moved out of the business, leaving it to William Sadler. The notice in the *Mercury* on 16 November 1842 stated that the 'partnership between ... Mary Wilson the younger, and William Ford Sadler, as Nursery and Seedsmen at Derby was dissolved ... by mutual consent'.[55] Sadler was to continue to run the business with his son-in-law, Joseph Wilson. The firm of Wilson and Sadler then seems to have lurched from crisis to crisis. Following the death of Mrs Wilson senior in 1847 they were forced to move the stock of their large nursery at Lady Grove, adjoining Derby Arboretum, as the land was to be sold for building purposes. Since the sale notice specifically stated that 'in consequence of the decease of Mrs Wilson, the elder, the land adjoining the Arboretum will have shortly to be sold for building purposes' it would appear that Mrs Wilson senior in fact owned the land on which the nursery stood and rented it out to the nursery.[56] The land was advertised as being in a very attractive and advantageous position: the 'site is altogether admirably adapted for Terrace Houses of a high class ... or for detached Villas, and the immediate contiguity of the celebrated Arboretum ... will give to the residences the increased value ...'.[57]

Plate 1.1 Herefordshire's water meadows were celebrated by Birmingham artist David Cox (1783–1859). Cox moved to Hereford in 1813 because it was the heartland of the picturesque and close to Wales. This image of pollard willows beside a feeder for the water system on the Lugg Meadows is from his *Treatise on Landscape Painting* (1813). Courtesy of the University of Birmingham

Plate 1.2 Thomas Gainsborough painted *Beech Trees at Foxley* in *c.*1760 for amateur artist Robert Price (1717–1761), the father of Uvedale Price. © Beech Trees at Foxley, Herefordshire, with Yazor Church in the Distance, 1760 (w/c on paper), Gainsborough, Thomas (1727–1788)/Whitworth Art Gallery, The University of Manchester, UK/ Bridgeman Images

Plate 1.3 Many contemporary artists, such as Thomas Hearne, followed in William Gilpin's footsteps and made a tour of the river Wye. *Goodrich Castle on the Wye*, Thomas Hearne, *c.*1785. Yale Center for British Art, Paul Mellon Collection. Digital image courtesy of Yale's Open Access Policy

Plate 2.1 Watercolour by William Shenstone of his ferme ornée, or ornamented farm, at The Leasowes, with his house in the distance. From William Shenstone's copy-book, reproduced with permission of Wellesley College, Margaret Clapp Library, Special Collections. English Poetry Collection, MS 34

Plate 2.2 The South Cascade at The Leasowes, depicted in a watercolour by Shenstone. From William Shenstone's copy-book, reproduced with permission of Wellesley College, Margaret Clapp Library, Special Collections. English Poetry Collection, MS 34

Plate 2.3 A gothic feature in the The Leasowes landscape: Shenstone created the Ruinated Priory from the remains of St Mary's Abbey at Halesowen and rubble from his farm. Shenstone's house can be seen in the background. R.W. Boodle, Worcestershire Scrapbook, Vol. II, 1903, by permission of the Library of Birmingham

Plate 3.1 *A View of the Upper Works of Coalbrook Dale, in the County of Salop* (George Perry and Francis Vivares, 1758) not only shows the Darby houses on the hillside but also illustrates in the foreground the cast-iron cylinder for which the Coalbrookdale company was famous. © The Ironbridge Gorge Museum Trust (AE185–769)

Plate 3.2 *The South West Prospect of Coalbrook-Dale, and the Adjacent Country* (Thomas Smith and Francis Vivares, 1758), showing the Darby gardens rising up the hillside. © The Ironbridge Gorge Museum Trust (AE185–773)

Plate 3.3 In William Williams' *Afternoon View of Coalbrookdale* (1777), visitors view the sublime nature of industry and landscape in the Severn Gorge. © Image supplied by Shropshire Council, Shropshire Museums

Plate 4.1 *Vauxhall Gardens, Saltley, 1850*, depicted on the eve of closure by J. Pedley. Photograph © Birmingham Museums Trust

Plate 5.1 The increasing variety of plants for the garden is illustrated in Jane Loudon's *The Ladies Flower-Garden of Ornamental Bulbous Plants* (1841). Reproduced by permission of the Cadbury Research Library: Special Collections, the University of Birmingham

*Right:* Plate 5.2 Curtis' *Botanical Magazine* (1787) illustrated many of the plants nurserymen used their skill to raise. Reproduced by permission of the Cadbury Research Library: Special Collections, the University of Birmingham

N.° 14

Published as the Act directs by W. Curtis Botanic Garden Lambeth Marsh 1787.

Sowerby del. fc.

Plate 6.1 Bricks moulded to emulate Italian terracotta in a drinking fountain (1894) at Burslem Park. Courtesy of Paul Rabbitts

Plate 6.2 Pulhamite cascade and rockery (*c.*1894) at Burslem Park, illustrating the illusory use of industrial materials. Courtesy of Paul Rabbitts

Plate 6.3 A Lion Foundry No. 23 cast-iron bandstand, Handsworth Park, Birmingham, which was acquired in 1903. Courtesy of Paul Rabbitts

*Right top* Plate 7.1 The grounds at Moseley Hall depicted by Humphry Repton before his suggested improvements. *Humphry Repton, Mosely* [sic] *Hall near Birmingham, a seat of John Taylor, Esqr.* (1792). Courtesy of the Frances Loeb Library, Harvard University Graduate School of Design

*Right bottom* Plate 7.2 Repton's suggested improvements for Moseley Hall revealed. *Humphry Repton, Mosely* [sic] *Hall near Birmingham, a seat of John Taylor, Esqr.* (1792). Courtesy of the Frances Loeb Library, Harvard University Graduate School of Design

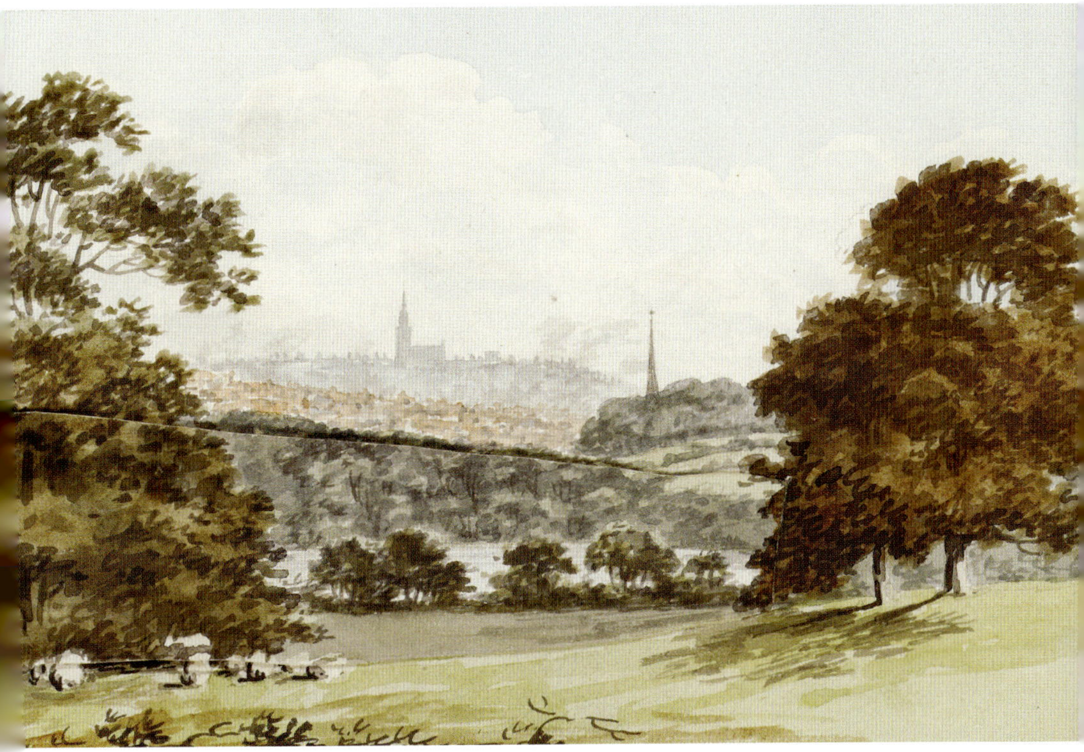

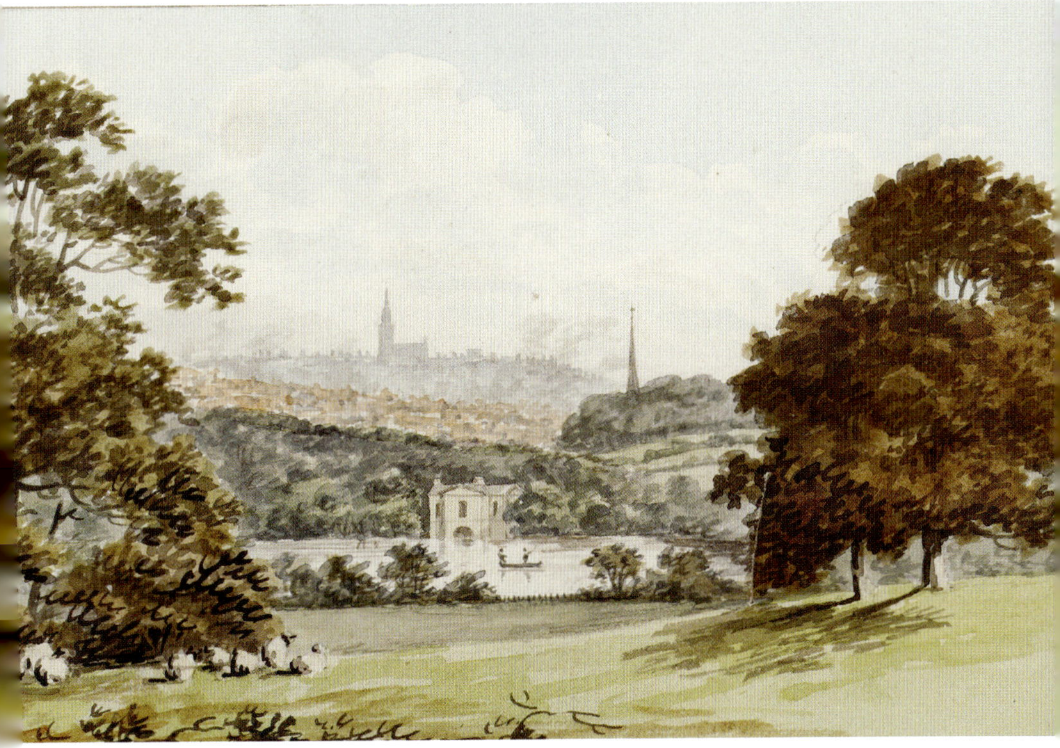

Uffculme - From Meadows.

Plate 7.3 A postcard showing the tall palm-house that was a distinctive feature of Richard Cadbury's Uffculme. Courtesy Mary Harding

Plate 8.1 Plan of *Cropwood Open-Air School*, Blackwell, by Bernard Sleigh (1922). Courtesy Birmingham Civic Society

*"That's fresh air,"* she said. *"Lie on your back and draw in long breaths of it"*

Plate 8.2 *The Secret Garden*, by Frances Hodgson Burnett (1911), illustrated by Charles Heath Robinson, explored the therapeutic effect of the garden on one child's health. Reproduced by permission of the Cadbury Research Library: Special Collections, the University of Birmingham

Plate 9.1 Extensive views from Milton's Seat of the parkland and country beyond at Hagley Hall, Worcestershire. © copyright Joe Hawkins

Plate 9.2 George Lyttelton, 1st Baron Lyttelton, the creator of Hagley's landscape. A portrait by Benjamin West, PRA, c.1772. Courtesy 12th Viscount Cobham

Plate 9.3 The restored Palladian Bridge at Hagley. © Joe Hawkins

George Rogers, who died in 1799, was an inn keeper and nurseryman.[58] He left his house and leases on his nurseries at Nun Garden and Handbridge, Chester, together with his nursery stock, to his wife Sarah, and after her death to her son John Gorton, who changed his name to Rogers.[59] John Rogers ran a nursery at Handbridge and a seed shop in Upper Bridge Street, Chester, dying at the age of 64 in May 1825. His widow Mary Rogers immediately announced that she would be carrying on the business.[60] She does not appear to have had children and presumably she was middle-aged by then. Thereafter she advertised the nursery and shop every year in the *Chester Chronicle* until 1842 and less frequently in the *Chester Courant*.[61] Her nursery stock of trees, shrubs and fruit bushes was extensive and in 1839 she stressed that 'Orders from 1 to 20,000 may be had at a short notice'.[62] With the ability to see a promising new market, in November 1840 she announced that 'Railway contractors will meet with a good opportunity this season of purchasing good Thorns [quickthorn] etc. etc.'.[63] These would be needed in large numbers by railway companies to form an impenetrable hedge along new railway tracks.

By 1842, when Mary Rogers had been running the business successfully in her name for 17 years, clearly problems arose. She advertised as usual in November 1842, adding that she was 'on the point of reducing her Establishment, and clearing a quantity of land … M.R. intends to carry on the Seed and Nursery Business as usual'.[64] Then there was the rather ominous announcement in 1843 that the nursery stock and household furniture of 'Mary Rogers, gardener etc' were to be sold at auction.[65] She may have been ill, or simply wanted to retire; she died in September 1846. Her considerable remaining nursery stock was auctioned in 1847 and purchased by Thomas Forrest, a nurseryman who leased the nursery grounds.[66] It clearly did not occur to the auctioneer that a woman might have owned the nursery, as he stated that the premises were 'late in the occupation of Mr Rogers, Nurseryman'.[67]

There is less information about another successful nurserywoman in Chester at the same period. Thomas Weaver, nurseryman, seedsman and gardener, took over Mrs Rogers' rented nursery at Handbridge, Chester in October 1801.[68] Thomas Weaver must have died in 1828, because by January 1829 his widow Hannah had taken over the business.[69] By 1839 she was stressing that this was an 'old established nursery' with a large stock of plants and seeds.[70] Her advertisements illustrate the difficulties of tracing nurserywomen, as she advertised as 'H. Weaver and Son' and then 'H. and J. Weaver'. Without the initial announcement of 1829 it would not be known that 'H. Weaver' was in fact a woman.[71] The business was clearly successful and was continued by her son, J. Weaver.

Sometimes mother and son partnerships in the nursery business could be problematic. Martha Littler was the widow of Joseph Littler, nursery- and seedsman, who ran his nursery at Over, near Winsford, Cheshire from at least 1815.[72] He sold the usual trees and shrubs but also seems to have specialised in bulbs, espaliered fruit trees and herbaceous plants, as advertised in October 1824.[73] He died very soon after this, perhaps unexpectedly, and his widow Martha announced that she intended to continue the business with the assistance of her son.[74] However, by September 1826 her son Joseph Littler had set up his own nursery business specialising in bulbs and seeds.[75] In late December 1826 Martha announced that she was running the Over nursery by herself.[76] In the event this turned out to be wise, because by July 1829 Joseph's business had failed and he was declared insolvent. He may have been a poor businessman, because he assigned all his goods to one creditor to whom he owed £300. Although absolved of any intention of fraud, it was noted specifically in the newspaper report that he owed a hefty £47 for drink.[77] Martha Littler continued alone, her last advertisement appearing on 2 November 1832.[78] Then sadly in June 1833 Martha Littler 'assigned and transferred all her estate and effects to Trustees' to arrange payment to her creditors.[79] She then vanished from newsprint, having run the nursery for nine years.

In other cases widows had no interest in continuing their husband's business. Jacob Moore (1756–1826) ran a business as nurseryman, seedsman and florist of Warstone Lane, Birmingham, from 1790 until his death late in 1826 at the age of 70.[80] The nursery was left to his wife, who decided to sell the business as soon as possible. Quickly she sold off 1200 hothouse plants in October 1827, probably because she lacked the necessary skill or resources to deal with this specialised aspect of the nursery.[81] Shortly afterwards, the nursery land and premises were announced as being on the market and suitable for building land.[82] In April 1828 'freehold building land, nursery ground and stock' were for auction and Mrs Moore was trying to sell off more nursery stock, which she offered at half price in May, as the land had to be cleared by the end of September for building.[83] Mrs Moore was about to move away when unsold stock at 'Mrs Moore's Nursery' was yet again offered for sale in September and November 1828, by which time she had been running the business for two years.[84] If she was about the same age as her deceased husband she would have been about 70 and the freehold nursery grounds would have fetched a good price for building plots to support her in her old age.[85] The final chapter came in March 1829, when E. Moore, her son, advertised that he had taken a shop in Constitution Hill, Birmingham, to sell garden seeds and grocery: 'And particularly solicits those Friends of his Mother who so kindly favoured her at the late Nursery, Wharstone Lane, to continue those favours to him (she having declined) [retired] as he is determined to sell good articles, and as cheap as possible.'[86]

Similarly, at Sparkbrook Nursery near Birmingham, where Michael Brookes ran a nursery and seeds business for 40 years until his death in 1826, his widow continued only reluctantly for another year, when the house, greenhouse and nursery grounds were put up for sale.[87] Mrs Palmer, widow of James Palmer, nurseryman of Duffield Road, Derby, also with a shop in Irongate, Derby, continued the business for a very short time. In October 1831 she asked past customers to continue their support 'during the period she may retain the Business in her hands' and while she settled her late husband's affairs.[88] In January 1832 she informed past customers that 'she has disposed of the Nursery and Seed business in favour of Mr John Palmer, whom she recommends as her successor'.[89] At the same time her son John announced he was taking over the business, but the nursery grounds were announced for lease just a month later.[90]

Often women would have a financial involvement with a family firm, and no doubt an active interest in its running, as suggested by an advertisement in 1828. Luke Pope (1740–1825) established a nursery at Smethwick, near Birmingham, in the early 1770s, with a second nursery at Handsworth in 1790.[91] His sons Luke and John became partners and after 1825 Luke junior ran the Smethwick Nursery; however, he died in November 1827, leaving his wife Mary as sole executrix. It was Mary who advertised to call in outstanding debts and who announced that the business had been taken over by Luke's sons.[92]

A search for nurserywomen using local newspapers has produced a handful of names for the nursery businesses operating across the region. At the very least it proves that women were involved with large businesses, but since smaller firms rarely used expensive newspaper advertisements there are no doubt unknown examples. This study used the British Newspaper Archive online, but given that there are not many complete chronological runs of a local paper and there are many yet to come on line this is in essence an introductory trial to find out more about nurserywomen over a 50-year period. The example of Mrs Spinks suggests that this approach could be applied to other professions and trades. Further research is needed for each case study here and this might be attempted at local history centres and record offices using trade directories, nursery catalogues, estate archives and probate wills.

### Notes

1. J. Harvey, *Early nurserymen* (Chichester, 1974). Also M. Hadfield, *A history of British gardening* (1960; 3rd edn London, 1979).
2. I acknowledge with thanks the permission granted by the British Newspaper Archive to quote from the newspapers accessed via the website <https://www.britishnewspaperarchive.co.uk>.
3. J. Pigot, *Directory of Derbyshire* (London, 1829), p. 125; S. Glover and T. Noble (eds) *The history, gazetteer, and directory of the county of Derby*, 2 vols, vol. ii (1829), pp. 425–6. Fluorspar is a

mineral that occurred in a range of colours and was cut and used for decorative purposes in the nineteenth century; at this time it was commonly referred to as spar.
4 *Derby Mercury*, 14 March 1811.
5 For information about grottoes see: H. Jackson, *Shell houses and grottoes* (Princes Risborough, 2001); B. Jones, *Follies and grottoes* (London, rep. 1979).
6 *Derby Mercury*, 14 March 1811.
7 *Derby Mercury*, 25 July 1811.
8 *Derby Mercury*, 25 July 1811.
9 *Derby Mercury*, 1 August 1811.
10 *Derby Mercury*, 21 April 1814.
11 *Derby Mercury*, 21 April 1814.
12 *Derby Mercury*, 13 July 1815.
13 *Derby Mercury*, 13 July 1815.
14 I am most grateful to Gareth Williams, Weston Park, for information and advice about the wallpaper.
15 *Derby Mercury*, 13 August 1818.
16 *Derby Mercury*, 24 June 1819.
17 *Derby Mercury*, 24 June 1819. Admission price was held at 1s per adult and 6d per child.
18 *Derby Mercury*, 30 September 1819; 3 July 1822.
19 *Derby Mercury*, 14 June 1824.
20 C. Bateman, *A descriptive and historical account of Alfreton* (Alfreton, 1812).
21 T.D. Ford, 'White Watson and his geological sections', *Proceedings of the Geologist's Association*, 71/4 (1960), pp. 349–63.
22 *Cheltenham Chronicle*, 22 July 1819.
23 *Derby Mercury*, 27 October 1758; 26 October, 2, 24 November 1759.
24 L. Harris and G. Jackson-Stops, 'When Adam delved: Robert Adam and the Kedleston landscape', *Country Life*, 181/10 (5 March 1987), p. 100.
25 Derby Record Office (DRO): 231/M/E/4836 Martin Leggett, head gardener to Leake Okeover, 28 January 1761.
26 *Derby Mercury*, 28 August and 4 September 1761; my thanks to Sue Gregory for compiling a Sandys family tree and tracing a marriage date for Charles and Anne. Anne Sandys was the daughter of John and Isabella Gell of Carsington, who was baptised in 1733, and was therefore a young widow of 28 when she took over the business. She had six children between 1754 and 1761: John (1754); John (1755–1796) – the first son must have died; William (1757, who became a gardener); Ann (1757–alive 1793); Charles (1759); and Charlotte (1761).
27 DRO: D5054/13/9 Sir Robert Burdett's account book. Entries, 31 July 1762 £2.10.6; 10 June 1765 £15.10.0.
28 *Derby Mercury*, 9 September, 2 November 1763.
29 *Derby Mercury*, 30 October, 13 November 1767.
30 *Derby Mercury*, 15 October 1773.
31 *Derby Mercury*, 12 February 1773.
32 *Derby Mercury*, 15 October 1773.
33 *Derby Mercury*, 15 October 1773. Haywood went on to set up his own nursery at Burslem by 1782 and retired in 1822: information supplied by Sue Gregory.
34 *Derby Mercury*, 16 February 1786.
35 I am grateful to Sue Gregory for details of Anne Sandys' will at Lichfield Record Office (LRO): LRO B/C/11 1793.
36 *Derby Mercury*, 22 April 1835.
37 Ayres established his nursery sometime after 1814 when he was still at Kedleston: *Derby Mercury*, 14 July 1814.

38  *Derby Mercury*, 18 May 1825.
39  *Derby Mercury*, 25 May 1825.
40  Glover and Noble, *History, gazetteer, and directory*, p. 65, lists Thomas as ornamental gardener and Thomas and John as nurserymen and seedsmen.
41  Information from Sue Gregory: LRO B/C/11 1825 the will of Thomas Ayres, 'Landscape Gardener', 18 June 1825. Probate was granted for £600.
42  *Derby Mercury*, 22 April 1835.
43  *Derby Mercury*, 29 April 1835.
44  *Derby Mercury*, 29 April 1835.
45  *Derby Mercury*, 17 October 1838; 17 February 1841.
46  *Derby Mercury*, 11 February 1763. Hodgkinson owned a house with stable and outbuildings in Wardwick, Derby: *Derby Mercury*, 1 January 1740.
47  *Derby Mercury*, 30 November 1786.
48  *Derby Mercury*, 31 August 1825.
49  A house was for sale in 1829 with the special attraction of being opposite this nursery: *Derby Mercury*, 4 February 1829.
50  *Derby Mercury*, 14 April 1830.
51  *Derby Mercury*, 23 July 1818. Wilson's planting at the Heights of Abraham, Matlock; 4 February 1824, pleasure grounds at Wood Villa, Uttoxeter, laid out by Wilson.
52  *Derby Mercury*, 22 August 1832.
53  *Derby Mercury*, 8 August 1838.
54  *Derby Mercury*, 29 August 1838.
55  *Derby Mercury*, 16 November 1842.
56  *Derby Mercury*, 15 December 1847.
57  *Derby Mercury*, 15 December 1847; 16 February 1848. The nursery grounds totalled 23,263 square yards, which increased to 25,691 by 15 November 1848.
58  Harvey, *Early nurserymen*, pp. 110–11.
59  Harvey, *Early Nurserymen*, pp. 169–70.
60  *Chester Chronicle*, 4 November 1825.
61  The story can be followed in: *Chester Chronicle*, 20 May, 4 November 1825; 10 November 1826; also adverts November 1827, November 1828, November 1830, March and November 1831, March and November 1832, November 1833, February 1835, March 1839, November 1838, 1839, 1840, March 1841 and 1842, November 1842; 3 February 1843; 2 October 1846; 17 January 1847; 5 February 1847.
62  *Chester Chronicle*, 22 March 1839.
63  *Chester Chronicle*, 13 November 1840.
64  *Chester Chronicle*, 18 November 1842.
65  *Chester Chronicle*, 3 February 1843.
66  *Chester Chronicle*, 5 February 1847.
67  *Chester Chronicle*, 15 January 1847.
68  *Chester Chronicle*, 23 October 1901. Thomas Weaver took over 'the gardens and nursery, lately in the occupation of Mrs Rogers, situated in Handbridgge'.
69  *Chester Chronicle*, 6 January 1829.
70  *Chester Chronicle*, 29 November 1839.
71  *Chester Chronicle*, 30 January 1829; 29 November 1839; 15 January 1841; 2 December 1842; 16 March 1849; 16 November 1849.
72  *Chester Chronicle*, 27 October 1815.
73  *Chester Chronicle*, 12 October 1824.
74  *Chester Chronicle*, 16 November 1824.

75  *Chester Chronicle*, 26 September 1826.
76  *Chester Chronicle*, 29 December 1826.
77  *Chester Chronicle*, 11 August 1829.
78  *Chester Chronicle*, 2 November 1832.
79  *Chester Chronicle*, 7 June 1833.
80  *Birmingham Journal*, 18 November 1826.
81  *Aris's Birmingham Gazette*, 1 October 1827.
82  *Aris's Birmingham Gazette*, 29 October 1827.
83  *Aris's Birmingham Gazette*, 7 April, 5 May 1828.
84  *Aris's Birmingham Gazette*, 22 September, 10 November 1828.
85  *Aris's Birmingham Gazette*, 5 May 1829.
86  *Aris's Birmingham Gazette*, 2 March 1829.
87  *Aris's Birmingham Gazette*, 23 October 1826; 8 October 1827.
88  *Derby Mercury*, 6 October 1831.
89  *Derby Mercury*, 4 January 1832.
90  *Derby Mercury*, 15 February 1832.
91  Harvey, *Early Nurserymen*, pp. 95, 104.
92  Harvey, *Early Nurserymen*, p. 104; *Aris's Birmingham Gazette*, 21 February, 21 March 1825; 5 November 1827; 11 February 1828.

## Bibliography
*Primary sources*
Derby Record Office (DRO)
    231/M/E/4836, Martin Leggett, head gardener to Leake Okeover, 28 January 1761
    D5054/13/9, Sir Robert Burdett's account book. Entries 31 July 1762 £2.10.6; 10 June 1765 £15.10.0.
Lichfield Record Office (LRO)
    B/C/11 1793, Will of Anne Sandys
    B/C/11 1825, Will of Thomas Ayres, 'Landscape Gardener', 28 June 1825

*Newspapers*
Accessed via The British Newspaper Archive online at <http://www.britishnewspaperarchive.co.uk>
*Aris's Birmingham Gazette*
*Birmingham Journal*
*Cheltenham Chronicle*
*Chester Chronicle*
*Chester Courant*
*Derby Mercury*

*Printed primary sources*
Bateman, C., *A descriptive and historical account of Alfreton* (Alfreton, 1812).
Glover, S. and Noble, T. (eds), *The history, gazetteer, and directory of the county of Derby*, 2 vols, vol. ii (Derby, 1829).
Pigot, J., *Directory of Derbyshire* (London, 1829).

*Secondary sources*

Ford, T.D., 'White Watson and his geological sections', *Proceedings of the Geologist's Association*, 71/4 (1960), pp. 349–63.

Harvey, J., *Early nurserymen* (Chichester, 1974).

Hadfield, M., *A history of British gardening* (1960; 3rd edn London, 1979).

Harris, L. and Jackson-Stops, G., 'When Adam delved: Robert Adam and the Kedleston landscape', *Country Life*, 181/10 (5 March 1987), pp. 98–101.

Jackson, H., *Shell houses and grottoes* (Princes Risborough, 2001).

Jones, B., *Follies and grottoes* (London, rep. 1979).

# 6

## Manufactured landscapes: Victorian public parks and the industrial imagination

*Katy Layton-Jones*

Conventional wisdom provides many explanations for the creation and design of public parks in late nineteenth-century Britain. Public health crises, industrial pollution and urban sprawl are identified as triggers for environmental reform, while philanthropy and civic ambition are acknowledged as having incentivised the urban elite to invest in increasingly expansive and elaborate landscaping schemes. This dualism of streets forged by capitalism and parks perceived as the fruits of charity and paternalism has fuelled a critical framework through which Victorian parks are interpreted as compensatory landscapes that atoned for the sins of the cities that surrounded them. Hazel Conway has described the urban parks of the nineteenth century as 'isolated elements, lungs and oases of green, which contrasted with their urban surroundings'.[1] In a purely topographical sense this claim has some validity, as parks provided a spatial interruption to the sprawl of regimented terraced housing, workshops and warehouses. However, public parks were not purely bucolic fantasies. When we venture into parks created during this period we encounter highly complex environments that often celebrate rather than denounce the materials, scale and socio-economic conditions of the industrial age. In parks across the West Midlands are bandstands, water fountains and shelters constructed from cast iron, as well as tea rooms and ornamental bridges built from red brick and decorated with glazed tiles. From the Pulhamite rockery in Burslem Park, Stoke-on-Trent (*c.*1894), to the glasshouse in Wolverhampton's West Park (1896), industrial raw materials and manufactures shaped, and continue to shape, the design and function of our public parks.[2] Using examples from across the region, this chapter examines the manner in which the aesthetics, materials and architecture of public parks were informed by the principles and processes of industrial production.

Although public parks are certainly neither commercial nor brownfield sites, during the nineteenth century they arose most rapidly and prolifically in industrial and commercial towns. As Paul Rabbitts has observed, 'the industrial iron age coincided with paternalist councils creating municipal parks for the industrial terrace-dwellers', and it was local corporations and town councils in the north of England and industrial Midlands that first issued calls for publicly funded parks and gardens.[3] As the nation's cities increased in size and density the contrast between town and country became more acute, prompting not only concerns about public health but also a conscious recognition of the psychological and political functions of green space. In 1833 Robert Slaney, MP for Shrewsbury, made the call that a 'Select Committee be appointed to consider the best means of securing open spaces in the immediate vicinity of populous towns, as public walks calculated to promote the health and comfort of the inhabitants'.[4] He argued that it was 'the duty of the legislature, to afford every accommodation and the means of rational enjoyment to the working classes, upon whom, in so great a degree, the prosperity of the country depended.'[5] Thus, to a great extent, we owe the existence of our Victorian parks to an awareness of the industrialised landscape and its aesthetic departure from the agricultural and natural landscapes of the past. Compounding the growing socio-political currency of parks in the nineteenth century was the appetite for political autonomy that defined the urban provinces from the late eighteenth century onwards. The progressive agenda of Chartism and reform fuelled the parks movement and, in turn, park landscapes helped to forge a meaningful narrative of social progress within sometimes rarefied political debates. In 1966 one of the earliest critical studies of the British parks movement described how 'having thoughtlessly allowed the Industrial Revolution to produce its two main end-products of the industrial town and the industrial worker, the Victorian aptitude for passionate reform was brought into play to attempt to improve at once both physical conditions and souls'.[6] It is perhaps then no coincidence that the Reform Act (1832) and the influential Select Committee on Public Walks (1833) occurred in close succession. The latter heard evidence from representatives from Walsall and Birmingham and, as evidence taken from Mr Theodore Price, magistrate of Birmingham, demonstrates, the Select Committee identified a direct correlation between industry-fuelled urbanisation and the need for parks and gardens:

> Select Committee: 'Is it not your opinion that a great proportion of the humbler classes, shut up for many hours every day in the week, having no other place to resort to on a Sunday except dusty or dirty thoroughfares, and no place but a public-house for recreation, are likely on such an account to be discontented and drunkards?'

Theodore Price: 'I think it would be very desirable and very beneficial, both for the health and morals, to have any place to which they might resort for exercise and recreation; anything like the parks'.[7]

Following the Select Committee, it was the manufacturing and commercial towns that pushed for the committee's recommendations to be implemented. When, in 1840, parliament finally committed public funds for the purpose of creating new green spaces, it was a meagre £10,000, leading the manufacturers and merchants of Liverpool, Leeds, Birmingham, Bradford, Manchester and Newcastle to donate hundreds of thousands of pounds of their own money. Thus, the wealth that paid for park creation, in the form of donations for capital expenditure projects and donations of land, originated in the profits of industrial production. In Birmingham's Botanical Gardens the distinctive alpine rock garden (1895) was financed by the Nettlefold family, local factory owners and screw manufacturers, while in Burslem Park Councillor Bowden donated the distinctive terracotta drinking fountains (1894) (Plate 6.1).[8] The goal for such philanthropists may have been to create naturalistic, sometimes rustic landscapes, but the means of financing them were modern and commercial. Equally, the original park *users* were embedded socially, economically and, therefore, culturally, in industry; they were not rural country bumpkins who ran scared from urbanisation and industrial premises. Rather, they were factory workers, dockhands and journeymen. It is therefore essential that we acknowledge that the minds that took pleasure in these new public green spaces, the minds that found in them opportunities for imaginative play and the indulgence of fantasy, were minds shaped by the industrial world. Furthermore, it would be naïve and certainly patronising to presume that parks were the only environments in which nineteenth-century urban society found satisfaction or interest. New docks, manufactories, museums, libraries, railways and coastal destinations all fed a public appetite for civic pride, diversion and novelty.[9] However, notwithstanding this competition for attention, parks were clearly welcomed and enjoyed across the industrial Midlands and the north of England. Given the central role played in town parks and gardens by industrial materials, and the wide spectrum of environments that appealed to urban residents, we must consider a more subtle interpretation of Victorian urban green spaces than as mere refuges or antidotes to a hostile industrialised landscape.

**Industrial materials**

The most conspicuous evidence in public parks of what we might deem the 'industrial imagination' can be found in the materials of their structures and artificial landscaping. In parks, the role of materials such as iron, red brick, concrete and commercially manufactured tile falls into two main categories, which might be usefully labelled the *illusory* and the *explicit*. In the illusory landscape feature industrial materials were used primarily to support the façade of nature and are thus concealed to perpetuate a fiction. Examples of the *illusory* category include concrete rock formations, cascades and even some cast ironwork that simulated organic forms. By contrast, in many Victorian parks and gardens industrial materials and modes of manufacture were celebrated, displayed or at least referenced explicitly in the landscape. It is with the illusory use of industrial materials that we are most familiar, and perhaps most comfortable, as it does not challenge the narrative of these sites as 'alternative' environments and refuges from reality. There are many examples of modern materials and manufacturing methods being used to such an effect in Victorian urban parks. Concrete-bottomed pools were constructed for the purpose of sailing model boats and increasingly sophisticated coal-fired stoves raised the temperature of public glasshouses to enable the cultivation of exotic specimens. Even the apparently modern macadamised roads and paths that delivered a smooth ride to horse riders, carriage passengers and, eventually, that most modern of urban characters, the cyclist, were laid out to mimic the meandering, serpentine tracks of rural England. Arguably the most effective and extreme examples of the illusory principle in action are Pulhamite 'rockeries'. Using a composite material similar to concrete, the resultant product was employed to especially good effect by James Pulham and Son, after which it acquired its moniker and became known variously as 'Pulham's Stone Cement' and, later, 'Pulhamite'.[10] Pulhamite rockeries were added to public parks and gardens in an attempt to emulate dramatic natural rock formations such as those found in the Alps, Snowdonia and the Peak District, as well as the grand man-made features of estate houses, such as the rockery and 'Strid' (a narrow chasm carrying rushing water) at Chatsworth House, Derbyshire. The intention was that through the manipulation of scale and appearance these false rockeries should 'illustrate' nature to an urban public unfamiliar with rugged and Romantic landscapes.[11] As an article in the *Nottingham Guardian* advised in 1879, such a feature 'should not look toy-like, too artificial or incongruous' and should instead appear permanent and embedded within the wider scheme.[12] The Pulhamite cascade and rockery at Burslem Park (opened 1894) is typical of this illusory use of industrial materials (Plate 6.2).

The use of such features to create false topography was a common device in urban parks and was often a consequence of economic necessity. Constructing features on site was cheaper than purchasing and transporting large, heavy materials, and arrangements could be built in the most confined spaces and to fit around existing features. Although naturalistic in design, Pulhamite rockeries and similarly illusory devices do testify to the ambition to reconstruct, manipulate and even improve upon nature in the service of man. In so doing, they were perhaps more indicative of the industrial mind-set than has been hitherto acknowledged. Furthermore, notwithstanding the impact and importance of such illusory features, the most surprising and revealing use of industrial materials in Victorian parks occurred when they were intentionally conspicuous, often comprising the signature landmark of the site.

Perhaps the most famous and distinctive instances of industrial manufactures within public parks and gardens take the form of ironwork bandstands, park furniture, water fountains and their canopies. The vast majority of these pieces were constructed from cast rather than wrought iron, and so could be manufactured relatively quickly and in multiples. Although fantastical and elaborate in design, they are industrial manufactures, pre-fabricated off-site and transported across the country via the network of railways and canals that underpinned industrial expansion and urbanisation. Thus, in material, function and transportation they were a far cry from the timber-framed cottages and stone grottos to be found in the rural playgrounds of the aristocracy, such as Stowe in Buckinghamshire and Stourhead in Wiltshire. Rusticated features – such as the lodge at East Park, Wolverhampton (1895–6), the tea rooms at West Park, Wolverhampton (1902) and the lodge at Small Heath Park, Birmingham (1878) – were of course also to be found in public gardens, but within the urban park the products of the industrial imagination were certainly as celebrated and valued as those which aped a bucolic past.[13]

Large cast-iron features were typically ordered from a catalogue or pattern book. As such, the chosen product was rarely unique, and versions of each model number were shipped around the world. A mere handful of factories were responsible for the vast majority of ironwork produced for Britain's parks and, of course, seaside resorts.[14] Birmingham had its own local company manufacturing decorative ironwork in the form of Henry Hope of Lionel Street, operational from 1875.[15] In addition, the Victoria Works of Bayliss, Jones and Bayliss, Wolverhampton (founded 1826), provided railings for a number of parks. Of one such product, the company claimed that 'where a cheap, strong, and unclimbable railing is required, it cannot be surpassed'.[16] The spear-like iron railings that encircle West Park, Wolverhampton, were produced at Bayliss, Jones and Bayliss's Cable Street works in 1880. However, despite the West Midlands' heritage of iron production, by the latter half of the nineteenth century the most prolific companies producing decorative cast-iron features were Scottish. Companies on the west coast of Scotland benefited particularly from the discovery of iron-rich black-band ironstone in 1802 and the ready availability of coal to fuel the furnaces. Two of the most influential manufactories responsible for supplying park features across the British Empire were Macfarlane and Co. of Glasgow, also known as the Saracen Foundry, and the Lion Foundry of Kirkintillock. Together these two firms

Figure 6.1 Detail of Walter MacFarlane No. 249 bandstand (1896) in East Park, Wolverhampton. Courtesy of Paul Rabbitts

were responsible for many of the bandstands, drinking fountains, benches and bridges installed in the West Midlands. In 1903 Handsworth Park in Birmingham (known also as Victoria Park) acquired a Lion Foundry number 23 bandstand (Plate 6.3). The elegant 'tracery' of the cast iron brackets beneath the roof is typical of this style of cast-iron ornament. It was certainly playful and elaborate, but this did not necessarily distinguish it from many structures encountered by urban populations on a daily basis. Railway stations, market halls, exhibition halls, railings, bollards, coal cellar plates and even post boxes were equally garnished with cast-iron flourishes, as at, for example, Burton Market Hall (opened 1883) and the Industrial Hall for the Wolverhampton Art and Industrial Exhibition (1902).[17] Conversely, the commercial character of cast-iron features was iterated by the relatively prominent position of makers' names and marks on the finished articles. As occurred with manhole covers and lamp posts, companies used the opportunity afforded by park furniture to announce their businesses, making bandstands and benches arguably the first form of commercial advertising to be permitted in public parks (Figure 6.1).

Cast iron was woven deeply into the urban fabric and, as such, was seen as not merely permissible but apposite for the urban park. In Wolverhampton's West Park in 1880, an iron bridge was constructed by the local firm Messrs. Bradney and Company to a design by the borough engineer, a man charged with

Figure 6.2 An iron bridge (1880) by local firm Bradney and Company at West Park, Wolverhampton. Photograph by Brianboru100. Wikimedia Commons

Figure 6.3 Cast-iron fountain made by Macfarlane and Co. at Hickman Park, Bilston (*c.*1911). Postcard printed with permission of Wolverhampton City Archives, P/2022

constructing bridges and thoroughfares across the urban realm (Figure 6.2). Similarly, the opening of Hanley Park in 1897 necessitated the construction of an iron bridge over the pre-existing Caldon Canal, which bisected the site. Although certainly more decorative than many of the other bridges on the commercial waterway, it was fabricated from the same material. This material connection between the streetscape and the park landscape supports a reading of the latter as being more deeply and intrinsically informed by the surrounding city than has hitherto been appreciated, a point reinforced by the frequent use of decorative ironwork railings to mark the point of transition from the street to the park. One of the consequences of the industrialised production of park features is that the same designs are to be found replicated in a range of locations. They have often acquired distinctive names, sometimes after the benefactor who donated them, or for a more general commemorative event, such as a Royal Jubilee, but they are all, essentially, the same mass-produced article. One particularly popular fountain pattern was found in the Macfarlane and Company catalogue for a period of at least 30 years. Versions made their way into at least two parks in the region: Handsworth Park and Hickman Park, Bilston (Figure 6.3).

When advertising the fountain, the company made implicit reference to the modern and urban character of the communities it would serve, arguing that the

> supply of drinking water to the outdoor population, and also to the lower animals, is now an acknowledged necessity of the changed circumstances of the times and the growing intelligence of the community, encouraging habits of temperance and humanity, and promoting the physical improvement of the people.[18]

Thus, although fanciful in decoration, the Macfarlane fountain was clearly marketed and recognised as a device of practical utility for a city of active, educated and even urbane citizens, a population far removed from the rural wandering denizens of picturesque sketches and watercolours.

Cast iron was a common component of another definitive feature of the Victorian municipal park – the ferrovitreous building. Glasshouses obviously represented a very clear departure from the industrial landscape of the Midlands and north of England in the sense that they created humid microclimates in which exotic, imported specimen plants could survive dark, wet days. Yet, as such weather was frequent in the industrial heartlands, the need for such structures was especially acute in those regions, meaning that winter gardens and conservatories were particularly sought after in manufacturing cities. Perhaps even more importantly, glasshouses, by their nature, protected delicate plants from the smoke-polluted atmosphere of the streets, a factor that had led to the failure of many city-centre botanic gardens in the early nineteenth century, when even hardy British specimens struggled to survive the smog and grime of the industrial city. Despite relocating from the city to the suburbs in the early 1830s, Liverpool Botanic Gardens continued to lose specimens to pollution on an annual basis. The combination of these factors made glasshouses particularly common in manufacturing towns and cities and, as such, arguably definitively 'industrial' buildings. The explosion in popularity of the glasshouse was also due in part to an event that conspicuously celebrated manufacturing, the Great Exhibition of the Works of Industry of all Nations (1851), and the glass structure that housed it.[19] The iron and glass that comprised that famous structure were produced in the Midlands. The iron components were manufactured at Woodside Works in Dudley and at Fox and Henderson of Smethwick, while the vast quantity of glass was provided by Chance Brothers of Smethwick. The Great Exhibition was a display of industrial products hosted in a vast industrially manufactured building, but it inspired the fashion for growing plants in smaller-scale public and domestic glasshouses that prompted an intimate encounter with nature.[20] This was not as antithetical as it may first appear. As Isobel Armstrong observes, the urban conservatory was 'not the pastoral antithesis of commercial glass, but its idealized double'.[21] Utility and fantasy were fundamentally combined in the glasshouse. While providing a practical horticultural solution to plant growers, the building itself created a spectacle of industrial materials and forms. Iron – wrought, or more commonly cast – became increasingly integral to their structural viability and affordability and, even when the superstructure was wooden, as was the case with the glasshouse in West Park, Wolverhampton (1896), the requisite quantities of flat glass panes necessitated industrial production. As such, glasshouses were perhaps more glazed works of civil engineering than architecture in the traditional sense.

There are other industrial materials that are perhaps less often associated with public parks, but which nonetheless testify to the impact of modern tastes and manufacturing techniques upon these landscapes; one of the most notable is red brick. The gradual recognition of Victorian houses as desirable 'period homes' in the late twentieth century has afforded this modest material a level of romantic nostalgia, and the vernacular style of many red-brick structures in public parks leads us to associate them primarily with domestic, somewhat suburban architecture. However, this was not the case in the nineteenth century. In addition to housing, red brick was the stuff of industrial warehouses, railway viaducts and municipal institutions. Bricks were a familiar, relatively low-value building material, but it was this very flexibility and ubiquity that made them invaluable in the park landscape. At the top end of the market bricks were moulded to emulate Italian terracotta, and so paid homage to the venerated, but equally urban, merchants of Renaissance city states. The expensive drinking

Figure 6.4 Carriage bridge (1875) crossing the south lake at Cannon Hill Park, Birmingham. Courtesy of Paul Rabbits

fountains in Burslem Park, donated by the Chair of the Parks Committee, testify to the extent to which civic leaders could so frame their contribution to park landscapes.

Elsewhere, brick and tile was employed much more conventionally to underpin the superstructure of the park landscape. Bridges, tunnels and gateposts were erected from brick and many of them remained unrendered, displaying the modest material of their construction honestly and openly. In Cannon Hill Park, Birmingham, a carriage drive was an integral component of John Gibson's original scheme. The long, sweeping road served to integrate the park into the wider urban infrastructure, albeit in a rather more genteel manner than the average urban thoroughfare. In order for the drive to traverse the extensive south lake, a bridge was required and subsequently constructed from red brick and stone (Figure 6.4). Incorporating a gothic arch as well as a carved stone panel and decorative brickwork, the bridge reflects much of that city's contemporary civic architecture, as well as myriad Victorian Neo-Gothic structures being erected across the country. It was certainly aesthetically considered, and the aesthetic chosen was that of the new urban powerhouses. In addition to red brick, other ceramic materials were employed to lend diversity and practical advantage to parks. Decorative tiles, particularly Minton tiles from Staffordshire, as well as majolica, can be found inside tea pavilions and shelters, and also, in some instances, as paving. The floor of the tea rooms in West Park, Wolverhampton (*c*.1902), is a particularly decorative example, but similar materials were also employed in park lavatories and conservatories. As with red brick, the presence of such materials might suggest the suburban villa rather than the manufactory that produced them, but it is certainly indicative of a confidently urban society that sought to celebrate rather than negate modernity.

**Industrial technology**

Perhaps the most unusual and overlooked industrial 'feature' of parks was the sometimes conspicuous and sometimes subtle evidence of modern technologies in the landscape.[22] The initial presence of machinery in parks was often due to pre-existing railways, such as the one that passed through Handsworth Park. Railways are actually a surprisingly common 'feature' of public parks, as the designation of parks on the then periphery of towns meant that they were frequently bisected by lines leading to the urban centre. There is no doubt that watching the trains was a great attraction for many early park users, especially children. However, the role of technology in parks quickly evolved alongside the ambitions of their designers, and mechanical and, later, electrical devices were employed to striking effect. By the 1870s engines were used to drive fountains, cascades, decorative windmills, lighting and floral clocks. In the closing years of the nineteenth century the role of machinery in parks grew alongside the popularity of fairground rides. In some instances, such as in Sutton Park, Sutton Coldfield, the ride took the form of its more perfunctory predecessor in the shape of a miniature railway. Requiring a significant financial outlay, these large features tended to be permanent, while elsewhere temporary rides were erected only during the high season. Contraptions including Hiram Maxim's Flying Machine, merry-go-rounds and early rollercoasters appeared in urban green spaces across Britain, ensuring that parks were anything but quiet sanctuaries from the noise and speed of modern life.[23] Yet, although the presence of machinery in parks certainly increased, urban public parks had never denied the urban and industrial nature of their location and the urban streets that encircled public parks were an intrinsic feature of their conception and design. Although sometimes obscured by trees to create the illusion that a park was larger in extent, in most instances surrounding streets, homes and even manufactories could be easily seen from within a park. Even when a park was laid out on the periphery of a town, as was the usual practice, the site would be rapidly encircled and the view became progressively more urban.

Figure 6.5 Engraving from the *Illustrated London News* of Wolverhampton's 1871 Royal Agricultural Show. Courtesy Katy Layton-Jones

## Industrial vistas

Much is made in garden history of the 'appropriated' or 'borrowed' view. The desirable view was traditionally rural, and country house estates relied upon them to a great extent, incorporating their parks and wider agricultural lands into the vistas from their parterres. The borrowed view was also utilised in public park design, but in this instance, rather than denying the town, external vistas confirmed the presence and proximity of the townscape and its resident industries.[24] For West Park in Wolverhampton, the urban skyline provided a diverse and attractive backdrop to a relatively flat piece of land that had been used previously for horse racing. In 1871 the town hosted the Royal Agricultural Show on the racecourse site that would become West Park. An engraving of the event, published in the *Illustrated London News*, reveals the proximity of the town and its visibility from the site of the future park (Figure 6.5). Natural topography clearly played a part in revealing the urban prospect, but, if not explicitly intended, the vista was neither denied nor concealed. In fact, at West Park the position from which the town was most visible proved one of the most popular vantage points for picture postcards (Figure 6.6). In Hanley Park, Stoke on Trent, the industrial character of the area was even more

Figure 6.6 Picture postcard (*c.*1910) of West Park, Wolverhampton. Courtesy Katy Layton-Jones

Figure 6.7 The Industrial Hall, Wolverhampton Art and Industrial Exhibition of 1902. Courtesy Katy Layton-Jones

apparent. The close proximity of the conservatory and the distinctive bottle furnaces of the neighbouring Brown Westhead and Moor works (later Cauldon Potteries) created an arresting scene.

On occasion, the architecture and trades of the wider city were brought intentionally into the confines of the park. In the wake of the 1851 Great Exhibition, trade fairs, shows and international exhibitions were hosted in a number of public green spaces, sometimes altering the form and perception of a site forever. In 1902 Wolverhampton again hosted a grand event on the West Park site, although, rather than an agricultural show, in this instance it was the Wolverhampton Art and Industrial Exhibition. In the event, art exhibits were housed primarily in the local art gallery, meaning that attention inside the park complex was focused primarily on the structure and contents of the temporary iron-framed Industrial and Machinery Halls (Figure 6.7).[25] Local firms, such as the lock manufacturers George Price and James Gibbons, exhibited and advertised their wares in guidebooks, bringing the wider town and its produce into the heart of the park.[26] Furthermore, the origin of industrial exhibits extended beyond local trades, as a correspondent for the *Manchester Guardian* observed: a 'large proportion of the exhibits illustrate, of course, local industries, but Manchester, Salford, Rochdale, and other Lancashire towns contribute a good share of the objects on view'.[27] Thus, although located in a park, the event made explicit reference to both a local and a national industrial project. The Wolverhampton Exhibition of 1902 made a considerable financial loss, although there is no evidence that this was in any way due to its being situated in a public park. In fact, there is no evidence at all of any public outcry that a green space was being invaded by a primarily industrial and commercially motivated event. Considering the event's apparent incongruity with so many of the values we presume were sought in public green spaces, we may need to reconsider the lexicon we use to discuss, evaluate and appreciate Victorian urban parks.

## Legacy

Clearly, public parks were not purely bucolic fantasies and so we need to reconsider the suitability of the rural–urban dichotomy and dispense with the paradigm of parks as 'antidotes' to the city. Nevertheless, we should proceed with caution. The dichotomy is powerful and has been forged at least partially in response to political and economic pressures. The recognition that public parks are special and distinct landscapes is just and has helped to protect urban green spaces, with varying degrees of success, since their creation. As the *Handsworth News* reported in 1887 upon the opening of the park, 'to all it means the preservation of a large and important plot of land from the ravages of the speculative builder'.[28] Today, public parks are at greater risk than ever. Their condition may have declined in the 1970s and 1980s, but today they face the very real threat of development. As Hazel Conway and David Lambert noted in 1993, parks 'often occupy land of potentially high development value, [and] the chance to turn them into much-needed revenue has tempted a number of local authorities to consider redeveloping them'.[29] As a non-statutory service they are particularly vulnerable to funding cuts, when other sources of income are increasingly sought to plug funding gaps. Moreover, the principles of historic conservation in Britain work on a hierarchy of age and rarity and, within such a matrix, Victorian parks have historically failed to score highly. In 1996 the introduction of the Heritage Lottery Fund's 'Urban Parks Programme' (and its successor 'Parks for People'), challenged this neglect of public parks and the scheme sought to recognise and reflect the high regard in which communities held their historic parks. There have been some substantial investments and striking successes as a result. Among numerous grants awarded in the Midlands are Handsworth Park's receipt of £4,996,500 in 2001 and Burslem Park's award of £2,194,000 in 2008.[30] It is therefore unsurprising that the public park's role as an alternative environment has been accentuated. However, there is a real possibility that, as a result, we have limited our understanding of urban parks and continue to risk turning them into caricatures of Victorian civic life; at the very least our interpretation of their design, value and legacy is impoverished. A more subtle and rich understanding of their purpose and meaning, and an acknowledgement of their industrial as well as environmental and civic character, could actually help us to defend these historic environments against what are certain to become sustained attempts to develop them.

## Notes

1. H. Conway, *People's parks: the design and development of Victorian parks in Britain* (Cambridge, 1991), p. 7.
2. Historic England, *National Heritage List for England* (NHLE), 1001329 and 1201899, <https://historicengland.org.uk/listing/the-list/>.
3. P. Rabbitts, *Bandstands of Britain* (Stroud, 2014), p. 6.
4. Commons and Lords Hansard, House of Commons Debate, 21 February 1833, vol. 15 cc1049–59.
5. *Ibid*.
6. G. Chadwick, *The park and the town: public landscapes in the 19th and 20th centuries* (New York, 1966), p. 19.
7. House of Commons Papers, No. 448, *Report from the Select Committee on Public Walks; with minutes of evidence*, 23 June 1833, minute 351, p.35.
8. 'Improvements at the Botanic Gardens', *Birmingham Daily Post* 2 July 1894, 4 and M. James, 'Nettlefold, John Sutton (1866–1930)', *Oxford Dictionary of National Biography* (*Oxford DNB*) (Oxford, 2011); online edn <http://www.oxforddnb.com/view/article/101218>, accessed 6 December 2016.
9. J. Stobart, 'Building an urban identity: cultural space and civic boosterism in a "new" industrial town: Burslem, 1761–1911', *Social History*, 29/4 (2004), p. 495.
10. English Heritage, *Durability guaranteed: Pulhamite rockwork – its conservation and repair* (Swindon, 2008), p. 3.

11  H. Taylor, 'Urban public parks, 1840–1900: design and meaning', *Garden History*, 23/2 (1995), p. 206.
12  'Making and planting rockwork', *Nottinghamshire Guardian*, 15 August 1879, p. 2.
13  Parks and Gardens UK, <www.parksandgardens.org>, accessed September 2015.
14  L. Pearson, *Piers and other seaside architecture* (Oxford, 2012).
15  H. Hope and Sons, *A short history of Henry Hope & Sons, 1818–1958* (Smethwick, 1958).
16  Advertisement for Bayliss, Jones, and Bayliss, in *The Engineer* June 1888.
17  J. Gloag and D. Bridgwater, *A history of cast iron in architecture* (London, 1948), esp. pp. 300 and 321–36.
18  *Walter Macfarlane & Company catalogue* (1911).
19  See I. Armstrong, *Victorian glassworlds: glass culture and the imagination 1830–1880* (Oxford, 2008), pp. 141–2. Joseph Paxton's building for the Great Exhibition was dubbed the 'Crystal Palace' by Douglas Jerrold in *Punch*, 13 July 1850.
20  J. Hix, *The glasshouse: the evolution of the glass building from its humble hothouse origins* (London, 2005).
21  Armstrong, *Victorian glassworlds*, p. 134.
22  Conway, *People's parks*, p. 5.
23  K. Layton-Jones, 'A legacy of ambivalence: industrial exhibitions, pleasure parks and urban green space', in Itzen and Müller (eds), *The invention of industrial pasts*, pp. 132–52, esp. pp. 136–43. See also the 'Spiral Toboggan' and 'Water Chute' depicted in H.J. Whitlock & Sons, *Views of the Wolverhampton Art and Industrial Exhibition* (Wolverhampton, 1902).
24  Report of the opening of Stanley Park in Liverpool. *Illustrated London News*, 28 May 1870.
25  'General View of the Buildings for the Great Exhibition which H.R.H. The Duke of Connaught is to open at Wolverhampton in May', *The Penny Illustrated Paper and Illustrated Times*, 1 March 1902, p. 133. See also Wolverhampton Archives and Local Studies, Wolverhampton Art and Industrial Exhibition, Photographs and Images (1902), DX-894/15/1 and Miscellaneous Items (1902), DX-894/15/2.
26  M. Filipova, 'The forefront of English commercial centres: Wolverhampton's exhibitions of 1869 and 1902', in Filipova (ed.), *Cultures of international exhibitions*, p. 145.
27  'The Wolverhampton Exhibition: preparations for the opening day', *The Manchester Guardian*, 29 April 1902, p. 12.
28  Report of the opening of Handsworth Park, *Handsworth News* (1887).
29  H. Conway and D. Lambert, *Public prospects: historic urban parks under threat* (London, 1993), p. 9.
30  Heritage Lottery Fund, Our Projects <https://www.hlf.org.uk/our-projects>, accessed August 2015.

## Bibliography
*Primary sources*
Wolverhampton Archives and Local Studies
    Wolverhampton Art and Industrial Exhibition, Photographs and Images (1902), DX-894/15/1 and Miscellaneous Items (1902), DX-894/15/2

*Printed primary sources*
Commons and Lords Hansard, House of Commons Debate, 21 February 1833, vol. 15, cc1049–59.
*The Engineer* (June 1888).
'General View of the Buildings for the Great Exhibition which H.R.H. The Duke of Connaught is to open at Wolverhampton in May', *The Penny Illustrated Paper and Illustrated Times* (1 March 1902).

House of Commons Papers, No. 448, *Report from the Select Committee on Public Walks; with minutes of evidence* (27 June 1833).
'Improvements at the Botanic Gardens', *Birmingham Daily Post* (2 July 1894).
'Making and planting rockwork', *Nottinghamshire Guardian* (15 August 1879).
'Opening of Stanley Park', *Illustrated London News* (28 May 1870).
*Punch, or the London Charivari* (13 July 1850).
Report of the opening of Handsworth Park, *Handsworth News* (1887).
*Walter Macfarlane & Company catalogue* (1911).
Whitlock & Sons, H.J., *Views of the Wolverhampton Art and Industrial Exhibition* (Wolverhampton, 1902).
'The Wolverhampton exhibition: preparations for the opening day', *The Manchester Guardian* (29 April 1902).

## Secondary sources

Armstrong, I., *Victorian glassworlds: glass culture and the imagination 1830–1880* (Oxford, 2008).
Chadwick, G., *The park and the town: public landscapes in the 19th and 20th centuries* (New York, 1966).
Conway, H., *People's parks: the design and development of Victorian parks in Britain* (Cambridge, 1991).
Conway, H. and Lambert, D., *Public prospects: historic urban parks under threat* (London, 1993).
English Heritage, *Durability guaranteed: Pulhamite rockwork – its conservation and repair* (Swindon, 2008).
Filipova, M. (ed.), *Cultures of international exhibitions 1840–1940: great exhibitions in the margins* (Aldershot, 2015).
Filipova, M., 'The forefront of English commercial centres: Wolverhampton's exhibitions of 1869 and 1902', in Filipova (ed.), *Cultures of international exhibitions*, pp. 137–62.
Gloag, J. and Bridgwater, D., *A history of cast iron in architecture* (London, 1948).
Heritage Lottery Fund, Our Projects <https://www.hlf.org.uk/our-projects>, accessed August 2015.
Historic England, *National Heritage List for England* (NHLE) <https://historicengland.org.uk/listing/the-list/>, accessed 4 November 2017.
Hix, J., *The glasshouse: the evolution of the glass building from its humble hothouse origins* (London, 2005).
Hope, H. and Sons, *A short history of Henry Hope & Sons, 1818–1958* (Smethwick, 1958).
Itzen, P. and Müller, C. (eds), *The invention of industrial pasts: heritage, political culture and economic debates in Great Britain and Germany, 1850–2010* (Augsburg, 2013).
James, M., 'Nettlefold, John Sutton (1866–1930)', *Oxford Dictionary of National Biography* (*Oxford DNB*) (Oxford, 2011); online edn <http://www.oxforddnb.com/view/article/101218>, accessed 6 December 2016.
Layton-Jones, K., 'A legacy of ambivalence: industrial exhibitions, pleasure parks and urban green space', in Itzen and Müller (eds), *The invention of industrial pasts*, pp. 132–52.
Parks and Gardens UK, <www.parksandgardens.org>, accessed September 2015.

Pearson, L., *Piers and other seaside architecture* (Oxford, 2012).
Rabbitts, R., *Bandstands of Britain* (Stroud, 2014).
Stobart, J., 'Building an urban identity: cultural space and civic boosterism in a "new" industrial town: Burslem, 1761–1911', *Social History*, 29/4 (2004), pp. 485–98.
Taylor, H., 'Urban public parks, 1840–1900: design and meaning', *Garden History*, 23/2 (1995), pp. 201–21.

# 7

## 'Almost in the country': Richard Cadbury, Joseph Chamberlain and the landscaping of south Birmingham

*Maureen Perrie*

In the mid-nineteenth century the outskirts of Birmingham contained a number of small landed estates that were still to all intents and purposes in the countryside. As they grew richer, the upper middle classes of Birmingham, like those of other industrialising cities, purchased estates in imitation of the gentry and aristocracy, but, perhaps to a greater extent than their counterparts elsewhere, they chose to acquire small properties in rural areas that were within easy commuting distance of their businesses in the city centre. The proliferation of such estates in the nineteenth century marked a discrete stage in the development of the city's hinterland that has been largely overlooked by historians of the urbanisation process. Garden historians, too, have tended to neglect the small rural properties of the upper middle classes in favour of the larger estates that surrounded the stately homes of the aristocracy.

This chapter examines three estates – Moseley Hall, Highbury and Uffculme – that were located in close proximity to one another on the southern outskirts of Birmingham (Figure 7.1). These estates were associated with three of the city's leading families. Moseley Hall was owned from the late eighteenth century by the Taylor family and leased in the 1880s by Richard Cadbury. Highbury was built for Joseph (Joe) Chamberlain in 1878, and Richard Cadbury built Uffculme on an adjacent site in 1890 after he decided to move from Moseley Hall.

The focus here will be on the landscaping of the estates' parkland, rather than the planting of their ornamental gardens. A major theme will be the relationship between city and countryside: I shall examine the attitude of the owners or designers of these estates towards their proximity to Birmingham and the balance they struck between convenience for commuting, on the one hand, and the desire for rural seclusion, on the other. I shall also explore the

'ALMOST IN THE COUNTRY'

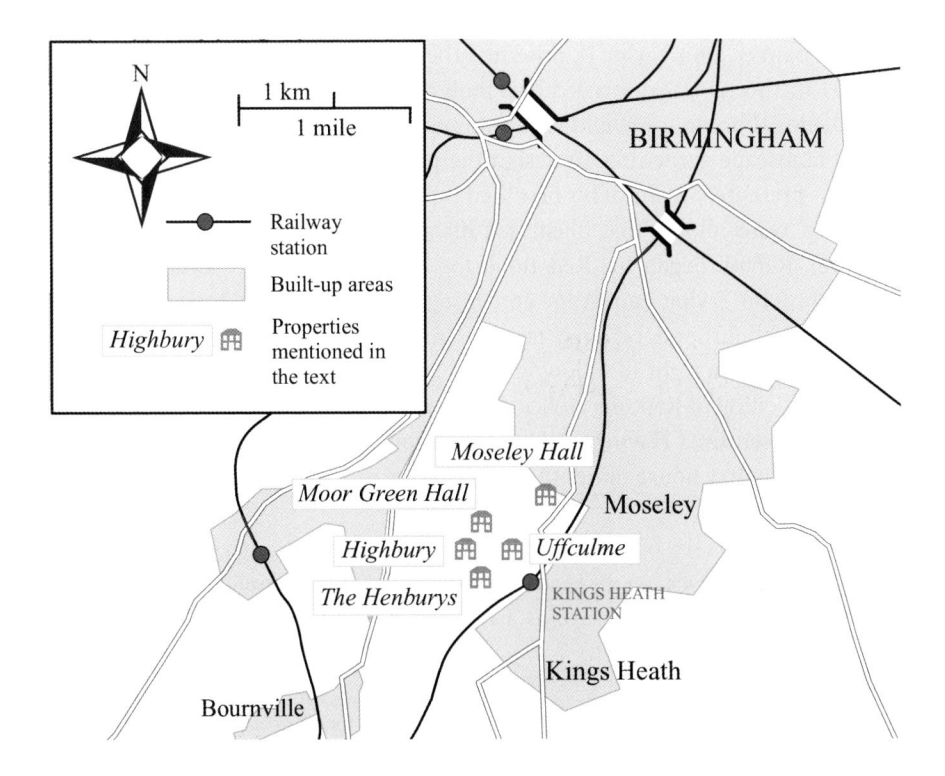

Figure 7.1 Small landed estates clustered on the southern outskirts of late nineteenth-century Birmingham. Map drawn by Catherine Glover

ways in which the estate-owners' attitudes changed as the built-up area of the city expanded, in a process of suburbanisation that threatened the rural character of their homes.

There is rich source material for all of these estates. For Moseley Hall, we have Humphry Repton's 'Red Book' of 1792, in which he set out his proposals for the 'improvement' of the landscape, and also the recollections of Richard Cadbury's daughter, Helen, who lived there as a child in the 1880s. Her biography of her father is a major source of evidence for Uffculme as well as for Moseley Hall, while the Chamberlain family's correspondence not only represents the main primary source for the landscaping of their Highbury estate but also provides supplementary information about neighbouring Uffculme.

## Moseley Hall, 1792–1891: Humphry Repton to Richard Cadbury

The Moseley Hall estate, some three miles south of the centre of Birmingham, was purchased by the manufacturer John Taylor in 1767 from the Grevis (Greaves) family, who had owned it since at least the seventeenth century. John Taylor's son, the banker John Taylor II, inherited the estate on his father's death in 1775. In 1791 the house was destroyed by a mob during the Priestley Riots, and when John Taylor II began to rebuild it he commissioned Humphry Repton, the rising star of landscape gardening, to design the park.[1] Repton's proposal for Moseley Hall was presented in one of his first 'Red Books', incorporating ingenious 'before and after' watercolours that illustrated his suggested improvements (Plates 7.1 and 7.2). Repton began his Red Book for Moseley Hall with some shameless flattery of John Taylor. Landscape gardening, he wrote, is 'very little understood in the neighbourhood of large manufacturing towns, where each individual feels that he has a right to follow his *own taste*, however absurd or ridiculous'.[2] Taylor's soliciting of Repton's advice, however, meant that he was 'excepted from this general censure'.[3] Having flattered his patron, Repton proceeded to praise his home as a country house rather than a suburban property:

> The Character and size of Mosely-hall, altho' its distance from Birmingham might induce me to treat it as a Villa, yet the landed property by which it is surrounded or contiguous makes it rather to be considered as a Family-seat in the Country, which is the real character it ought to assume.[4]

The Moseley Hall estate was already laid out as parkland, enclosed by a wall, so that Repton had relatively few suggestions to make in relation to the landscaping. He recommended that the wall be screened by tree plantations, and that to the south 'the hedge should be taken away to unite the lawns and show the trees in the hedgerows to more advantage'.[5] Elsewhere he proposed that in order to improve the approach to the house some adjoining land currently leased to a tenant farmer and used as arable, should be taken back into the park and converted into pasture.[6] These recommendations were very much in line with Repton's general principles of landscaping, which involved the removal of hedges and the grassing over of arable to convert agricultural land into parkland.

Repton's main concern in his Red Book for Moseley Hall was with the view of Birmingham from the house. This view looked northwards across a pool, to which the ground sloped steeply downward. Because of this, Repton warned,

> we must use the utmost caution in taking away any trees, however they may appear to intercept the prospect; for in so populous a neighbourhood, scarce a branch can be lopped off, that will not let into view some red house or scarlet tiled roof. The Town of Birmingham tho' in some points of view it may be a beautiful object, must be introduced only in part, and instead of removing that ridge of hill, and the trees to the North-west – I should rather advise that a few more be placed upon the lawn, so as to hide more of the gaudy red houses.[7]

Repton clearly found the red bricks and tiles that characterised Birmingham buildings to be particularly objectionable from an aesthetic point of view, since he referred to them twice more in his report. 'To the north-west', he wrote, 'Sir H[enry] G[ough] Calthorps woods, and lawns, make a very beautiful feature, and this view will be much improved by taking away the hedge to set a few trees at liberty, and also some more may be scattered to hide the red part of the town.'[8] He found a spot, further down the slope towards the pool, from which Birmingham looked more 'picturesque' than it did from the house, since

> we must be so low down the hill, as not to see much of that flaming red part of the town, but merely St Philip's church and the neighbouring houses dimly seen thro' the intermediate smoke, which gives it that misty tone of colour so much the object of Landscape-painters. The spire [of St Martin's] rising out of the trees is another charming feature.[9]

In Repton's proposals for the landscaping of estates such as Moseley Hall that were situated on the outskirts of cities he often incorporated townscapes into the views from the park. At Catton Park in Norfolk, his very first commission (1788), he designed a vista towards Norwich that culminated at the spire of the city's cathedral.[10] And at Brandsbury, near Willesden in Middlesex, for which he compiled his first Red Book (1789), he proposed the creation of a view towards London that focused on the dome of St Paul's Cathedral and the twin towers of Westminster Abbey, which he described as 'objects which heighten the value of this peaceful situation by the charm of contrast'.[11] In some circumstances, therefore, Repton considered that proximity to a city could enhance the aesthetic potential of a park by providing views of distant urban landmarks that offset the rural scene in the foreground. Although designing views of commercial or industrial cities such as Birmingham 'presented more difficulties' than in the case of cathedral cities such as Norwich and Hereford,[12] Repton did not shrink from the challenge. He did not try to screen Birmingham entirely from the view from Moseley Hall, but aimed to hide only the redbrick buildings, focusing instead on church spires. Even the smoke of the city added to the picturesqueness of the view.

It is not clear how many of Repton's proposed improvements were actually carried out at Moseley Hall. When the new house was completed it was occupied by John Taylor II, and after his death in 1814 it provided a home for his widow and subsequently for other members of his family. From the 1870s it was let out to tenants.[13] In 1883 the estate was leased by Richard Cadbury of the chocolate-making dynasty. Richard and his brother George had recently relocated their factory from the city centre to a new site at Bournville, and Richard's move to Moseley from Edgbaston was primarily inspired by his desire to live closer to his business. He was also influenced by the proximity of Moseley to the Highgate district, where he was involved in an adult literacy project. According to Helen Cadbury, Richard represented Moseley Hall to his family as a home in the countryside. 'Great was the delight of the children at the thought of living in the country', she wrote. 'Their father brought home descriptions of the spreading lawns, the trees and woods, the open fields and beautiful pool, with its tree-shaded island.'[14] They left Edgbaston's suburban setting ('the pretty roads of Edgbaston, lined with houses and gardens') for rural Moseley, with its village green:

> Close by the green, and sloping steeply from the road at right angles, was the entrance to Moseley Hall. Tall wooden gates, flanked by a little lodge on each side, were thrown open under the shade of spreading trees, and showed a vista of the long drive, winding between woods and fields, down-hill and up again, with glimpses of the pool in the bottom of the valley.[15]

In contrast to Humphry Repton, who almost a century earlier had designed picturesque views of Birmingham city centre from Moseley Hall, the Cadburys revelled in the seclusion of their new home:

Figure 7.2 View from Moseley Hall towards St Anne's Church in a photograph from Helen Cadbury Alexander's biography of her father, *Richard Cadbury of Birmingham* (1906). Courtesy the University of Birmingham

The views from the windows were very beautiful; not a house was in sight anywhere. From the dining-room, drawing-room, and library you looked across a downward slope of lawn and field on to the cool, shining waters of the pool, from which the eye rose again up a green hillside to the thick belt of trees fringing the top of the hill. Above all soared the spire of St Ann's Church.[16]

Trees had now grown up to block the view of the city, and the only visible spire was that of the nearby St Anne's Church in Moseley, which had been built in 1874 (Figure 7.2).

Richard Cadbury does not seem to have done any landscaping during the eight years he spent at Moseley Hall. His daughter refers to his 'hobby of gardening', but this apparently involved only such activities as pruning and weeding, which he carried out before breakfast; he also 'took a great interest in his little farm' – evidently a small dairy farm on the estate.[17] In 1890, when his lease was shortly due to expire, Richard learned that the Taylors planned to sell the estate or cut it up for building purposes. He therefore decided to buy the house with 20 acres of land and donate it to the city as a children's convalescent home, while looking for a new home for himself elsewhere. In reaching his decision, Richard was influenced by 'the peace and beauty of country surroundings' that Moseley Hall offered the sick children, while '[t]he fact of its being within easy reach of the town was an added advantage'.[18]

The site that Richard Cadbury chose for his new home, Uffculme, was in the Moor Green district of south Birmingham (between Moseley and Kings Heath), where it immediately adjoined Joe Chamberlain's Highbury estate, which had been established more than a decade earlier.

## Highbury, 1878–94

In 1878, when he purchased the land for Highbury, Joe Chamberlain – who had made his reputation as a reforming mayor of Birmingham – had only recently been elected as the member of parliament for the city. Joe's decision to build a house in Moor Green was influenced by the fact that his brother Arthur already lived nearby. In 1863 Joe's father, Joseph Chamberlain Senior, gave up the family's cordwaining business in Islington and moved to Birmingham, where Joe had been his representative since 1854 in the screw-making firm of Nettlefold and Chamberlain. Joseph Sr leased Moor Green Hall from the Taylor family of Moseley Hall.[19] Joe's son Austen recalled his grandfather walking across the fields from Moor Green Hall to Moseley, where he took an omnibus or trap into town to his brass-foundry business of Smith and Chamberlain.[20] These new transport links made Moor Green Hall convenient for Joseph Sr to commute to his business premises in the city centre, but it was also a pleasant country home for his wife Caroline. Caroline's daughter Clara

Figure 7.3 Highbury, Joseph Chamberlain's Venetian Gothic house at King's Heath, c.1906. Postcard courtesy Elaine Mitchell

Ryland told Austen Chamberlain in 1914 – by which time the area had become very built up – that her mother 'enjoyed far more than my father our beautiful new house with its lovely old garden and views, and the pleasure of having a carriage of her own, and of making many country drives in the then beautiful country which surrounded us'.[21] These drives went as far as the Lickey Hills in search of spring flowers, and in summer Clara and her mother made 'delightful excursions … to all the neighbouring lanes for wild roses'.[22]

Joseph Chamberlain Sr died in 1874, and his wife the following year; the lease of the Moor Green Hall estate was taken over by their son Arthur, who was also a partner in Smith and Chamberlain. Arthur Chamberlain was married to Louisa Kenrick, the twin sister of Joe's second wife Florence, who died in 1875 leaving him twice widowed with six children.[23] In the circumstances, the presence of his close family at Moor Green Hall made the site Joe chose for Highbury particularly attractive. It was also conveniently situated for Kings Heath station, from which he could travel to Westminster when parliament was in session.

The house at Highbury was built in 1878–80 (Figure 7.3). It was designed by the Birmingham-based architect John Henry Chamberlain – no relation of Joe – in the Venetian Gothic style that characterised many of his other private and public commissions in the city. The grounds were designed by Edward Milner, a landscape gardener from Dulwich Wood in Surrey, who had already acquired a reputation as a fashionable designer of modest-size

Figure 7.4 Landscaping at Highbury displays the curvilinear features favoured by designer Edward Milner. Reproduced by permission of the Cadbury Research Library: Special Collections, the University of Birmingham

estates for *nouveaux riches* industrialists. Milner had begun his career as an apprentice to Joseph Paxton at Chatsworth; he later worked with Paxton on the Crystal Palace after its transfer to Sydenham in 1852, before setting up his own practice. According to his great-granddaughter, Alice Hodges, 'As a designer of parks and grounds, Milner was not an innovator: he followed in the tradition of Repton – Loudon – Paxton.'[24] Edward Milner's eldest son, Henry Ernest Milner, worked as an assistant to his father and continued the practice after Edward's death in 1884. In 1890 Henry Milner published a book entitled *The Art and Practice of Landscape Gardening* that set out the principles that had guided his work and that of his father. He described his gardening philosophy as 'natural picturesqueness', and favoured the imitation of the effects of water on landscape, with undulations and curvilinear features, rather than straight lines, which were 'very rarely found' in Nature (Figure 7.4).[25]

The landscaping of Highbury was fairly typical of Edward Milner's work. The original site was *c*.25 acres of former agricultural land, from which Milner had the field boundaries removed, while retaining some of the hedgerow trees to create an impression of maturity in the parkland. Soon after the design plan was drawn up for the estate, Joe Chamberlain purchased an additional seven acres, which he used as the site for some farm buildings. The decision to conduct farming activity – which was a very common practice on Birmingham suburban estates of this kind – required the erection of additional iron railings in the parkland to contain the livestock.[26] In 1888, when Joe wrote to his American fiancée Mary Endicott to describe her new home, he explained that, 'in the drive the railings separate the gardens proper from the Fields where the cows and horses pasture. I suppose roughly that the House and gardens occupy about 12 acres and the fields about 18.'[27] In 1893 the parkland was extended by 42 acres when Joe rented the western part of the adjacent Henburys estate from Richard Cadbury, who had purchased it the previous year (see below).

This account of Highbury will focus on the landscaping of the parkland, but the property had most of the other elements characteristic of English country estates at the time. The house itself was built on a ridge, with stables to the rear. The garden front, which had extensive views towards open country to the south, had a terrace with a parterre; to the east of the house, and linked to it by a conservatory, there was an extensive range of glasshouses, where Joe raised orchids and many other varieties of exotic flowers and fruit. The ornamental gardens included a rose garden and a fern rockery; for recreation there were tennis courts which doubled as croquet lawns. The productive areas included a kitchen garden and an orchard, as well as the farm. One of the more unusual features of the estate was a terraced platform, about half-way down the steep slope in front of the house, which afforded fine views over the parkland (Figure 7.5).[28]

The parkland itself comprised meadow and pasture, with a circuit path round the external boundaries of the estate. There were water features of the kind favoured by Edward Milner: two small pools near the house, and on the southern boundary of the estate an extensive lake, with cascades at either end, rustic bridges linking the larger of the two islands to the parkland, and a rustic-style boathouse (Figure 7.6).[29]

Another decorative element of the Highbury parkland was the livestock it contained. This comprised not only the ornamental fowl – a pair of swans on the lake and, even more exotically, a pair of storks – but also the sheep and cattle that grazed on the pasture. Farm animals had been regarded as an essential feature of landscaped parkland since the eighteenth century, and they were valued by the Chamberlains for their aesthetic as well as their productive merits. Austen Chamberlain had taken over responsibility for the Highbury farm from the late 1880s, and his choice of breeds of cattle seems to have been made largely on the basis of their attractiveness. For his dairy herd he specialised in Jersey cows, and he and his siblings frequently commented on their 'prettiness'.[30] The parkland was laid out in such a way that the cattle could

Figure 7.5 A terraced platform at Highbury afforded views over the parkland. Reproduced by permission of the Cadbury Research Library: Special Collections, the University of Birmingham

Figure 7.6 Oak Tree Pool, one of a number of water features at Highbury. Reproduced by permission of the Cadbury Research Library: Special Collections, the University of Birmingham

be viewed from the house; a journal article about Highbury noted that 'from the terrace one catches a glimpse of the little farm lying in the valley below, and of a drove of Jersey cows, beautiful creatures, looking from afar off like deer, with their glossy, lustrous fawn coats'.[31] (The comparison with deer may have been intended as a flattering reference to the deer parks that characterised large aristocratic estates.) When his farming activities expanded onto the former Henburys land, Austen acquired a small herd of West Highland cattle, and one suspects that his choice of that breed reflected not only their hardiness, which allowed them to over-winter in the open, but also what one visitor described as their 'extremely romantic and characteristic appearance' that was 'as pleasing to the eye as that of the Jerseys themselves'.[32] Sheep too enhanced the landscape: Joe's eldest daughter, Beatrice, wrote to her younger half-brother Neville in the spring of 1894 that Austen's lambs 'look most truly rural on the slope of his new field'.[33]

But the fact that the parkland was used for livestock farming had some negative consequences as far as the aesthetics of the estate was concerned, and these required creative solutions. Soon after her marriage to Joe in 1888 Mary Chamberlain ordered an ornamental dairy to be built on a site where it would screen the view of the farmyard from the house.[34] In November 1893 his youngest sister, Ethel, reported to Neville that a rhododendron border that they had planted on their new land had been successful in hiding 'the muddy slough made by the cows at the gate'.[35] The former Henburys land also had a number of outhouses (sheds or 'hovels', as they are described in the correspondence) to provide shelter for the livestock, and planting was done in the fields in order to screen them from view from the house.[36]

The disagreeable sight of these farm buildings was, however, a minor irritant to the Chamberlains in comparison to the construction of Richard Cadbury's new house in close proximity to their own.

**Uffculme, 1890–1914**
At the time when Joe Chamberlain bought the land for Highbury it was bordered on the east by the Firs estate, owned by the Taylor family but leased to tenants. In 1890 the southern part of The Firs (13 acres out of 31) was purchased by Richard Cadbury as the site for his new home, after his decision to leave Moseley Hall.[37] Uffculme was only about a mile further from the city centre than Moseley Hall, and the site was chosen by Richard and his wife for reasons of convenience. 'Had it been merely a personal question they would have moved several miles out into the country,' Helen Cadbury wrote, 'for the town was fast pushing its long arms into the direction of Moseley and King's Heath.'[38] But, because of his voluntary work commitments in the Highgate district, Richard did not want to move too far out of town, and he settled on

Figure 7.7 Uffculme, where Richard Cadbury designed both house and gardens. Photograph from Helen Cadbury Alexander's biography of her father, *Richard Cadbury of Birmingham* (1906). Courtesy the University of Birmingham

Moor Green, which was 'still almost in the country'.[39] He built his house on the same piece of high ground as Highbury, with views that extended as far as the Lickey Hills and Rednal.[40] The Cadburys moved into their new home shortly before Christmas 1891.[41]

Unlike Joe Chamberlain, who had employed a well-regarded local architect for Highbury, Richard Cadbury designed the Uffculme house himself, in a neo-Jacobean style. Its most distinctive feature was a tall palm-house that was almost the full height of the mansion itself (Plate 7.3). The Chamberlains were not at all impressed by their new neighbour, describing the Cadburys' house in their correspondence as 'hideous' and 'a beast of a place'.[42] They were particularly horrified by its height, and planned to plant trees on top of a 'gigantic mound' in order to hide it, though Mary feared that this would help only in the summer, and that they would be 'doomed' in the winter.[43]

At the end of 1892 Richard Cadbury inflicted another aesthetic outrage on his neighbours. It had been the Cadburys' practice at Moseley Hall to stage all kinds of charitable and philanthropic function in their house and grounds. The largest of these were huge temperance demonstrations, sometimes numbering as many as 20,000–30,000 people, which took place in the meadows each summer. Refreshment tents were erected in the fields to cater for the visitors.[44] At Uffculme, Helen Cadbury tells us, 'Instead of tents for the summer field-parties, a large, open tea-shed was erected in the fields across the road, and proved a great convenience.'[45] The Chamberlains were horrified by this edifice, which was apparently a permanent structure. Beatrice described it as 'a hideosity, for all the world like a band stand', adding that, 'We should not see it much in summer, but it is awful in winter.'[46]

Just as Richard Cadbury had chosen to design his house himself, he also designed the gardens without the services of a landscape architect (Figure 7.7). According to his daughter, 'The laying out of the grounds gave scope to his artistic and botanic interests. The undulations of the land lent themselves to beautiful effects.'[47] She adds that

> The rockeries at Uffculme were Richard Cadbury's chief delight, and on the arrangement of these he spared no energy. Many a time he would go down and work away with the men, guiding and directing all the details. A piece of marshy ground at the foot of the hill was transformed into two pretty ponds at different levels, with a bridge across the little waterfall that united them.[48]

The Chamberlains, however, found the gardens at Uffculme rather less delightful. In September 1891 Austen complained to Neville that 'the garden is about as badly laid out as possible'.[49] When the grounds had been planted up, the Chamberlains were no more complimentary. On 4 January 1894 Beatrice reported to Neville that 'Papa had an interview with Mr Cadbury yesterday … & declares that he told him in so many words that his garden looked like a tea garden & that the man, who laid it out, was not accustomed to laying out gentlemen's places!'[50] Writing to Neville the next day, Austen also reported Joe's conversation with Richard: 'Father had a friendly interview with him the other day & appears to have told him many plain truths about his plain garden.'[51]

The snobbery revealed in the Chamberlains' correspondence about Uffculme is perhaps somewhat surprising, since the Cadburys' social position, as successful Birmingham businessmen, was very similar to that of the Chamberlains themselves. There were, however, clear differences in taste and lifestyle between the Chamberlains and the Cadburys, which extended to their tastes in landscape gardening: Joe shared the mainstream nineteenth-century predilection for parkland, while Richard was more individualistic. These differences became even more evident when Richard Cadbury acquired the adjoining Henburys estate.

The Henburys estate, which first appeared on a map in c.1760, dated back to the mid-seventeenth century and originally comprised a residence with grounds and a farm.⁵² It was typical of small rural estates on the periphery of the city that were at first occupied by middle-class Birmingham families only in the summer months; from the eighteenth century, as transport links with the city improved, they lived in them all year round. When the Henburys estate was sold in 1826 it was described as consisting of 45 acres of meadow and pasture. The house was situated in the centre of the estate; as well as a farmhouse near the turnpike road, the extensive outbuildings of the main residence included a cow-house and a piggery. In 1836 the Birmingham to Gloucester railway cut through the southern part of the estate, depriving it of five acres of land; some time later, the remaining land south of the railway was sold and the farmhouse was demolished. In subsequent years, six additional fields were purchased to the west of the original estate and adjoining it. By 1886 the Henburys had increased in size to 65 acres.

Henbury House itself was set in more than three acres of ornamental gardens, which included a rectangular pool with a curved end and a stone obelisk situated on rising ground from which there were extensive views over the neighbouring countryside. Not much is known about the landscaping of the estate, but the 1840 tithe map suggests that some field boundaries had been removed in the meadow nearest the house to create the appearance of parkland. In 1848 the Henburys was purchased by Walter Lyndon, an edge-tool manufacturer, and in 1875 it was inherited by his son George. In 1892, when George Lyndon learned that the Grange estate, on the far side of the railway line, was to be put up for sale for building purposes, he sold the Henburys to Richard Cadbury, who bought it in order to prevent it too from being sold off for speculative development.

In 1893 Richard Cadbury agreed to lease the western part of the Henburys (*c.*42 acres) to his neighbour Joe Chamberlain. The Cadburys retained the eastern part of the estate, including the house with its surrounding gardens, and some land that may have been used by the Lyndons as paddocks for the racehorses they bred. Richard Cadbury subsequently used the fields to pasture the cattle from his small dairy farm.⁵³

Joe Chamberlain invited Henry Milner to come down to Highbury at the beginning of January 1894 in order to advise him on the layout of the paths on his new land, and on the planting to be done there. He also hoped that Richard Cadbury would agree to consult Milner on the landscaping of the Uffculme grounds. Even before Milner arrived, Joe himself offered Richard advice on the design of his new land. Following their meeting on 3 January at which Joe had been so rude about Richard's taste in gardening, he wrote to his neighbour, suggesting a modification to the surveyor's original plan. In relation to the boundary between the two parts of the Henburys, which the plan had shown as a straight line, Joe informed Richard that 'as a straight line is always exceedingly ugly to look upon, I thought that it might be materially improved by substituting a curve ...'. 'If the curve were agreed to', he continued,

> I should then suggest that it should be laid out with a mound and plantation with trees and shrubs entirely similar to the one which I have made here to mask the road on the northern boundary of Highbury. Such a plantation would be very pretty from your house, and would, I think, entirely screen my ground from your prospect.

The decision could, however, he added, be left until Henry Milner's visit to Highbury: 'he may perhaps have some other suggestion.'[54]

Henry Milner came to Highbury in the middle of January, but Richard Cadbury does not seem to have agreed to consult him. He went ahead with marking his boundary in a straight line, much to the Chamberlains' horror. Hilda reported to her brother Neville on 24 January that she and Mary had walked over the new ground on the previous day and had seen a truly shocking sight:

> Imagine Mr Cadbury has begun putting up his bank along his boundary. It is to be 3ft high and about 3ft in width! Think of the effect of this from his drawing-room windows, running in a straight line across his field. The man is really mad! No wonder he did not take to the idea of having Mr Milner![55]

In the following months the Chamberlains continued to express their dismay at their neighbour's taste in landscaping. In March Beatrice complained to Neville that Mr Cadbury had 'made a continuous straight border with regular planting of the most ineffective description' along his boundary.[56] In October Hilda reported that her father had 'marked out a new border against the road on our side to break the line' of what she sarcastically described as 'Mr Cadbury's beautiful fence'.[57]

The purchase of the Henburys estate meant that the Cadburys now had two houses on their land. Their eldest son, Barrow, had married in 1891, just before the family left Moseley Hall, and Richard hoped that he and his wife Geraldine would occupy the Lyndons' old house. The young couple, however, remained in Edgbaston, and Richard then considered demolishing the Lyndons' house.[58] In the end he did not demolish it completely, but reduced it considerably in size and knocked down some outbuildings and glasshouses, while retaining the ornamental planting in the pleasure gardens.[59]

After Richard Cadbury died in 1899 his widow, Emma, continued to occupy Uffculme until her own death in 1907, when Barrow acquired the estate. Barrow and Geraldine Cadbury adapted Uffculme House for use as an Adult School, and in 1911 they built an Open-Air School in the grounds for children with tuberculosis. Thus, in spite of several decades of urban growth, the Moseley–

Kings Heath area was clearly felt to have a sufficiently unpolluted atmosphere at this time to benefit children with lung infections.[60]

In contrast to Highbury, the landscaping of the Uffculme estate before 1914 owed nothing to professional landscape architects: the grounds developed somewhat haphazardly, with little regard for current fashions in garden design. Unlike the Chamberlains (see below), Richard Cadbury did not seem to experience too much concern about the increasingly suburbanised nature of Moor Green. When he decided to move from Moseley Hall, he was fully aware that the site of his new house was in an area that was being rapidly built up, but he chose it for practical reasons of proximity both to his business and to his voluntary work. In some respects he regarded the closeness of his home to some of the more deprived districts of Birmingham as an advantage: it provided him with opportunities for charitable activity. When living at Moseley Hall Richard had encouraged his children to befriend poor households in the nearby inner-city district of Balsall Heath and invited 'ragged children from the slums' to pick bluebells in his woods, and at both Moseley Hall and Uffculme he invited under-privileged families to functions in the house and grounds.[61] In any case, Richard Cadbury was wealthy enough to mitigate any potential inconvenience caused by urban sprawl. When the prospect of speculative building loomed closer to Uffculme, he could afford to purchase the Henburys estate as a buffer against the developers; and in 1897 he acquired a house that really was in the country. He bought Wynd's Point, high in the Malvern Hills, jointly with his brother and business partner George (who had a south Birmingham estate of his own, the Manor House at Northfield), and it was used by their families, friends and associates for weekend and holiday visits.[62]

**Highbury and the western Henburys, 1894–1914**
As we have seen, George Lyndon had decided to sell the Henburys because of the prospect of the development of the Grange estate, beyond the railway line, for speculative building. After Joe Chamberlain leased the western part of the Henburys, the railway marked the new southern boundary of his land. He planned to screen it with a line of trees and proposed doing this in the autumn of 1894, after preparing the ground over the summer.[63] The Chamberlains soon learned, however, that work on the housing development was due to begin in the winter of 1894/5, and they became anxious that their trees would not grow up quickly enough to hide the buildings.[64] In March 1895 Joe complained to Mary that

> A building Company intends to run roads from Dads Lane to King's Heath, parallel to the railway, and to put up small houses, one row to have their backs directly on to the

railway and overlooking Highbury! Pleasant! – especially as I shall not be surprised if the continued frost has killed half the shrubs and trees.[65]

The younger Chamberlains too expressed their dismay. Hilda described the prospect of the new building as 'horrible', while Austen referred to the builders of homes for his future constituents as 'brutes' and Ethel categorised them as 'beasts'.[66] Joe's planting along the railway line was, perhaps surprisingly, of deciduous trees rather than evergreens. Within ten years they had grown up sufficiently to screen Kings Heath from view when the trees were in leaf in the summer, but the suburb was clearly visible from Highbury house in the winter.[67] The Chamberlains' neighbours were no longer only the owners of nearby mansions such as Uffculme and Moor Green Hall, but also the occupants of the redbrick terraced houses of Kings Heath.

The Chamberlains' share of the Henburys estate mainly comprised land that had previously been used for agriculture and had not been landscaped as parkland by the Lyndons. Most of the fields were meadow or pasture, with an eight-acre arable field in the far south-eastern corner. According to Austen Chamberlain, the main issue was to integrate the landscaping of the Henburys land with that of the original Highbury estate. On 15 January he wrote to Neville: 'The difficulty is to make it now look like part of one property with our own after trying for more than 10 years to shut it out as much as possible.'[68] When Henry Milner came down to Highbury he advised the Chamberlains on ways to achieve this, and these soon created great controversy within the Chamberlain household. The main debate concerned the destruction of the hedges on the Henburys land that marked the field boundaries and their replacement with iron railings, as had been the case at Highbury. Even before Milner's arrival Austen proposed cutting down the hedgerows: Beatrice reported to Neville on 23 December that he wanted to pull down hedges, adding that, 'at present the railway, the road and a lower hedge make three parallel lines, which greatly disturb his mind.'[69] Austen's mind was disturbed, presumably, by the ugliness of the straight lines, on which he clearly shared the views of his father and Henry Milner. He may also have accepted the argument, put forward by Milner in his book on landscape gardening, that no features of an estate should be allowed to cut across the line of vision from the house towards the boundary, since anything at right angles to the sightline made distances seem shorter.[70]

When Henry Milner came down for his consultation visit in mid-January, it became clear that on the matter of the hedgerows there was a sharp division of opinion between Austen, Joe and Milner, on the one side, who wanted to replace the hedges with iron railings, and Mary and Hilda, in particular, on the other side, who wanted to keep the hedges. Beatrice informed Neville that 'Mary is against bringing the new fields too much into the garden, lest we lose the country look & get nothing instead, but Papa and Austen want to open it up and make it "park like".[71] Ethel confirmed that 'Mary wants to keep the hedges to preserve the countrified look and have the new land rather as farm than park', adding, 'She is afraid the iron railings and planting will make it look suburban and like all the houses in Edgbaston which have a few fields.'[72] Hilda, too, argued that hedges created a rural ambience: 'they help the illusion that we are in the depth of the country, whilst the palings make it look like "grounds".' And she added, 'Now if it really were all country round about it might be desirable to have those fields as part of the grounds, but as matters stand is it not a trifle suburban.'[73]

In the end Joe and Austen got their way, and the removal of hedges on the former Henburys land began.[74] Nevertheless, the short-lived rebellion of the Chamberlain womenfolk against the introduction of iron railings reflected a significant moment in the history of landscaped parkland. Like all fashions, landscape gardening had begun at the higher levels of society, in this case on large aristocratic estates in the eighteenth century, and had quickly moved down the social scale: to smaller country estates, and even to the growing suburbs. At the end of the nineteenth century upper-middle-class owners of small estates on the outskirts of Birmingham, such as Joe Chamberlain, still favoured landscaped parkland, and Joe regarded his employment of a metropolitan landscape gardener such as Henry Milner as a status symbol to be recommended to his neighbours. For the women of his household, however, the 'parkland' look already seemed suburban, and they advocated the retention of traditional fields with hedgerows to create the impression that they were still living in the real countryside, in spite of the growth of speculative building all around them.

Although the Chamberlains' landscaping of the former Henburys land continued to display the features of parkland design advocated by Henry Milner, Milner's style of work was already falling out of fashion. His 1890 book was the object of sharp criticism in Reginald Blomfield's *The formal garden in England*, published in 1892.[75] Blomfield mocked Milner's claim that his interference with nature was 'natural-like', and accused him of deception in his attempts to make estate grounds appear much bigger than they were.[76] Blomfield was a fierce opponent of the entire English school of landscape gardening initiated in the eighteenth century by Lancelot 'Capability' Brown, and he sought to rehabilitate the older style of formal gardening that had preceded it. From the end of the nineteenth century formal gardens began to be reintroduced on English country estates, at least in the immediate surroundings of the house. This fashion was even followed at Highbury, where between 1899 and 1904 the Chamberlains created a number of new gardens on former pasture land that they took out of the park near the house, on the western edge of the original estate. These new gardens included a 'Dutch' garden densely planted with spring bulbs, a formal 'Italian' garden, a new rockery and shrubbery and even a 'tea garden'.[77] All of these innovations involved geometrical features and straight lines of the kind that Joe Chamberlain had found so ugly only a decade earlier. The rest of the estate, however, remained as landscaped parkland at the time of Joe's death in 1914, when Highbury passed into institutional use.[78]

The fashion for landscape gardening was of long duration in south Birmingham: John Taylor II was at the forefront of the trend when he commissioned Humphry Repton in 1792, and Joe Chamberlain continued to favour the style even after it had passed its peak of popularity when he employed Henry Milner in 1894. Between these dates the city expanded and estate-owners' attitudes towards it changed. Where Repton had designed a picturesque vista of the distant townscape for his patron, the Chamberlains were anxious to screen the encroaching suburbs from their view.

Throughout the period we have considered, the businessmen of south Birmingham situated their semi-rural homes within highly attractive parklands. Most of these estates have now disappeared, but some have survived to the present day, and sufficient evidence remains to enable us to reimagine their landscapes as they existed in the late nineteenth century.[79] Their history serves to remind us that it was not only undeveloped agricultural land but also the designed parkland of the city's upper middle classes that was overtaken by the constant expansion of the suburbs.

**Notes**

1  On the early history of Moseley Hall see, for example, P.D. Ballard, 'A commercial and industrial elite: a study of Birmingham's upper middle class, 1780–1914', PhD thesis, 2 vols (Reading, 1983), vol. ii, pp. 473–4.
2  Harvard University, Graduate School of Design, Frances Loeb Library: H. Repton, *Mosely Hall near Birmingham, a Seat of John Taylor, Esq<sup>r</sup>*, 1792, seq. 7 in the digital version <http://nrs.harvard.edu/urn-3:GSD.loeb:10897498>, accessed 5 November 2017.
3  *Ibid.*
4  *Ibid.*, seq. 12.
5  *Ibid.*, seq. 14.
6  *Ibid.*, seq. 31 and sketches at seq. 35–6.
7  *Ibid.*, seq. 18.
8  *Ibid.*
9  *Ibid.*, seq. 40 and sketches at seq. 42–3.
10 S. Daniels, *Humphry Repton: landscape gardening and the geography of Georgian England* (New Haven and London, 1999), pp. 79–81, 208.
11 Cited in *ibid.*, p. 218.
12 *Ibid.*, p. 208.
13 Ballard, 'Commercial and industrial elite', vol. ii, pp. 473, 548.
14 H.C. Alexander, *Richard Cadbury of Birmingham* (London, 1906), p. 213.
15 *Ibid.*, p. 214.

16 *Ibid.*, pp. 215–16.
17 *Ibid.*, pp. 227–8.
18 *Ibid.*, pp. 244–5. Moseley Hall, much extended and renovated, remains standing today as a community hospital. A dovecote, cow-house and ice-house that survive from the eighteenth-century estate are now cared for by the Moseley Society. When the Taylors sold off the rest of the estate for building purposes at the end of the nineteenth century, a group of local businessmen purchased the pool and some surrounding parkland in order to create a private park: this survives as Moseley Park and Pool.
19 Ballard, 'Commercial and industrial elite', vol. ii, pp. 552–3.
20 A. Chamberlain, *Notes on the families of Chamberlain and Harben* (n.p., 1915), p. 51.
21 *Ibid.*, p. 61.
22 *Ibid.*
23 Beatrice and Austen by his first wife Harriet Kenrick; Neville, Ida, Hilda and Ethel by Florence Kenrick, who was Harriet's cousin.
24 A. Hodges, 'A Victorian gardener: Edward Milner (1819–1884)', *Garden History*, 5 (1977), p. 70.
25 H.E. Milner, *The art and practice of landscape gardening* (London, 1890), pp. 2–6, 31–2.
26 P.D. Ballard, *Highbury Park, Moseley, Birmingham: historic landscape appraisal* (Birmingham City Council, 2009), pp. 24–42.
27 University of Birmingham, Cadbury Research Library, Special Collections (UoB/CRL/SC), Chamberlain papers, JC28A/1/25, Joe to Mary, 29 May 1888. References prefaced AC (Austen Chamberlain), BC (Beatrice, Ida, Hilda and Ethel Chamberlain), JC (Joe Chamberlain) and NC (Neville Chamberlain) are to collections in this archive.
28 Ballard, *Highbury Park*, p. 37. The viewing platform survives, having been restored after severe vandalism in 2011.
29 Ballard, *Highbury Park*, pp. 32–3, compares photographs of Highbury with designs of rustic features in Henry Milner's book.
30 M. Perrie, 'Hobby farming among the Birmingham bourgeoisie: the Cadburys and the Chamberlains on their suburban estates, c.1880–1914', *Agricultural History Review*, 61 (2013), p. 123.
31 UoB/CRL/SC, Chamberlain papers, JC4/12/7, F.H. Low, 'Mr Chamberlain's Garden', cutting from an unidentified periodical, March 1897, pp. 736–7.
32 J. Long, 'Mr Austen Chamberlain, M.P., as a farmer', *The Rural World*, 6/314 (21 December 1894), p. 911.
33 UoB/CRL/SC, Chamberlain papers, NC1/13/2/24, Beatrice to Neville, 3 April 1894.
34 UoB/CRL/SC, Chamberlain papers, AC4/3/114, Mary to her mother, Mrs Endicott, 8 Nov. 1889.
35 UoB/CRL/SC, Chamberlain papers, NC1/14/64, Ethel to Neville, 17 Nov. 1893.
36 UoB/CRL/SC, Chamberlain papers, NC1/15/3/11–12, Hilda to Neville, 20 March 1894; NC1/13/2/22, Beatrice to Neville, 21 March 1894.
37 Ballard, 'Commercial and industrial elite', vol. ii, pp. 553–4.
38 Alexander, *Richard Cadbury*, p. 245.
39 *Ibid.*, p. 254.
40 *Ibid.*, p. 256.
41 *Ibid.*, pp. 249, 254.
42 UoB/CRL/SC, Chamberlain papers, AC4/3/182, Mary to Mrs Endicott, 27 Feb. 1891; AC5/3/18, Austen to Neville, 19 Sept. 1891.
43 UoB/CRL/SC, Chamberlain papers, AC4/3/182, Mary to Mrs Endicott, 27 Feb. 1891; AC4/3/225, Mary to Mrs Endicott, 6 Nov. 1891.
44 Alexander, *Richard Cadbury*, pp. 221–2.
45 *Ibid.*, p. 257.

46  UoB/CRL/SC, Chamberlain papers, BC/A/2/1/71, Beatrice to Neville, 11 Dec. 1892.
47  Alexander, *Richard Cadbury*, p. 256.
48  *Ibid.*, p. 257.
49  UoB/CRL/SC, Chamberlain papers, AC5/3/18, Austen to Neville, 19 Sept. 1891.
50  UoB/CRL/SC, Chamberlain papers, NC1/13/2/11, Beatrice to Neville, 4 Jan. 1894.
51  UoB/CRL/SC, Chamberlain papers, AC5/3/70, Austen to Neville, 5 Jan. 1894.
52  The following account of the Henburys estate is based on Ballard, *Highbury Park*, pp. 15–24.
53  *Ibid.*, pp. 23, 44.
54  Library of Birmingham, Archives and Heritage, Cadbury Collection, MS 466.292/3–4, Joe Chamberlain to Richard Cadbury, 8 Jan. 1894. In making these suggestions, Joe was echoing ideas put forward by Henry Milner in his book. See Milner, *Art and practice*, pp. 6, 32–3, 35.
55  UoB/CRL/SC, Chamberlain papers, NC1/15/3/6, Hilda to Neville, 24 Jan. 1894.
56  UoB/CRL/SC, Chamberlain papers, NC1/13/2/22, Beatrice to Neville, 21 March 1894.
57  UoB/CRL/SC, Chamberlain papers, NC1/15/3/28, Hilda to Neville, 24 Oct. 1894; see also AC5/3/90, Austen to Neville, 28 Oct. 1894.
58  UoB/CRL/SC, Chamberlain papers, NC1/13/2/11, Beatrice to Neville, 4 Jan. 1894; AC5/3/70, Austen to Neville, 5 Jan. 1894.
59  Ballard, *Highbury Park*, p. 44. The remaining part of the house was demolished in 1965: *ibid.*, p. 62.
60  Uffculme House today is used by the National Health Service as a conference and training venue; the buildings of the Open-Air School are now occupied by Uffculme Special School for autistic children. For Uffculme see chapter in this volume by Clare Hickman.
61  Alexander, *Richard Cadbury*, pp. 222–3, 225, 257.
62  *Ibid.*, pp. 282–6.
63  UoB/CRL/SC, Chamberlain papers, NC1/15/3/7, Hilda to Neville, 14 Feb. 1894.
64  UoB/CRL/SC, Chamberlain papers, AC5/3/89, Austen to Neville, 17 Oct. 1894.
65  J.L. Garvin, *The life of Joseph Chamberlain*, vol. ii (London, 1933), pp. 626–7 (Joe to Mary, 6 March 1895).
66  UoB/CRL/SC, Chamberlain papers, NC1/15/3/50, Hilda to Neville, 12 April 1895; AC5/3/105, Austen to Neville, 12 April 1895; NC1/14/112, Ethel to Neville, 12 April 1895.
67  Ballard, *Highbury Park*, p. 47.
68  UoB/CRL/SC, Chamberlain papers, AC5/3/71, Austen to Neville, 15 Jan. 1894.
69  UoB/CRL/SC, Chamberlain papers, NC1/13/2/10, Beatrice to Neville, 23 Dec. 1893.
70  Milner, *Art and practice*, pp. 6, 34, 75, 115–16.
71  UoB/CRL/SC, Chamberlain papers, NC1/13/2/13, Beatrice to Neville, 19 Jan. 1894.
72  UoB/CRL/SC, Chamberlain papers, NC1/14/73, Ethel to Neville, 19 Jan. 1894.
73  UoB/CRL/SC, Chamberlain papers, NC1/15/3/5, Hilda to Neville, 20 Jan. 1894.
74  UoB/CRL/SC, Chamberlain papers, NC1/14/75, Ethel to Neville, 10 Feb. 1894.
75  R. Blomfield, *The formal garden in England* (1892; 3rd edn, London, 1901), pp. 7–11, 13–14, 16.
76  *Ibid.*, p. 9.
77  These gardens have been described by Ballard, and illustrated with photographs from the Chamberlain papers; see Ballard, 'Commercial and industrial elite', vol. ii, pp. 877–84; P.D. Ballard, '"Rus in urbe": Joseph Chamberlain's gardens at Highbury, Moor Green Birmingham, 1879–1914', *Garden History*, 14 (1986), pp. 66–72; Ballard, *Highbury Park*, pp. 49–53.
78  Highbury Hall, as the house is now known, is at present used primarily as a wedding venue. The Highbury Heritage Trust (now the Chamberlain Highbury Trust) was established in 2015 to restore the Hall and estate.
79  Most of the former grounds of the Highbury, Uffculme and Henburys estates now comprise Highbury Park, a wonderfully informal green space.

## Bibliography

*Primary sources*

University of Birmingham, Cadbury Research Library, Special Collections (UoB/CRL/SC)
> Chamberlain Papers. References prefaced AC (Austen Chamberlain), BC (Beatrice, Ida, Hilda and Ethel Chamberlain), JC (Joe Chamberlain) and NC (Neville Chamberlain) relate to collections in this archive. Correspondents referred to by first name only have the surname Chamberlain. The regular letters written by his siblings to Neville in 1891–7, while he was working on the family's sisal plantation in the Bahamas, are a particularly valuable source of information on the history of the estate.

Library of Birmingham, Archives and Heritage
> Cadbury Collection, MS 466.292/3–4, Joe Chamberlain to Richard Cadbury, 8 Jan. 1894

Harvard University, Graduate School of Design, Frances Loeb Library
> Repton, H., *Mosely Hall near Birmingham, a Seat of John Taylor, Esq$^r$*, 1792

*Secondary sources*

Alexander, H.C., *Richard Cadbury of Birmingham* (London, 1906).

Ballard, P.D., 'A commercial and industrial elite: a study of Birmingham's upper middle class, 1780–1914', PhD thesis, 2 vols (Reading, 1983).

Ballard, P.D., '"Rus in urbe": Joseph Chamberlain's gardens at Highbury, Moor Green Birmingham, 1879–1914', *Garden History*, 14 (1986), pp. 61–76.

Ballard, P.D., *Highbury Park, Moseley, Birmingham: historic landscape appraisal* (Birmingham City Council, 2009).

Blomfield, R., *The formal garden in England* (1892; 3rd edn, London, 1901).

Chamberlain, A., *Notes on the families of Chamberlain and Harben* (n.p., 1915).

Daniels, S., *Humphry Repton: landscape gardening and the geography of Georgian England* (New Haven and London, 1999).

Garvin, J.L., *The life of Joseph Chamberlain*, vol. ii (London, 1933).

Hodges, A., 'A Victorian gardener: Edward Milner (1819–1884)', *Garden History*, 5 (1977), pp. 67–77.

Long, J., 'Mr Austen Chamberlain, M.P., as a farmer', *The Rural World*, 6/314 (21 December 1894), p. 911.

Milner, H.E., *The art and practice of landscape gardening* (London, 1890).

Perrie, M., 'Hobby farming among the Birmingham bourgeoisie: the Cadburys and the Chamberlains on their suburban estates, c.1880–1914', *Agricultural History Review*, 61 (2013), pp. 111–34.

# 8

## Care in the countryside: the theory and practice of therapeutic landscapes in the early twentieth century

*Clare Hickman*

In 1945 Jane Whitney, when writing her biography of Geraldine Cadbury, visited the Cropwood Open-Air School in Blackwell and described how 'the sleep-time garden might be the envy of princes, with its fountain in the midst of a green lawn, so that the children took their naps amid the soothing, somnolent plash of falling water' (Figure 8.1).[1] This evocative description of a princely garden gives an indication of the attention and importance given to gardens associated with such institutions in the early decades of the twentieth century. Cropwood, opened in 1922, was just one of a number of open-air schools and hospitals operating at this time in Blackwell, near Bromsgrove, in the West Midlands. The open-air approach to treating chronic diseases such as

Figure 8.1 Sleep-time garden for children at Cropwood Open-Air School, Blackwell, near Birmingham. Detail, *Cropwood Open Air School*, Bernard Sleigh, 1922. Courtesy Birmingham Civic Society

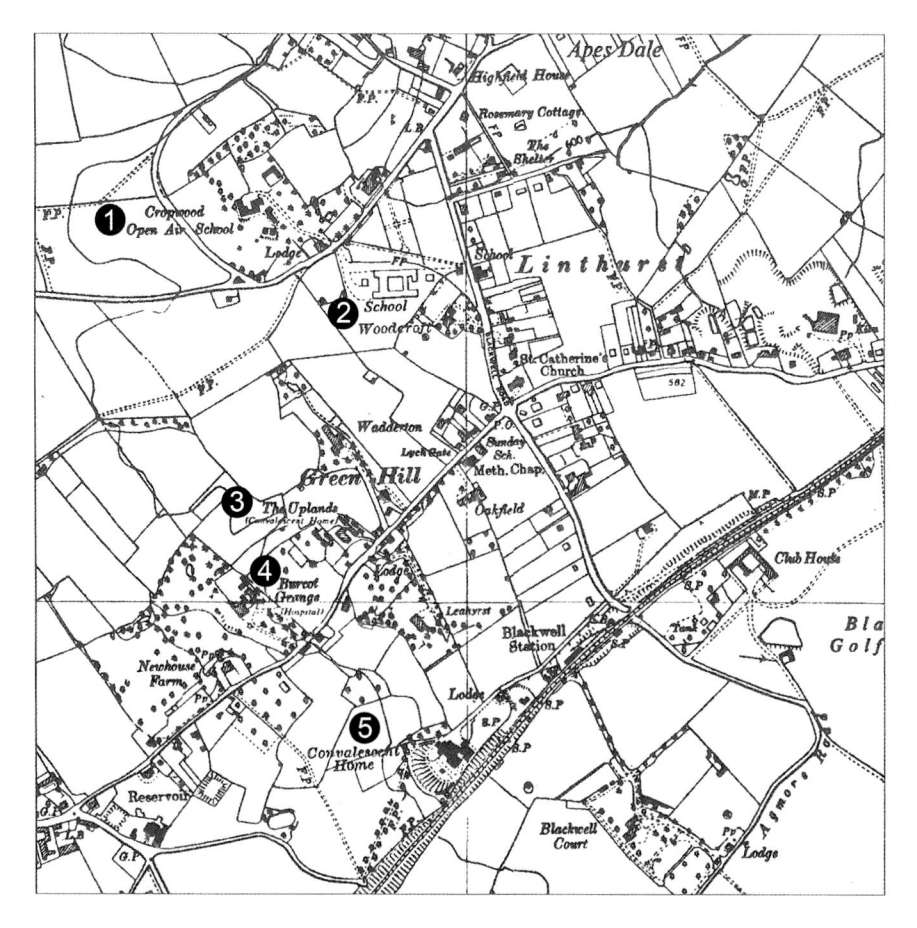

**KEY – Annotated 1954 Ordnance Survey Map**

1. Cropwood
2. Hunter's Hill
3. The Uplands
4. Burcot Grange
5. Blackwell Convalescent Home (formerly Birmingham and Midland Counties Sanatorium)

Figure 8.2 Cluster of open-air institutions in the Blackwell area close to Birmingham. Detail of 1954 Ordnance Survey Map © Crown Copyright and Landmark Information Group Ltd (2015). All rights reserved (1954)

| Initial name of institution | Dates of operation | Type when opened |
|---|---|---|
| Birmingham and Midland Counties Sanatorium (subsequently Blackwell Convalescent Home) | 1873–1984 | Adult convalescent home |
| Cropwood Open-Air School | 1922–amalgamated with Hunter's Hill in 1980 | Residential school for girls |
| The Uplands | 1923–1967 when it became a reception centre | Children's convalescent home |
| Hunters Hill Open-Air School | 1933– Currently Hunters Hill Technology College | Residential school for boys |
| Burcot Grange | 1936–1990 | Annexe to the Birmingham and Midland Eye Hospital |

Figure 8.3 Therapeutic institutions in the Blackwell area funded through enlightened philanthropy and patronage.

tuberculosis became popular in the late nineteenth and early twentieth century in Britain. It encouraged patients to spend as much time as possible in the fresh air and sunshine, as both were considered to have curative properties. The 1937 Ordnance Survey map depicts a cluster of these establishments – along with Cropwood, there were Hunters Hill Open-Air School, opened in 1933; The Uplands, a Children's Convalescent Home opened in 1923; Burcot Grange, an annexe to Birmingham and Midland Eye Hospital, opened in 1936; and the Birmingham and Midland Counties Sanatorium, opened on this site in 1873, and which became known as Blackwell Convalescent Home (Figures 8.2 and 8.3). This chapter will explore this cluster but focus in detail on the gardens associated with Cropwood and Blackwell Convalescent Home. In particular, it aims to unpick the design and use of these gardens in relation to contemporary medical and social ideas. In so doing, it will illustrate a growing research area that connects garden history and histories of health care. Historians who have explored this connection in relation to designed green spaces include myself and Sarah Rutherford.[2] Medical historians, particularly Andrew Scull and

Figure 8.4 The south aspect of Blackwell Sanatorium, showing the conservatory and gardens. Undated postcard reproduced by permission of Historic England Archive

Linda Bryder, have discussed the hospital landscape in relation to issues such as economics and national efficiency.[3] Similarly, cultural geographers have taken an interest in the concept of 'therapeutic landscapes', including Chris Philo on asylums, Hester Parr on mental health and space and Wil Gesler, who originally coined the term.[4]

For this consideration of open-air institutions and their landscapes a wide range of primary source material has been analysed, including institutional prospectuses and reports, published medical accounts, personal descriptions of visits (Jane Whitney's biography of Geraldine Cadbury included detailed eye-witness accounts) and postcards (which have yielded photographic evidence as well as patient accounts). As with similar studies, the main limitation has been the general lack of contemporary patient and children's voices. Some of this has been overcome by drawing on the rich oral histories collected and published by Frances Wilmot and Pauline Saul, which give a valuable, albeit selective, insight into the children's experiences of the institutions.[5] Such varied source material has been utilised so that the design, use and experience of the gardens can be explored from a range of perspectives.

**Location, location, location**

As this geographical clustering of medical institutions attests, Blackwell as a location was considered to have suitable environmental characteristics. One determining factor seems to be that it retained its rural nature while still being in close proximity to the urban centre of Birmingham. The institutions in Blackwell were all in some way designed to give children and adults a rural respite and place of recovery, away from the unhealthy urban conditions of the city. Blackwell itself also had good road and rail links, which meant that there was easy access for patients and visitors.

The earliest of these institutions was Blackwell Convalescent Home, established in 1866 for paying patients. Initially the sanatorium was based in an existing domestic building but after a few years nine acres of land near Blackwell Station were purchased from the Midland Railway. On this land a purpose-built home was constructed, which opened on 16 April 1873 for a maximum of 60 patients (Figure 8.4). In 1876 a subscription fund was established by the gentlemen of Worcester to help with the immediate costs of completing the building as well as to ease the financial burden for poorer patients of staying in the home.[6] In 1921 the Home became known as the Blackwell Convalescent Home for Birmingham and the Midland Counties.[7]

An undated prospectus for the Home indicates that its location was considered important in relation to patient recovery, or at least seen as a useful marketing device to family members and local physicians who might refer patients:

> Send your convalescent to Blackwell on the sunny southern slopes of the Lickey Hills to regain health and strength. The Home stands in its own grounds of 12 acres on a gravel soil, high on the S/W foothills of the Lickey Hills, with the ground sloping rapidly away below it. The windows look right over the length and breadth of Worcestershire, across the Severn Valley to the Malvern Hills, 20 miles away, with a view, in clear weather of the Mountains of Wales, from which the prevailing S/W wind blows.[8]

The writer of the prospectus clearly linked health and strength to the environmental conditions found at Blackwell. This was in line with national trends. According to Harriet Richardson, 'most convalescent homes were situated in the countryside or by the sea, where rest, graduated exercise, fresh air and wholesome food could help overcome the debility resulting from illness or surgery.'[9]

Similar arguments regarding location are also evident in Whitney's description of Cropwood, which, according to her, stood 'on a high hill overlooking miles of country, the view on a fine day compassing the borders of Wales and the Malvern Hills, seventy-five miles clear across beautiful undulating hills and valleys. The whole atmosphere of the place was full of happiness and clean sunshine.'[10] Her description is somewhat romanticised, but it does chime with the Cropwood prospectus, which stated that 'it stands on high ground near to the Lickey Hills and the air is pure and health giving.'[11] The terms used to describe the environmental conditions emphasised the cleanliness and purity of the air and the health-giving properties of the sunshine, which presumably contrasted with the dirty and impure surroundings of the patients' homes, and therefore also their lives, in inner-city Birmingham. This medical–moral discourse is one that is often used in relation to the environment at this time, and will be returned to later in this chapter.

These descriptions, with their emphasis on the height of the location above sea level, the magnificent views and the wind direction, point to a shared philosophy regarding where such institutions should be placed. As many of these accounts are found in advertisements aimed at potential subscribers (who contributed to institutional funding) as well as patients and their families, it suggests there was a general shared understanding of the potential therapeutic influence of the environment. In particular, this was seen as beneficial for convalescing patients as well as those with chronic conditions and children deemed to be weak or pre-tubercular.[12] It should also be noted that similar advertisements highlighting the environmental conditions were produced for tuberculosis sanatoria during this period and that they also espoused open-air philosophies.[13]

However, there were other factors at play, which were more philanthropic than environmental in nature. Both Cropwood and Hunters Hill schools owe their origins to Geraldine and Barrow Cadbury, who were both practising Quakers and part of the wider Cadbury chocolate manufacturing dynasty.[14] The Cadburys had already established a day school based on the open-air principles at Uffculme near Moseley, designed by Barry Peacock in 1911.[15] It was also Peacock who adapted the Cadburys' home at Cropwood into a residential open-air school for girls in 1922. The later Hunters Hill school for boys was built on part of the Cropwood site.

The Cadburys' interest in the open-air method was related to personal experience as well as being one that followed contemporary trends. When their own son, Paul, aged 12, became ill with tuberculosis in 1907 they consulted the doctor Sir Thomas Barlow, who recommended 'educating him at home in the country and ensuring that he had plenty of good food and fresh air'.[16] Following this advice, the Cadburys adapted Paul's bedroom at their country estate of Cropwood so that he had one wall completely open to the air. As his health improved enough for him to return to conventional education, his parents appear to have felt that this method of treatment should be made available to those from more impoverished backgrounds. After initially building Uffculme open-air school in the grounds of their family home at Moseley, they went on to donate the whole of their Cropwood estate for educational use.

Similarly, Burcot Grange was gifted to the Birmingham & Midland Eye Hospital by Mr and Mrs Rushbrooke in 1936. Like Barrow Cadbury, Frederick

Rushbrooke was a successful businessman and started what is now the ubiquitous chain of Halford bicycle shops. It is not why he donated the Grange, but the cluster of institutions near Blackwell seem to have developed through a combination of patronage and a belief in the area's suitability as a therapeutic environment.

**Open-air therapies**
All the institutions based in Blackwell appear to have practised open-air therapies to a greater or lesser extent. This therapeutic approach ensured that patients spent as much time as possible in the fresh air and sunshine, as both were considered to have curative properties. According to the historian F.B. Smith, the vogue for open-air sanatoria began in Germany around 1860, 'inspired by a mixture of traditional cure-taking at spas, nature worship, and a new physiology of lung weakness'.[17] After Robert Koch discovered the tuberculosis bacillus in 1882, the theory that disease was caused by germs gradually became standard.[18] While men such as Koch tried to develop specific serum therapies in the 1890s, inspired by the highly successful smallpox vaccine, other doctors developed therapeutic approaches in response to a new understanding of natural immunity. According to Paul Weindling, these doctors 'emphasised the importance of strengthening the body's natural resistance to disease rather than promoting "artificial immunity" through mass immunisation'.[19] Therefore the use of open-air therapies in the specialist institutions and convalescent homes in Blackwell could be seen as a way to strengthen the body's natural immunity.

This theory was expressed in a paper published in *The Medical Officer* in 1909, which also argued that open-air therapies were gaining popularity in Britain:

> In fact the 'fresh air cure' has become almost a household word, and many people seem to look upon fresh air as a kind of specific or panacea for phthisis[20] in the same sense as we look on opium as a specific for pain. To my mind, this is quite an erroneous view; what the fresh air does is to increase metabolism and thus increase the resisting power of the individual to the tubercle bacillus.[21]

As Roger Cooter has argued, while bacteriology theories still permitted air to be thought of as a reservoir of harmful agents, as in earlier theories of disease caused by miasma (or bad air) that had been popular among Victorians such as Florence Nightingale, they also allowed more emphasis to be placed on air as curative or constitutionally restorative in and of itself.[22] This emphasis on the therapeutic nature of air led to gardens being considered a fundamental element of the therapeutic regime.

## Blackwell convalescent and medical institutions

As convalescent homes and other specialist institutions such as sanatoria became popular at the end of the nineteenth century, there was also a change in the perceived importance of gardens for patients within general hospitals. As the eminent physician John Syer Bristowe argued in 1871 in relation to the building of the new St Thomas's Hospital in London:

> as regards airing courts for patients; there is no doubt that these are desirable, but they are far more important for a sanatorium, or a convalescent institution, than for a general Hospital; because … when that stage has been reached, at which out-of-door exercise or air is desirable, the patients have to be discharged to make room for more pressing cases of disease.[23]

This emphasises how the perception of the therapeutic value of gardens shifted, so that they became seen as more important for longer-term residential patients rather than short-stay hospital cases. This also reflects the growing medicalisation of general hospitals and a change in the locus of patient recovery for chronic conditions and after immediate hospital-based treatment.

According to Harriet Richardson,

> A fundamental factor governing the design of convalescent homes was the mobility of the patients, who were neither expected, nor encouraged, to remain in their beds during the day. As a result, day-rooms, dining-rooms and attractive grounds were common features in the earlier homes.[24]

These elements were easily adapted to serve the open-air therapeutic approach as it was more widely introduced at the start of the twentieth century. The Blackwell Convalescent Home for Birmingham and the Midland Counties Report of 1932 records that:

> As the Conservatory was in need of repair a suggestion was put forward that it should be converted into an Open-Air Ward, which would be of advantage to patients, particularly those received from the Queen's Hospital. This conversion has been carried out and is hoped will be appreciated by and be beneficial to the patients.[25]

There is no clear evidence of the extent to which open-air therapies were carried out at the Home, but this implies that they thought it was important for at least some convalescent patients.

It is difficult to find patient accounts of what the regime was like in the Home. However, on a postcard illustrated with a photograph of the back of the Home with its outside shelter and glazed day rooms sent to Mr and Miss Morris on 24 June 1959, Auntie Rose wrote

Have spent three happy weeks here among the 100 patients. This place stands in lovely grounds 15 miles from Worcester overlooking the Malverns. Have spent most of the time sitting in sun lounge and walking or sitting in the grounds. Am feeling much better but cannot walk far yet.[26]

This suggests that spending time outside either sitting or walking in the grounds still formed an important element of the daily life of the convalescent, despite the decline in the use of open-air therapies after the Second World War.

Similarly, at the Uplands the children 'had a field to romp and play in, swings and other amusements, a large play-hut for wet or cold days and beautiful grounds'.[27] This indicates that similar open-air ideas were being practised here; the particular importance of the huts, fields and grounds for the recovery of children will be discussed in relation to the open-air schools below.

There is little evidence for the design of the grounds at the Blackwell Home, but it is possible to delineate some of the features from postcards that show the rear of the house. The earlier postcard, which is undated, shows a conservatory adjoining the right side of the house, a steeply sloping garden planted with trees and shrubs and a steep flight of steps that descends to a gate in the foreground of the photograph.[28] The conservatory was still present in the later photograph, but there was also a new area with large glass windows in the centre of the building, possibly a day room or dining room (Figure 8.5). The postcard also shows a flight of steps descending from this new room to a terrace. The steps have a hedge to their left that is cut into an ornamental

Figure 8.5 A postcard of Blackwell Sanatorium, showing additional glassed areas. Courtesy Mary Harding

shape, which suggests that the gardens were designed to be attractive as well as functional.

The 1937 Ordnance Survey map depicts an avenue of trees running diagonally across a field at the base of the steep slope by the Home. There is also a footpath marked through the centre of this field that led directly from the sanatorium. Part of the convalescent regime included exercise and it is likely that the patients would have been encouraged to walk further than the immediate grounds around the Home. The same map also shows a number of pine trees to the north-west of the Home, which may reflect the German and Alpine precedents of open-air therapy.

Within this cluster there was also an institution with a more directly medical remit. Burcot Grange, a Victorian timber-framed country house with ornamental gardens, was used as an annexe to the Birmingham & Midland Eye Hospital (located in Church Street, Birmingham) and provided accommodation specifically for women and children. However, like the other institutions in Blackwell, its rural location – or at least the removal of its patients from their poor urban living conditions – was considered as important as the medical care it offered. The hospital's 1938 Annual Report suggested that children might need to stay longer at the Grange for reasons other than the eye treatments available: 'Not only is the condition given all necessary treatment, but every effort is made to effect improvement in the general health and physique of the children.'[29] This is used in the Report as an argument to extend the length of stay of children in the hospital and is clearly related to more general concerns about their overall state of health. The Annual Reports also include three photographs of the gardens at Burcot Grange. Two of the photographs show walks through what appear to be rockeries and past drifts of daffodils. The final photograph shows the lily ponds and terraces, and what appears to be a conservatory attached to the house (Figure 8.6). The gardens may well relate to the earlier history of the house as the residence of Mr Rushbrooke, who donated the house and gardens, but the conservatory is perhaps an indication that similar therapeutic practices relating to sunshine and air were also being conducted.

**Cropwood open-air school**

On 17 June 1922 Cropwood open-air school was opened and the buildings, along with 75 acres of land, were formally handed over to the Birmingham Education Department. Cropwood was developed as a residential school for children from deprived areas in inner-city Birmingham who had been diagnosed with a physical ailment that would benefit from open-air treatment. According to Whitney, the decision to admit them to the school was 'made by the doctors who have treated them for measles or scarlet fever, or some other debilitating childhood disease, usually combined with malnutrition.'[30]

Figure 8.6 Burcot Grange, Blackwell, from the 1938 *Annual Report* of the Birmingham and Midland Eye Hospital. By permission of the Library of Birmingham, HC EY/1/3/14

Figure 8.7 Children's garden Cropwood Open-Air School, Blackwell, near Birmingham. Detail from *Cropwood Open Air School*, Bernard Sleigh (1922). Courtesy Birmingham Civic Society

Unlike the previous examples, there is more explicit evidence that the gardens at Cropwood were an integral part of the school regime. A detailed plan of the house and grounds survives which clearly depicts a great variety of garden features (Plate 8.1). These include the sleep-time garden described by Whitney above, a children's garden, outdoor classrooms, a treehouse, a rose pergola, an outdoor swimming pool, the children's playing lawn, a tennis court, arbours and a small farm with vegetable garden (Figure 8.7). The purpose of the features is clearly related to the outdoor philosophy of the school.

The artist who created the plan, Bernard Sleigh, was a leading member of the Birmingham Guild of Handicraft and the Bromsgrove Guild of Applied Art, so the Arts and Crafts style is perhaps to be expected.[31] However, the choice of style also perhaps reflects the shared ideals of the wider Cadbury family. For example, the Bournville model estate created by Barrow's uncle, George Cadbury, is described by the latest Pevsner architectural guide as 'perhaps the fullest expression of arts and crafts ideals'.[32] Gardens were central to the design of the village and 'Cadbury himself placed an emphasis on the advantages to a family's health and economics of a well-kept garden'.[33] Although much of the architectural credit for the estate may be due to the architect, William Alexander Harvey, interesting comparisons can also be made with the idealised factory in a garden as typified in promotional literature.[34] As John Bryson and Philippa Lowe have argued, these advertisements 'emphasized the wholesome quality of the environment in which chocolate was manufactured' and also used gardens to 'signify tranquility and nature, whereas a factory is associated with connotations of noise and pollution'.[35]

In both the plan of the school and the advertisement the buildings were given less prominence than the landscape surrounding them. The link between ideas of purity and the garden setting of the factory at Bournville perhaps also has parallels with the fairytale image of the school estate, with its tree house and sleep-time garden. This parallel between the setting of the Bournville factory and the Cropwood estate also supports Linda Bryder's argument that 'the open-air school movement in fact harked back to a sentimental pre-industrial Golden Age.'[36] The gardens at Bournville similarly give the impression of an earlier, more rustic time, belying its reality as a modern factory.[37]

The parallels with Bournville are unsurprising given the close Cadbury family network. Common interests regarding the influence of the environment on health were certainly shared by Geraldine Cadbury and her niece Elizabeth Taylor Cadbury. For example, Helen Smith has argued that Elizabeth felt that '"physical deterioration" as well as drunkenness and infant mortality were the result of debilitating urban conditions' and that Bournville was contributing to the amelioration 'of the public health risks caused by the urban environment'.[38] This parallels Geraldine Cadbury's work with open-air schools and their intake of impoverished and sickly inner-city children; the significant role played by such women deserves further attention.

Geraldine's personal involvement certainly should not be underestimated; beginning with Uffculme, she seems to have been involved in much of the design and implementation of the schools. In line with open-air design principles, the classrooms were built with doors and windows that would open outwards so that there were no walls on three sides when they were in full use. According to Whitney, 'her ingenuity not only put hot-water radiators on the wall side of the classroom, but ran them under the sides that might be opened, so that the entering air might be tempered by the upward flow of air. I believe this system is quite original with her'.[39] Once Cropwood became her focus she 'involved herself in every detail of the design'.[40] Whitney recorded how

> Geraldine Cadbury herself chose and bought every article of furniture for Cropwood and all the clothes for the fifty-two little girls who were the first pupils – green serge dresses and figured crêpe frocks from Liberty's, camp-beds for the outdoor afternoon sleep, even their lesson-books and story-books.[41]

The gardens as outside spaces were obviously integral to the open-air approach conducted at the schools. Whitney is again a useful voice, as she records her visits to the schools in the 1940s. It is worth including at length her detailed description of the important role played by the gardens at Uffculme open-air school, also established by Geraldine and Barrow Cadbury:

> their lessons in these open classrooms give a sort of camping-out holiday feeling to the place. The play in the open air is so free. The trees and hedges help keep it rural and simple. There is nothing of the playground about it. I saw one group in the lower meadow having organized games, and another group just rolling about on the grass like little ponies, running about, playing tag, two or three boys kicking a football. The ground being on two levels, with an apple orchard on the higher ground right by the school, and a meadow on the lower ground, with a grassy slope between, gives a special charm, and greatly adds to the feeling of space. Gardening is also one of the children's occupations, and they have recently won prizes for their products in a local show.[42]

The romantic idyll proclaimed in such descriptions and depicted in Sleigh's plan is also reflected in some of the later oral histories collected in the 1990s from those who had attended the open-air schools as children. For example, Mrs Elsie Kite, who had been Head Girl at Cropwood 1936–9, recounted how

> The school grounds were lovely with large cedar trees along the drive. There was an orchard full of apple trees … . There was a tennis court and a pergola with roses covering the top,

and beds of red poppies each side leading to the swimming pool. There were fir trees all round the classrooms. The smell from the trees was supposed to be good for you.[43]

The outdoor approach included time set aside for sleeping during the day as an integral therapeutic element to help children recover from the ailments that had led to their admission, which mirrored the time spent by patients with tuberculosis sleeping on balconies.[44] The importance of outdoor sleep can be seen in the plan of Cropwood, with its sleep-time garden. At Uffculme, Whitney recorded how 'besides the food there is a daily rest in the healthy-building scheme. Each child sets up its own light cot, either in a huge airy shed, three sides of which can be opened completely to the air, or out on the grass under the apple trees.'[45]

Activities undertaken by the children were described by Whitney as follows: 'handicrafts are a great feature of the educational scheme, and open-air games and swimming are, of course a main feature of the children's natural and free-looking life.'[46] These activities reflected wider ideas regarding the way the school should operate. In 1915 the Inspector of Educational School Gardening for Somerset, G.W.S. Brewer, wrote that:

> The chief points about school work associated with the garden are the facts that children are brought into touch with actualities; they work and breathe the fresh air amidst surroundings they themselves largely help to shape … . As to the garden itself for the

Figure 8.8 A class of schoolgirls having lessons in the open air, c.1925–35. Courtesy Wellcome Library, London CC BY 4.0

open-air school, I would have it to embrace not only land for vegetable culture, but also borders for flowers and shrubs, a rock garden, fruit, Nature study, and geographical plots, and if by any means possible a nice sweep of lawn.[47] (Figure 8.8)

Similarly, Arthur Beasley recalled that, during his stay at Hunter's Hill in 1933, 'lessons were not so academic as a normal school but we were involved in a lot of activities including handicraft and nature study, gardening, country walks etc.'[48] These accounts are in line with Bryder's argument that the 'schools were seen as character-building institutions, training in "natural" living'.[49]

These are all very seductive images; however, we should remember that this was an open-air school in Britain. As Whitney recorded on hearing about the cots: '"How nice", I say, "out in the sunshine!" "Yes", said the headmistress dubiously, "or under the grey sky". They had been out that very day under the soft, chill, grey sky, with a brisk breeze and flying autumn leaves.'[50] At Uffculme, even with its innovative heating system, Whitney noted the cold:

> it was a breezy day, and the room I first went into was open fully on two sides and partially open on the third. I was dressed in overcoat and fur, and inclined to shiver. The children were mostly very poorly clad, with bare arms and legs and cotton frocks (in the case of girls).[51]

As the children were meant to be exposed to the open air all year round, it also led to events such as this recorded by Maurice Hicks, who had been at Hunter's Hill in 1935–8: 'I remember many mornings, in the winter, waking up to find the bottom of the bed covered in snow.'[52]

Within the rich oral histories and log-book accounts recorded by Frances Wilmot and Pauline Saul there are recurring accounts of children thinking about or actually running away. For some children it seems to have been a welcome break from the hardship of inner-city life, but others felt incredibly homesick and struggled with the different food and cold showers. Others were removed and taken home by their families on visiting days. However, oral accounts suggest that for other children the rural experience was positive.

There are some indications that the children also had agency of their own and could develop this natural-living approach outside of the proscribed boundaries: Beasley described how

> myself and three friends had a den in the top field under the hawthorn hedge. Looking back now, this den was quite amazing. We had dug down into the earth about four or five feet, covered this with tree branches, and put grass turf on top of this. We had a hidden trap door to enter and for light we had wax tapers stuck in the earth wall![53]

There was a strong moral element attached to education in the open air, which reflected wider concerns around the perceived connections between physical deterioration, moral depravity and urban poverty. For example, at Cropwood in the 1920s it was noted that children lost weight when they went home in the summer holidays. This was 'attributed to the loss of regular meals, rest, exercise and an irregular life led in the holidays'.[54] There are clear parallels with Geraldine Cadbury's work with young offenders. In her 1938 book *Young Offenders Yesterday and Tomorrow*, she praised the 'aims of the farm colony set up at Stretton-on-Dunsmore in Warwickshire in 1818, which hired out boys from county gaols to work on local farms, with the aim of reforming rather than punishing them'.[55] Geraldine was not alone in holding this idea. As well as advocating farming as part of the curriculum in open-air schools, in 1915 James Campbell also noted that in his work at reformatory schools for boys he had found that 'the boy benefits morally by work in his garden, and his physical improvement is decidedly apparent'.[56] He went on to emphasise the strength of the moral element of gardening: 'A careful study of boys and their gardens at Stoke Farm Reformatory School goes to show that as a reforming influence the garden – the boy's own garden – is a powerful aid.'[57]

The Headmistress at Uffculme definitely relayed a moral narrative to Whitney when she visited:

> It's often just the crowded conditions in the slum areas where they live that make children difficult. One of the greatest releases they find here is space. They've plenty of room! A child may get in wrong with the children of the neighbourhood, and find itself involved in constant fights, and get a bad name. But when the child comes here, if it doesn't like its companions, it can get away from them. It can try going by itself, for a while, [ …], or it can choose a congenial set of companions to play with.[58]

The rural environment was thus also seen as a space away from immoral influences.

The restorative powers of the garden for both the mind and the body are also literary themes in the period. In *The Glory of the Garden*, written by Rudyard Kipling and first published in his *A School History of England* in 1911, there were moral overtones to the act of gardening, which reflected those of the Reformatory school.

> There's not a pair of legs so thin, there's not a head so thick,
> There's not a hand so weak and white, nor yet a heart so sick,
> But it can find some needful job that's crying to be done,
> For the Glory of the Garden glorifieth every one.[59]

According to Anne Helmreich, this poem uses the 'metaphor of England as a garden to reinvigorate the value and benefits of hard work'.[60] Helmreich has also argued that the

> fears of a disintegrating domestic order and a declining international profile drove the desire to equate gardens with Englishness. In visualizing England as a garden and promoting the garden as a symbol of the nation, artists, architects, designers, and writers were responding to a growing perception that nature and the English rural landscape, as well as the nation itself, were no longer immutable.[61]

The most famous example of the therapeutic powers of a garden for the health of a child in a literary work is arguably Frances Hodgson Burnett's *The secret garden*, published in 1911 (Plate 8.2). In line with open-air ideals, it was being indoors that caused Colin's character to become weak and sickly:

> So long as Colin shut himself up in his room and thought only of his fears and weaknesses and his detestation of people who looked at him and reflected hourly on humps and early death, he was a hysterical, half-crazy little hypochondriac who knew nothing of the sunshine and the spring, and also did not know that he could get well and stand upon his feet if he tried to do it.[62]

One of the first factors in the hypochondriac Colin's recovery was the opening of the windows so that he could breathe in the fresh air. The heroine, Mary, also described how Dickon, her friend who spent all his time outdoors and was close to nature, felt about fresh air: 'He says he feels it in his veins and it makes him strong and he feels as if he could live for ever and ever.'[63] The strong message in this didactic children's book is that fresh air and being outdoors in a garden is good both mentally and physically. This reflected contemporary medical advice. In 1910, David Chowry-Muthu, an Indian physician who established the Hill Grove Sanatorium in the Mendips and the Tambaram Sanatorium in India, argued that open-air therapy was a 'natural treatment' and suggested that, 'the secret of its widespread interest in Europe is due to the discovery – if discovery it may be called – that fresh air, hitherto regarded as an enemy to be shut out and barred, is really a friend, and one of Nature's best gifts to man.'[64] Like many, he related the concept of open-air therapies to a time before industrialisation and urbanisation: 'man, by building towns and manufacturing dirt and disease, is undoing Nature's work, and ... to put himself right again he must go back to Nature, and lead an open-life in the green fields and meadows, and breathe the sweet fresh air.'[65]

This brings us back again to medical–moral discourses. It suggests that if the dirty air of the town was the problem, the clean air of the countryside was

Figure 8.9 A postcard of Blackwell Sanatorium, illustrating the influence of the Arts and Crafts movement on the architecture of the therapeutic institutions in the area. Courtesy Mary Harding

the obvious solution. These concepts were certainly still popular in the 1940s and were reflected by Whitney in her description of the perceived limitations of Uffculme open-air school, which only took day pupils. According to her, as soon as Uffculme was established Geraldine Cadbury began to worry about children 'who needed the kind of care, for a short period, which would preclude their going back to dirty and germ-laden homes at night'.[66] Similarly, when Whitney described the children who attended the later, residential Cropwood, she stated that 'most of the children who come to this school are from the poorest districts in Birmingham. They have lived all their lives in stuffy, overcrowded, often dirty homes. The change is tremendous.'[67]

**Garden cities and the open-air movement**
These medical ideas concerning the value of fresh air and sunshine influenced other broader movements in Britain, including the development of the Garden City ideal and modernist architecture, although in the case of the Blackwell institutions and Bournville the architectural influence seems to have been predominately the Arts and Crafts rather than the Modernist movement (Figure 8.9).[68] According to Margaret Campbell, 'Britain retained an architectural loyalty to the Arts and Crafts movement … despite many innovative features.'[69] Although the innovative features Campbell is discussing here relate to

the Edward VII sanatorium built according to open-air principles to treat tuberculosis, similar modernist features, including purpose-built pavilions and folding doors, could be found at the institutions based in Blackwell.

The ideals of the Arts and Crafts movement and their relationship to open-air principles are worth exploring a little more. John Ruskin, as a founder of the movement, was particularly admired by the Cadbury family; not only did Geraldine and Barrow have a portrait of him in their photograph album, but the Bournville School of Arts and Crafts was originally called Ruskin Hall. In 1865 Ruskin had postulated an idealised city full of gardens and with easy access to the countryside. He discussed how one could improve the houses that existed already and then

> the building of more – strongly, beautifully, and in groups of limited extent, kept in proportion to their streams, and walled round, so that there may be no festering and wretched suburb anywhere, but clean and busy streets within, and the open country without, with a belt of beautiful garden and orchard round the walls, so that from any part of the city perfectly fresh air and grass, and sight of far horizon, might be reachable in a few minutes' walk.[70]

Sharing similar views with Ruskin, William Morris, another leading instigator of the Arts and Crafts movement, wrote *News from nowhere* (1890), a utopian vision set in the future where everyone lived in the countryside. Within this text he made constant references to similarities between this future world and the medieval period.[71] In this world where people have returned to a pre-industrial way of life there were also echoes of the new open-air philosophy, with outdoor work being recommended as a method 'to clear the cobwebs' from the brain.[72] One of the characters inhabiting this land explained to the protagonist that

> these children do not all come from the near houses, the woodland houses, but from the countryside generally. They often make up parties, and come to play in the woods for weeks together in summer-time, living in tents, as you see. ... the less they stew inside houses the better for them.[73]

Similarly, the protagonist often comments on how healthy and young the people look in comparison with those of the industrialised society he has left. For example, the children in the forest were described as being 'especially fine specimens of their race',[74] while, 'as to the women themselves, it was pleasant indeed to see them, they were so kind and happy-looking in expression of face, so shapely and well-knit of body, and thoroughly healthy looking and strong.'[75] Throughout the novel Morris argues that a life of physical labour in a rural setting with as much open air as possible was the reason for the health, youth and beauty of the fictional population. This can be seen as being related to both the fear of ill-health caused by urbanisation and industrialisation and the myth that rural living created a stronger, healthier population.

These ideas were espoused by many in the medical profession. Benjamin Ward Richardson, physician, sanitary reformer and prolific writer, described his utopian city, *Hygeia*, just ten years after Ruskin had laid out his. Within this vision, which he argued was based on the latest scientific principles, gardens and open spaces were given an important, if somewhat less romantic, role:

> The acreage of our model city allows room for three wide main streets or boulevards, ... . They are planted on each side of the pathways with trees, and in many places with shrubs and evergreens. All the interspaces between the backs of houses are gardens. ... other public buildings, as well as some private buildings such as warehouses and stables, stand alone ... . They are surrounded with garden space, and add not only to the beauty but to the healthiness of the city.[76]

Ebenezer Howard, the visionary behind the Garden City movement, was heavily influenced by Ward Richardson, as well as Morris and Ruskin, among others, and argued in the 1890s that although the country 'is the source of all health, all wealth and all knowledge' it needed to be combined with society as symbolised by the town.[77] The solution to the problems caused by urbanisation was to bring the countryside into the towns in the form of gardens – the *rus in urbe* ideal. However, in his 1902 Garden City plan he still placed 'children's cottage homes', a 'farm for epileptics', 'asylums for blind and deaf' and 'convalescent homes' in rural areas between fruit farms, allotments and cow-pastures, which highlights the importance placed on the pastoral nature of the environment for such institutions.

Some of the medical profession appear to have viewed the garden city as a potential weapon in their ongoing war against the degeneration of the population. In 1919 Dr Leonard Hill, Director of Applied Physiology of the National Institute for Medical Research, argued that garden cities were the solution, rather than the building of more houses on the edges of existing towns, as they could help create a more vigorous and happy nation. He wrote that 'it is open air and exercise, good feeding and well-regulated rest, which have converted weedy citizens into robust soldiers, which restore the weakly in open-air schools, and the consumptive in sanatoria.'[78] The idea that there had once been an English golden age of health before the development of the towns, when people were employed on the land, also embraced broader fears that the British race was degenerating in terms of physical and moral health. During recruitment for the Boer War, doctors had reported that there was a low level of physical fitness in the general population. These concerns in turn led to the investigation of the health of the population by the 1904 Interdepartmental Committee on Physical Deterioration.[79] The concerns regarding efficiency, morality and the future health of the nation certainly affected the development of school architecture throughout the country, as Tom Hulme has already shown.[80] Open-air institutions were one attempt to manage the perceived deterioration caused by urbanisation, by moving the weaker members of society to rural situations where it was hoped that access to sunshine and fresh air would revitalise their bodies and stem the degeneration of the labouring classes.

The cluster at Blackwell provides us with a snapshot of much wider medical, moral and national concerns. The institutions look back towards a golden age of rural living but at the same time argue that they are progressive in their approach to convalescence and health. The gardens are essential spaces for the successful implementation of open-air therapies and are therefore given prominence in eye-witness descriptions, patient accounts and other promotional literature. The gardens also reflect social and cultural concerns regarding urbanisation and industrialisation and relate to fears that the population was degenerating. The post-Second World War decline in open-air institutions is symptomatic of changes in medical understanding, particularly with the discovery of antibiotics, as well as other changes in housing conditions and welfare. Combining cultural, medical and garden history methodologies enables therapeutic landscapes to be viewed as more than just spaces for air, sunshine and exercise. This broad approach could provide a fruitful way to reconsider the role of other institutional, industrial and urban landscapes. Concerns around our health and wellbeing have always been woven into the fabric of everyday life and are, therefore, also fundamental influences on our use and design of gardens.

## Notes

1  J. Whitney, *Geraldine S. Cadbury 1865–1941: a biography* (London, 1948), p. 93.
2  C. Hickman, 'Cheerful prospects and tranquil restoration: The visual experience of landscape as part of the therapeutic regime of the British asylum, 1800–1860', *History of Psychiatry*, 20/4 (December 2009), pp. 425–41; Hickman, 'An exploration of the National Health Society and its influence on the movement for urban green spaces in late-nineteenth century London', *Landscape and Urban Planning*, 118 (2013), pp. 112–19; Hickman, 'The "Picturesque" at Brislington House: the role of landscape in relation to the treatment of mental illness in the early nineteenth-century asylum', *Garden History*, 33/1 (2005), pp. 47–60; Hickman, *Therapeutic landscapes: a history of English hospital gardens since 1800* (Manchester, 2013); S. Rutherford, 'The landscapes of public lunatic asylums in England, 1808–1914', PhD thesis, 3 vols (Leicester, De Montfort University, 2003); Rutherford, *The Victorian asylum* (Oxford, 2008).
3  A. Scull, *The most solitary of afflictions: madness and society in Britain 1700–1900* (New Haven and London, 1993); L. Bryder, *Below the magic mountain: a social history of tuberculosis in twentieth century Britain* (Oxford, 1988); Bryder, '"Wonderlands of buttercup, clover and daisies":

tuberculosis and the open air school movement in Britain, 1907–39', in Cooter (ed.), *In the name of the child*, pp. 72–95.
4   C. Philo, *A geographical history of institutional provision for the insane from medieval times to the 1860s in England and Wales* (Lewiston, NY, 2004); H. Parr, *Mental health and social space: towards inclusionary geographies?* (Malden, 2008); W. Gesler, *Healing places* (Lanham, MD, 2003).
5   F. Wilmot and P. Saul, *A breath of fresh air: Birmingham's open-air schools, 1911–1970* (Chichester, 1998).
6   'The Blackwell Sanatorium', *Worcester Journal*, 15 July 1876, p. 7.
7   Its name changed again in 1952, when it became the Blackwell Recovery Hospital.
8   Worcestershire Archive and Archaeology Service (WAAS): b499.8/B.A.10134/20 *Prospectus for Blackwell Convalescent Home for Birmingham and the Midland Counties*, stuck in a scrapbook from Blackwell Convalescent Home for Birmingham and the Midland Counties, n.d.
9   H. Richardson, *English hospitals 1660–1948: a survey of their architecture and design* (Swindon, 1998), p. 183. See Richardson for more details on the relationship between spa towns and convalescent homes.
10  Whitney, *Geraldine S. Cadbury*, p. 91.
11  Birmingham Archives and Heritage (BAH): MS617/234a City of Birmingham Education Committee, *Cropwood Residential Open-Air school, Blackwell Prospectus*.
12  For more information on the open-air movement and tuberculosis see Bryder, *Below the magic mountain* and '"Wonderlands of buttercup, clover and daisies"'. The role of gardens as part of the wider movement is also discussed in Hickman, *Therapeutic landscapes*.
13  Hickman, *Therapeutic landscapes*, pp. 152–205.
14  See M. Waterson and S. Wyndham, *A history of the Barrow Cadbury Trust: constancy & change in Quaker philanthropy* (London, 2013), for more detail on Geraldine and Barrow Cadbury and their family history.
15  The building is now listed Grade II by Heritage England.
16  Waterson and Wyndham, *Barrow Cadbury Trust*, p. 33.
17  F. Smith, *The retreat of tuberculosis, 1850–1950* (Kent, 1988), p. 97.
18  P. Weindling, 'From infectious to chronic disease: changing patterns of sickness in the nineteenth and twentieth centuries', in Wear (ed.), *Medicine in society*, pp. 303–16.
19  *Ibid.*, pp. 313–14.
20  This was the term sometimes given to the pulmonary form of tuberculosis.
21  A. Warner, 'Open-air recovery schools', *The Medical Officer* (25 December 1909), p. 469 (originally a paper given at Leicester).
22  R. Cooter, 'Open-air therapy and the rise of open-air hospitals', *The Bulletin for the Social History of Medicine*, 35 (1984), p. 44.
23  J. Bristowe, *An introductory address on the future of St Thomas's Hospital, delivered at the hospital in the Surrey Gardens on the occasion of the opening of the session of its medical and surgical college*, 1 October 1862 (London, 1862), p. 13.
24  Richardson, *English hospitals*, p. 183.
25  WAAS: b499.8/B.A.10134/20 *Blackwell Convalescent Home for Birmingham and the Midland Counties Report*, 1932, stuck in a Scrapbook, p. 2.
26  Historic England Archive (HEA): National Buildings Record Index Number 100767 Postcard, 24 June 1959. From Auntie Rose to Mr and Miss Morris.
27  P. Maskell, *Best of health: 130 years of the BHSF 1873–2003* (Birmingham, 2003), p. 17.
28  HEA: National Buildings Record Index Number 100767 Postcard, n.d.
29  Birmingham and Midland Eye Hospital, *Report of the year's work of the Birmingham and Midland Eye Hospital* (1938).
30  Whitney, *Geraldine S. Cadbury*, p. 91.

31  See R. Cooper, 'Bernard Sleigh, artist and craftsman, 1872–1954', *The Journal of the Decorative Arts Society 1850–the Present*, 21 (1997), pp. 88–102. As well as being heavily influenced by William Morris and Edward Burne Jones, he corresponded with Walter Crane, who viewed gardens as utopian and socialist spaces: see M. O'Neill, 'Walter Crane's floral fantasy: the garden in Arts and Crafts politics', *Garden History* 36/2 (2008), pp. 289–300.
32  A. Foster, *Pevsner architectural guides: Birmingham* (New Haven and London, 2005), p. 22.
33  N. Pevsner and A.Wedgewood, *The buildings of England: Warwickshire* (Harmondsworth, 1974), p. 156.
34  For promotional literature on Bournville see Connecting Histories website at <http://www.search.connectinghistories.org.uk>, accessed 10 June 2015.
35  J. Bryson and P. Lowe, 'Story-telling and history construction: rereading George Cadbury's Bournville Model Village', *Journal of Historical Geography*, 28/1 (2002), p. 26.
36  Bryder, '"Wonderlands of buttercup, clover and daisies"', p. 72.
37  For more on the Bournville gardens see the work of H. Chance and in particular 'The angel in the garden suburb: Arcadian allegory in the "Girls' Grounds" at the Cadbury factory, Bournville, England, 1880–1930', *Studies in the History of Gardens & Designed Landscapes*, 27/3 (2007), pp. 197–216.
38  H. Smith, 'Elizabeth Taylor Cadbury (1858–1951): religion, maternalism and social reform in Birmingham, 1888–1914', PhD thesis (University of Birmingham, 2012), p. 77.
39  Whitney, *Geraldine S. Cadbury*, p. 89.
40  Waterson and Wyndham, *Barrow Cadbury Trust*, p. 40.
41  Whitney, *Geraldine S. Cadbury*, p. 92.
42  *Ibid.*, p. 90.
43  Wilmot and Saul, *A breath of fresh air*, p. 122.
44  The design and use of balconies and sun loungers for patients with TB is discussed in M. Campbell, 'What tuberculosis did for modernism: the influence of a curative environment on modernist design and architecture', *Medical History*, 49 (2005), pp. 463–88.
45  Whitney, *Geraldine S. Cadbury*, p. 89.
46  *Ibid.*, p. 92.
47  G. Brewer, 'School gardening and open-air schools', in T.N. Kelynack (ed.), *The year book of open-air schools and children's sanatoria*, vol. i (London, 1915), p. 162.
48  Wilmot and Saul, *A breath of fresh air*, p. 97.
49  Bryder, '"Wonderlands of buttercup, clover and daises"', p. 90.
50  Whitney, *Geraldine S. Cadbury*, p. 89.
51  *Ibid.*, p. 87.
52  Wilmot and Saul, *A breath of fresh air*, p. 133.
53  *Ibid.*, p. 98.
54  *Ibid.*, p. 67.
55  Waterson and Wyndham, *Barrow Cadbury Trust*, p. 33.
56  J. Campbell, 'School gardening in reformatories for boys', in T.N. Kelynack (ed.), *The year book of open-air schools and children's sanatoria*, vol. i (London, 1915), p. 91.
57  *Ibid.*, p. 96.
58  Whitney, *Geraldine S. Cadbury*, p. 88.
59  R. Kipling, *Rudyard Kipling's verse: definitive edition* (London, 1940), pp. 732–3.
60  A. Helmreich, *The English garden and national identity: the competing styles of garden design, 1870–1914* (Cambridge, 2002), p. 36.
61  *Ibid.*, pp. 7–8.
62  F. Burnett, *The secret garden* (1911; Harmondsworth, 1982), p. 239.
63  *Ibid.*, pp. 168–9.
64  D. Muthu, *Pulmonary tuberculosis and sanatorium treatment: a record of 10 years' observation and work in open-air sanatoria* (London, 1910), pp. 83–4.

65  *Ibid.*
66  Whitney, *Geraldine S. Cadbury*, p. 90.
67  *Ibid.*, p. 91.
68  See Campbell, 'What tuberculosis did for modernism'.
69  *Ibid.*, p. 467.
70  J. Ruskin, *Sesame and lilies* (London, 1904), p. 199.
71  W. Morris, *News from nowhere* (1890; 9th edn, London, 1907), p. 24.
72  *Ibid.*, p. 18.
73  *Ibid.*, p. 29.
74  *Ibid.*
75  *Ibid.*, p. 14.
76  B. Richardson, *Hygeia, a city of health* (1876; reprinted Gloucester, 2008), pp. 12–13.
77  E. Howard, *Garden cities of tomorrow* (1902; London, 1946), p. 48. For Richardson's influence see in particular R. Beevers, *The garden city utopia: a critical biography of Ebenezer Howard* (Abingdon, 2002), p. 30.
78  As quoted in Bryder, '"Wonderlands of buttercup, clover and daisies"', pp. 84–5.
79  E. Fee and D. Porter, 'Public health, preventive medicine and professionalization: England and America in the nineteenth century', in Wear (ed.), *Medicine in society*, p. 271.
80  T. Hulme, '"A nation depends on its children": school buildings and citizenship in England and Wales, 1900–1939', *Journal of British Studies*, 54 (2015), pp. 406–32.

## Bibliography

*Primary sources*

Birmingham Archives & Heritage (BAH)
> MS617/234a, City of Birmingham Education Committee, *Cropwood Residential Open-Air school, Blackwell Prospectus*

Worcestershire Archive and Archaeology Service (WAAS)
> b499.8/B.A.10134/20 *Blackwell Convalescent Home for Birmingham and the Midland Counties Report*, 1932
> b499.8/B.A.10134/20, *Prospectus for Blackwell Convalescent Home for Birmingham and the Midland Counties*, n.d.

Historic England Archive (HEA)
> Index Number 100767, Postcard, 24 June 1959. From Auntie Rose to Mr and Miss Morris
> Index Number 100767, Postcard, undated

*Printed primary sources*

Anon, *The Medical Officer* (12 July 1919).
Birmingham and Midland Eye Hospital, *Report of the year's work of the Birmingham and Midland Eye Hospital* (1938).
'The Blackwell Sanatorium', *Worcester Journal*, 15 July 1876.
Brewer, G., 'School gardening and open-air schools', in T.N. Kelynack (ed.), *The year book of open-air schools and children's sanatoria*, vol. i (London, 1915), pp. 158–62.
Bristowe, J., *An introductory address on the future of St Thomas's Hospital, delivered at the hospital in the Surrey Gardens on the occasion of the opening of the session of its medical and surgical college*, 1 October 1862 (London, 1862).
Campbell, J., 'School gardening in reformatories for boys', in T.N. Kelynack (ed.), *The year book of open-air schools and children's sanatoria*, vol. i (London, 1915), pp. 90–96.

Howard, E., *Garden cities of tomorrow* (1902; London, 1946).
Kelynack, T.N. (ed.) *The year book of open-air schools and children's sanatoria*, vol. i (London, 1915).
Morris, W., *News from nowhere* (1890; 9th edn, London, 1907).
Muthu, D., *Pulmonary tuberculosis and sanatorium treatment: a record of 10 years' observation and work in open-air sanatoria* (London, 1910).
Richardson, B., *Hygeia, a city of health* (1876; reprinted Gloucester, 2008).
Ruskin, J., *Sesame and lilies* (London, 1904).
Warner, A., 'Open-air recovery schools', *The Medical Officer* (25 December 1909).
Whitney, J., *Geraldine S. Cadbury 1865–1941: a biography* (London, 1948).

*Secondary sources*

Beevers, R., *The garden city utopia: a critical biography of Ebenezer Howard* (Abingdon, 2002).
Bryder, L., *Below the magic mountain: a social history of tuberculosis in twentieth century Britain* (Oxford, 1988).
Bryder, L., '"Wonderlands of buttercup, clover and daisies": tuberculosis and the open air school movement in Britain, 1907–39', in Cooter (ed.), *In the name of the child*, pp. 72–95.
Bryson, J. and Lowe, P., 'Story-telling and history construction: rereading George Cadbury's Bournville Model Village', *Journal of Historical Geography*, 28/1 (2002), pp. 21–41.
Burnett, F., *The secret garden* (1911; Harmondsworth, 1982).
Campbell, M., 'What tuberculosis did for modernism: the influence of a curative environment on modernist design and architecture', *Medical History*, 49 (2005), pp. 463–88.
Chance, H., 'The angel in the garden suburb: Arcadian allegory in the "Girls' Grounds" at the Cadbury factory, Bournville, England, 1880–1930', *Studies in the History of Gardens & Designed Landscapes*, 27/3 (2007), pp. 197–216.
Cooper, R., 'Bernard Sleigh, artist and craftsman, 1872–1954', *The Journal of the Decorative Arts Society 1850–the Present*, 21 (1997), pp. 88–102.
Cooter, R. (ed.), *In the name of the child: health and welfare 1880–1940* (London, 1992).
Cooter, R., 'Open-air therapy and the rise of open-air hospitals', *The Bulletin for the Social History of Medicine*, 35 (1984), pp. 44–6.
Fee, E. and Porter, D., 'Public health, preventive medicine and professionalization: England and America in the nineteenth century', in Wear (ed.), *Medicine in Society*, pp. 249–75.
Foster, A., *Pevsner architectural guides: Birmingham* (New Haven and London, 2005).
Gesler, W., *Healing places* (Lanham, MD, 2003).
Helmreich, A., *The English garden and national identity: the competing styles of garden design, 1870–1914* (Cambridge, 2002).
Hickman, C., 'Cheerful prospects and tranquil restoration: The visual experience of landscape as part of the therapeutic regime of the British asylum, 1800–1860', *History of Psychiatry*, 20/4 (December 2009), pp. 425–4.
Hickman, C., 'An exploration of the National Health Society and its influence on the movement for urban green spaces in late-nineteenth century London', *Landscape and Urban Planning*, 118 (2013), pp. 112–19.

Hickman, C., 'The "Picturesque" at Brislington House: the role of landscape in relation to the treatment of mental illness in the early nineteenth-century asylum', *Garden History*, 33/1 (2005), pp. 47–60.

Hickman, C., *Therapeutic landscapes: a history of English hospital gardens since 1800* (Manchester, 2013).

Hulme, T., '"A nation depends on its children": school buildings and citizenship in England and Wales, 1900–1939', *Journal of British Studies*, 54 (2015), pp. 406–32.

Kipling, R., *Rudyard Kipling's verse: definitive edition* (London, 1940).

Maskell, P., *Best of health: 130 years of the BHSF 1873–2003* (Birmingham, 2003).

O'Neill, M., 'Walter Crane's floral fantasy: the garden in Arts and Crafts politics', *Garden History* 36/2 (2008), pp. 289–300.

Parr, H., *Mental health and social space: towards inclusionary geographies?* (Malden, 2008).

Pevsner, N. and Wedgewood, A., *The buildings of England: Warwickshire* (Harmondsworth, 1974).

Philo, C., *A geographical history of institutional provision for the insane from medieval times to the 1860s in England and Wales* (Lewiston, NY, 2004).

Richardson, H., *English hospitals 1660–1948: a survey of their architecture and design* (Swindon, 1998).

Rutherford, S., 'The landscapes of public lunatic asylums in England, 1808–1914', PhD thesis, 3 vols (Leicester, De Montfort University, 2003).

Rutherford, S., *The Victorian asylum* (Oxford, 2008).

Scull, A., *The most solitary of afflictions: madness and society in Britain 1700–1900* (New Haven and London, 1993).

Smith, F., *The retreat of tuberculosis, 1850–1950* (Kent, 1988).

Smith, H., 'Elizabeth Taylor Cadbury (1858–1951): religion, maternalism and social reform in Birmingham, 1888–1914', PhD thesis (University of Birmingham, 2012).

Waterson, M. and Wyndham, S., *A history of the Barrow Cadbury Trust: constancy & change in Quaker philanthropy* (London, 2013).

Wear, A. (ed.), *Medicine in society* (Cambridge, 1992).

Weindling, P., 'From infectious to chronic disease: changing patterns of sickness in the nineteenth and twentieth centuries', in Wear (ed.), *Medicine in society*, pp. 303–16.

Wilmot, F. and Saul, P., *A breath of fresh air: Birmingham's open-air schools, 1911–1970* (Chichester, 1998).

# 9

## Finding my place: rediscovering Hagley Park
*Joe Hawkins*

In May 2012 I was invited to oversee the restoration of Hagley Hall's largely forgotten Georgian landscape park, situated just inside the northern tip of Worcestershire. Still the seat of the Lyttelton family, the imposing Hall, built after the shaping of the gardens to match the park's eighteenth-century eminence, was designed by amateur architect Sanderson Miller (1716–1780) and constructed between 1754 and 1760, replacing an older house that stood nearby.[1] Behind the Palladian mansion's austere façade, a richly decorated rococo interior reflected a deep connection with its rural setting and its original owner's love of nature.[2] The following study presents recent advances in understanding the design and reception of and the reasons behind the appearance of Hagley Park's eighteenth-century landscape (Figure 9.1). It details the methodology used in a quest to authentically inform a restoration programme sympathetic to the period. Hagley's status as a pioneer location in the evolution of the eighteenth-century English landscape garden is recognised by its listing in the twenty-first century as an English Heritage Grade I registered park, a designation judging it to be of exceptional national interest.[3]

At Hagley there was no formal landscape to sweep away in the early eighteenth century, when the regular symmetries of gardens previously modelled on French and Dutch designs were widely rejected. Instead, inspired by the arts of painting and poetry, this Georgian landscape was coaxed gently from a medieval deer park, utilising its natural hillside topography, ancient trees, watercourses, green dales and deep wooded vales. Sloping away from the Clent Hills before abruptly rising to the Iron Age hillfort on Wychbury Hill, the park has extensive vistas to the south and west to the Malverns, the Clee and Abberley Hills, the Wrekin and, on a clear day, as far as the Black Mountains of Wales and Hay Bluff (Plate 9.1).

Hagley's main period of development, following a complex history and eventual re-emparkment by Sir Charles Lyttelton from 1693, occurred

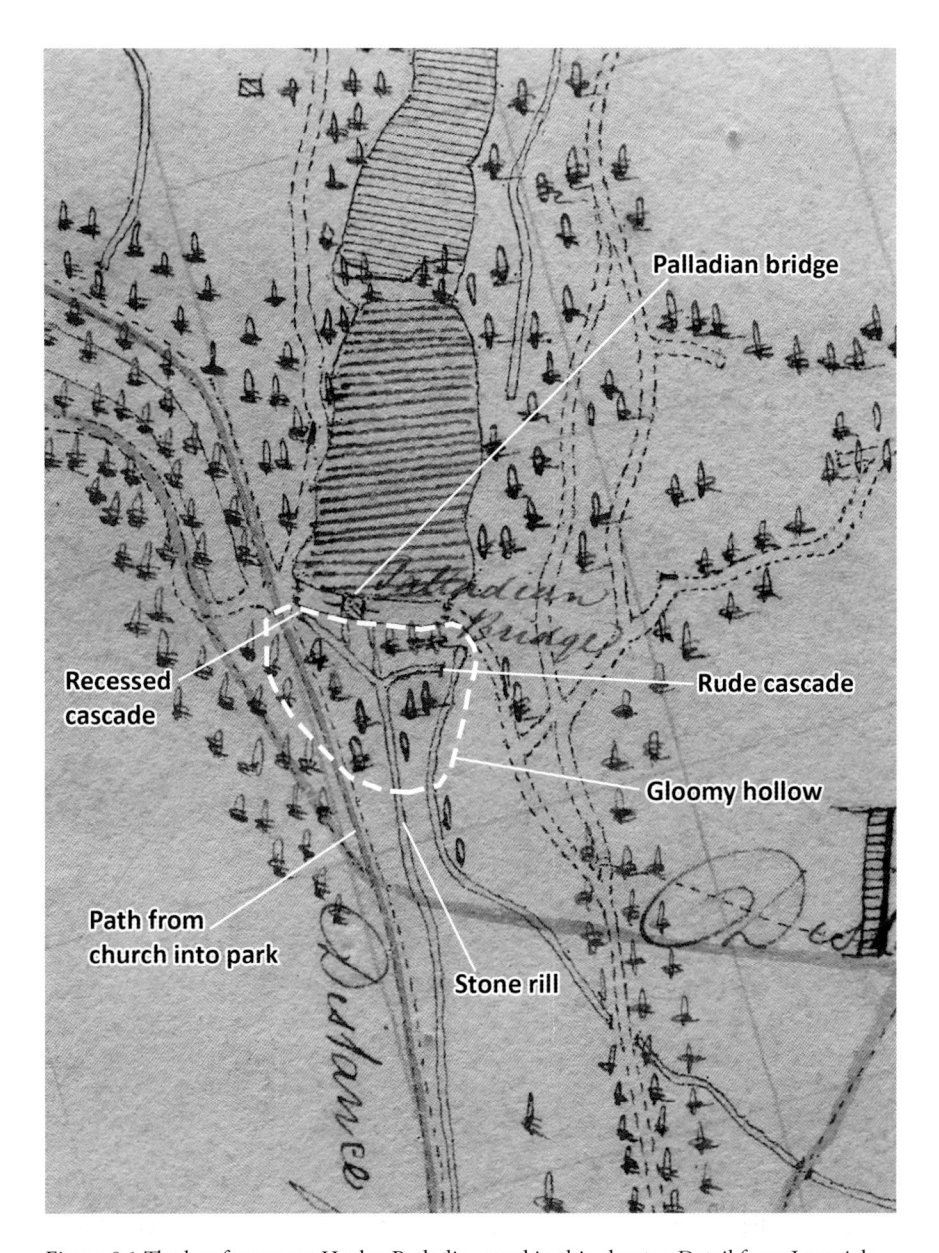

Figure 9.1 The key features at Hagley Park discussed in this chapter. Detail from Jeremiah Matthews' 1826 survey of Hagley with overlay by the author. Courtesy Joe Hawkins and Hagley Archive

Figure 9.2 Architectural features at Hagley, such as a ruined castle and temple, provided visual diversions and talking points for visitors. *A View in Hagley Park, belonging to Sir Thomas Lyttelton Bart*, Francis Vivares after Thomas Smith of Derby, 1748. Yale Center for British Art, Paul Mellon Collection. Digital image courtesy of Yale's Open Access Policy

from 1747 under the guidance of Sir Charles's grandson George Lyttelton (1709–1773) (Plate 9.2), who, seeking solace after the premature death of his beloved wife Lucy, invested his energy in creating a place that may also be read as a memorial to her loss.[4] The park contained memorials to Alexander Pope (Pope's Seat, Pope's Walk, Pope's Urn), while the addition of further monuments in memory of lost friends, including the poets James Thomson (1700–1748) and William Shenstone (1714–1763), ensured the park became a landscape for quiet contemplation. The park's pathways led through contrasting scenes intended to affect the senses, provoke moods and inspire the imagination. Its architectural features – temples, seats, urns, a ruined castle and an obelisk – were positioned along the route as visual entertainments to stimulate thought and prompt conversation through associations raised in the visitor's mind (Figure 9.2). George Lyttelton's poetic and aesthetic sensibilities and his literary knowledge gave the park a philosophical dimension. Many of the seats and temples were adorned with tablets inscribed with Latin verses from Roman authors such as Horace and Virgil, often extolling the delights and virtues of the country over the corruptions and vanities that were found in courtly or city life.

Hagley Park was visited, viewed and reviewed to great acclaim by some of the century's most enlightened minds. Early in its creation the English poet, critic and family friend Alexander Pope visited and contributed designs for three garden buildings. The owner of Prior Park, Ralph Allen (1693–1764), supplied stone for a monument at Hagley, the Prince's Pillar, which was apparently a gift from Frederick, Prince of Wales. Writing to Allen, Pope announced: 'among other places I have been at Sir Tho. Lyttlton's, where your Pillar is impatiently expected, & where I have designed three buildings'.[5] Similarly, Scottish poet James Thomson's first visit inspired verse that praised both the park's natural beauty and its creator's virtuous nature; in his 1744 revision of the nature poem *The Seasons* he declared:

O LYTTELTON, the Friend! thy Passions thus
And Meditations vary, as at large,
Courting the Muse, thro' HAGLEY-PARK you stray,
Thy British Tempe! There along the Dale,
With Woods o'er-hung, and shag'd with mossy Rocks,
Whence on each hand the gushing Waters play,
And down the rough Cascade white-dashing fall,
Or gleam in lengthen'd Vista thro' the Trees,
You silent steal;[6]

The art historian and critic Horace Walpole visited in 1753 and wrote: 'I wore out my eyes with gazing, my feet with climbing, and my tongue and vocabulary with commending'.[7] As its reputation grew, Hagley's landscape began to attract international visitors. John Adams and Thomas Jefferson, the second and third American presidents, along with Russian counts and Italian princes, made pilgrimage to witness the beauties to be found in Hagley's 'hallow'd' shades.[8]

Despite its broad appeal, Hagley's moment of glory was relatively brief and following George Lyttelton's death in 1773 the park's overall appearance began to change. A period of gentle decline grew into increasing neglect, particularly from the middle of the nineteenth century, when unrestrained nature impacted heavily on its features, eventually bringing the designed landscape to the brink of disappearance. During this period, the park's architectural features fell into disrepair; some were vandalised, others completely removed, and the meanders of its once well-trodden pathways disappeared beneath an accumulation of decades of leaf-litter and encroaching vegetation. Untended silt-traps became blocked, together with sluices, drains and culverts – some of which collapsed – and the park's pools became congested and stagnant. Seasonal rains from the catchment area of the Clent Hill slopes caused the breaching of dams and some lower cascades were buried. Many of the park's notable mature trees were harvested for timber, while open spaces were utilised for the quick cash crop of softwood plantations. Elsewhere, self-set weed-trees grew unchecked, gradually obscuring the park's internal views and extensive outward vistas.

Beneath this mantle of decay, and sheltered from any major subsequent design intervention, the apparent transience of the park's life was sustained by a constant recurrence of references to the park's reputation in landscape history research. In 2006 the impetus to revive Hagley's former glories was born when Christopher Lyttleton inherited the estate.[9] In 2007 the Garden History Society published a supplement to its journal dedicated to the eighteenth-century park and in 2011 this document underpinned a conservation management plan alongside additional studies in topography, archaeology, hydrology and ecology.[10] With a vision in place, funding was sought and obtained, and restoration of the park began.[11] The traditional picture of the landscape was predominantly informed by period accounts, but I approached Hagley's history anew. My MA in Garden History at the University of Bristol stressed the importance of directly experiencing the landscape as well as engaging with original primary sources. One advantage of this approach was the abundance of written descriptions. Spanning more than a century, these commentaries, whether celebratory, critical or indifferent, not only presented a timeline for the park's original design and development but also revealed a historiography of its aesthetic reception. Each account offered a subjective response to the landscape on the part of the respective authors and their narratives were usually drawn from their direct experience of the physical terrain guided by their personality, specialisms, understanding and the intended audience for their text. Collectively, these accounts not only corroborate detail but, through the identification, comparison and collation of their idiosyncrasies, create a comprehensive portrait of place. An assiduous comparison of these, allied with my deepening familiarity with the park's terrain, inspired a strategy to distil descriptive content into distinct regions, thereby establishing a literary map that allowed a sensory re-engagement with past-experienced space to be created in the present day. The prime objective in finding the 'where' of these textual topographical depictions was to detect and recover the park's lost physical aspects and to recognise and reawaken those attributes that were still close at hand.

Standing as a testament to and validating the strategy of this sense-driven approach were two buried cascades, unknown to recent research, that were rediscovered in the first two months following the start of the restoration. These and subsequent finds challenged how previous authors had described the landscape's original shape and appearance and enabled me to inform the restoration process with new and verifiable detail. This ensured a greater authenticity in the presentation of the restored park. Following these successes, all archival evidence was viewed through a similar lens and a stronger idea of the

Figure 9.3 Section of Jeremiah Matthews' 1826 survey of the Park at Hagley. Courtesy Joe Hawkins and Hagley Archive

park's eighteenth-century appearance emerged. Letters, diaries, account books, title deeds (muniments), charters, indentures and personal recollections were scrutinised to enrich the restoration of the landscape. Visual evidence existed in the form of engravings, collections of rough sketches, various nineteenth-century watercolours and the Hagley archives' collection of twentieth-century photographs. These sources assisted in revealing the park's appearance. One informative source in the collection was an 1826 survey of the park, which marked pathways, architecture, watercourses, timber densities and lawn extent (Figure 9.3). This source provided the closest representation of the entire estate and one that was more substantial than the less detailed nineteenth-century maps and later ordnance surveys.

Once the shape of the park was understood, the next issue to be resolved was why it had taken this shape. To answer this it was essential to appreciate George Lyttelton's inspirations, aspirations, attitudes and interests. A detailed exploration focusing on Lyttelton's formative experiences, his patronage and his commissions, as well as the wider connections of the Lyttelton family, was undertaken before applying these observations across a wider chronology of garden history and the cultural and aesthetic background to the park's creation and development. Tracing these ideas of the park's many contributory intellects not only confirmed George Lyttelton's role in the park's development but also suggested a continuity in the family's aesthetic and spiritual values.

Creating a narrative through period descriptions was key to understanding the park's creation. Much of the original archive was lost in the fire that destroyed the current Hall's library on Christmas Eve 1925, so my study had to draw from a wider range of primary source material. To gain a fundamental understanding of the park's creation, sources for the earlier history of the park were also consulted, as well as consideration of cultural ideas that permeated, shaped and gave it its identity. The persistence of older traditions has relevance to the progression of the landscape's aesthetic development. The target date of the restoration was set at about 1770, the zenith of the park's development.

This quest to detect the park's historic appearance began by following in the footsteps of eighteenth-century poet Thomas Maurice, whose 1776 account of his visit was the first to present a glimpse into the park's past and stimulated the first major rediscovery: an unknown cascade. Maurice, as a preliminary to his poetic tribute to Hagley, left St John the Baptist's Church, then the starting point for most visitors, and followed a narrow path 'from hence along the lawn to a gloomy hollow; whose steep banks are covered with large rocky stones, as if rent asunder by some violent concussion of nature. The gushing cascade, on either side, adds to the solemnity of the scene.'[12]

By 2012 the gloom perceived by Maurice was all but gone, although a hint of his experience was still discernible in a remnant of an earlier, more extensive planting development referred to by Sir Charles Lyttelton.[13] In a letter to Charles Hatton dated 17 December 1699 Sir Charles wrote:

> I have last week planted out about 40 horse chestnuts which I raised in a vista which goes through my garden and if your lordship will send me & can well spare 100: of those you so kindly offered me I shall not only continue that a great deal further but be able to plant another walk which I have in my design.[14]

Perhaps Sir Charles' decision to select this tree species for his vista was inspired by the lower pond's original name of Horse pool.[15] Whatever the catalyst for his choice, the line of his planted vista coincided with a development referred

Figure 9.4 The ruined Palladian Bridge and, from left to right, a mature horse chestnut and two yew trees shown in a mid-twentieth-century photograph. Hagley Archive, courtesy 12th Viscount Cobham

to by William Shenstone in a letter to Richard Jago almost 50 years later, when Shenstone informed him that the Lytteltons were 'to build a rotundo to terminate the visto' in their park'.[16] Recent archival material corroborates this reading of these early accounts. A mid-twentieth-century photograph shows a mature horse chestnut on the southern flank of the scant remains of the Palladian bridge, although this tree has since disappeared (Figure 9.4). On the south-eastern bank of the pool, now called the Lily Pond but known previously as the Palladian Pool, in front of the Palladian bridge, another contemporary mature specimen still stands as did another further east until 2014. One of a pair of horse chestnuts sited to the west, part of Sir Charles' original vista planting in the hollow behind the bridge, completes a line from the site of the original Hagley Hall, ascending along the line of the southern banks of the central vale of pools through to the site of the Rotunda.[17]

Three-quarters of a century after Sir Charles' embellishments, the pair of trees behind the bridge would have assisted in providing Maurice's perceived summer gloom. In the twenty-first century the effects of *pseudomonas*, a bleeding canker disease that has affected the horse chestnut nationwide, necessitated the removal of the most northerly of the remaining trees, limiting the contribution of the species to the ambience of the original scene behind the bridge to a single tree. This last remaining specimen on the south side illustrates the deep shade cast by the species, with little vegetative ground cover beneath its spreading limbs. Amplifying this shade, and the gloom witnessed by Maurice, were two yew trees that stood high on the eastern bank of the hollow. They must have been planted to give shelter and to screen out the back wall of the 'Alcove' seat, where the effect of their evergreen dark foliage, when viewed from the park's more easterly ascents, would frame by contrast and accent the building's appearance.

The Reverend Richard Pococke's 1751 description records no engagement with Maurice's gloomy hollow, perhaps convincing us that the spectacle was a later development. However, Pococke's account does illustrate the choice of paths available to the visitor not far from the church:

> Ascending up the valley there is a walk on each side, one winds up to the prospect and also along the side of the hanging ground. Going into the other to the left we came to a head, which is a bay to the water above, and on this is a rustick seat of bricks opening to the water above it in form of a Venetian window.[18]

This observation removes any notion that there was an intended circuit route in the landscape, which allows us to understand that the visitor was presented with a variety of connected and contrasting scenes to enjoy at their leisure.

Although there is no visual record of Pococke's 'rustic seat of bricks', its description as a 'Venetian window' suggests a Palladian semblance of order to its design, although it appeared to have been a sheltered seat rather than Thomas Pitt's subsequent more delicate and decorous architectural thoroughfare.[19] While the appearance of the original structure is, as noted, unknown, Resta Patching, a visitor in 1755, followed the same route as Maurice and noted that 'Our first Rest was an Alcove', which reveals the construction to be a recess and thus at least a shelter with side-walls.[20] More clues come from William Toldervy in 1762, when he described the feature as 'a whimsical Brick Building, with wicker Chairs on it'.[21] Again, we are given a clue in the latter part of his comment, the final two words hinting at a raised construction that would increase the visibility of movement beneath the surface of the pool at the near bank.

Perhaps Alexander Pope was the seat's designer, as the terminology used to describe it is very similar to the 'rustic seat of stone' he witnessed in the 1720s when visiting Sherborne, another landscape on which he is known to have advised.[22] George Lyttelton conveyed a better idea of this 'rustick seat' in a letter to Elizabeth Montagu regarding the development of the building.[23] He described Thomas Pitt as being 'very busy in converting the brick building at the end of my Pools in the Park into the semblance of a Bridge *at his own expense*. There is an Architect for you!'[24] This conversion of the original building shows that the Palladian bridge's portico and balustrades were an addition that presented a new façade to the original 'rustic seat'. The two yews planted behind this seat disguised the rear of the building and created a bold contrast between two distinct moods in the landscape: according to Joseph Heeley, the visitor was transported 'from gloom and melancholy, into the roseate bowers of paradise'.[25] The poetic mood cultivated in the design of Hagley reflects Edmund Burke's observation on architectural contrast in his influential essay of 1757:

> to make an object very striking, we should make it as different as possible from the objects with which we have been immediately conversant; when therefore you enter a building, you cannot pass into a greater light than you had in the open air; to go into one some few degrees less luminous, can make only a trifling change; but to make the transition thoroughly striking, you ought to pass from the greatest light, to as much darkness as is consistent with the uses of architecture.[26]

While he experienced that transition in reverse, passing from dark to light, Heely's prose was intended to provoke both a physical and an intellectual response. Evidence suggests that this design at Hagley is at least contemporary with Burke's advice. Two late nineteenth-century photographs show the dark backdrop of yew still shading the bridge (Figures 9.5 and 9.6). The second of these images also shows with more clarity the wooden bench behind the front balustrade, probably a replacement for Toldervy's wicker chairs and more in keeping with the light and delicate air of Pitt's Palladian bridge.

The passage of time and ravages of nature have moderated the contribution of these two yews to the scene behind the bridge, as just a single tree remains. While the mid-twentieth-century photograph illustrating the horse chestnut to the south of the Palladian bridge (Figure 9.4) shows two yew trees still in place above the much-diminished bridge structure, by 2012 one mature yew stump, partially uprooted, sat diagonally slightly lower down the bank, revealing an abrupt end to the extant yew's contemporary companion. With its southern root-flare wrenched from the ground and pointing upward, its position and cleanly cut stem was clear evidence of a wind-blown tree that, falling north, had for a time blocked the major thoroughfare into the park. Its side branches were also likely to have damaged the ceramic drains from the outfall chamber of the pool above, resulting in scours behind the wall to the right of the cascade race before it was cut away and removed to allow access into the park. Like the horse chestnuts, these yews would have left the gloomy hollow bare-earthed and dark, or 'devoid of verdure', as described by Heely on a visit preceding that of Maurice.[27]

Comparing Heely's observations with those of Maurice brings a greater depth to our understanding of later perceptions of the area. Heely recorded his

Figure 9.5 A late nineteenth-century photograph shows the Palladian Bridge still shaded by a backdrop of yew. Hagley Archive, courtesy 12th Viscount Cobham

Figure 9.6 The wooden bench on the Palladian Bridge, identified from this late nineteenth-century photograph. Hagley Archive, courtesy 12th Viscount Cobham

Figure 9.7 The brick culvert and stone rill revealed during excavations at Hagley Park. © Joe Hawkins

experiences of Hagley twice: a second extended account, *Letters on the Beauties of Hagley, Enville and The Leasowes*, was written following what he considered to be plagiarism of his initial observations recorded in *A Description of Hagley, Envil and the Leasowes*.[28] Maurice followed a similar route to Heely into the park, but Heely's first account gives us a more substantial account: 'From the Church, a narrow path, by the side of a small pebbly chirping rill, leads along the lawn, to a rude, solitary hollow, seemingly marked so by some violent concussion of nature.'[29] His later work, the *Letters* describes, after exiting the church, how he 'came to a narrow easy waving path, by the side of a pebbly rill, that led me to a rude gloomy hollow, with every appearance of its being left by some violent concussion, or inundation'.[30] Heely added an extra detail to Maurice's introductory route in both of his accounts: namely, the rill that ran down from the gloomy hollow. Today the route of this pebbly rill is still visible in the two parallel lines of stone that once constrained its course along the narrow lawn-edged path noted by Maurice.

By 2015 silting of the rill and inundations from storms had caused the watercourse to create its own meander, collapsing some stones and eroding banks on either side to interrupt its original linear character, which must have been part of Sir Thomas Lyttelton's original improvements to the drainage of the park. It had a connection via a brick-built conduit to the bypass culvert that ran, and still runs, through the southern side of the entire pond system (Figure 9.7). The original rill would have been a way of taking the water past the old hall or hunting lodge in times of heavy rain, its brick bottom and straight course ensuring that an unimpeded flow conveyed any storm water past the old house as quickly as possible, although it seems to have had only limited success. In a letter dated 13 June 1748 to his son Charles, Sir Thomas noted that his remedy for a frequently flooded house was not always effective:

> we had the most furious storm of thunder &c yesterday I ever remember, it rain'd incessantly with the utmost violence for four hours my cellars & all the ground floor fill'd with water I was in terrible apprehensions for the Ponds in the Park the water run over all the dams not withstanding the great drains lately made.[31]

With no mention of the rill in Pococke's account, it seems that it was modified after the new Hall was completed in 1760. The bypass culvert was then diverted and became the supply for the serpentine that wound across the park, providing water via sluices to wash out the sewage from beneath the new Hall before joining forces with the Gallows brook on the southern extremity of the park pales. With the danger of flooding removed, large rounded pebbles were placed along the rill's course and intermediate spill-stones restricted the faster flow, energising the water's aural qualities to produce a sensory entertainment designed to attract the visitor's attention, as it certainly had with Heely. After following the course of the rill to the gloomy hollow, Heely's initial description continued:

> The abrupt, steep and hanging banks, devoid of verdure, large rocky stones, as if rent from the bowels of the earth, and the naked roots of old trees, promiscuous, tottering, hollow, impending; and the dashing cascade among massy stones and burnt cinders, strike the mind, and add to the wildness of the scene.[32]

His later extended account in the *Letters* recorded a very similar scene:

> surrounded by steep abrupt banks, devoid of verdure – trees of an amazing height, some in the bottom as if slipped down the sides, confusedly jumbled together, their roots exposed, creeping along, and over the ground huge stones, seemingly rolled or driven there, by some violence, in the utmost disorder – rocky cascades – and the dribbling of springs.[33]

Both Heely and Maurice's later observations of 'banks covered with large rocky stones' were strangely absent from the scene in 2012, as was any plurality of cascades. Maurice's account directly echoes the terminology used by Heely, although he is more succinct: 'To that lone Dell, beneath the deepen'd shade,

Figure 9.8 The source of the 'rude cascade' uncovered at Hagley Park. © Joe Hawkins

Where down the valley bursts the rude cascade.'[34] Maurice's perception of a 'rude cascade', enriching Heely's original description of 'rocky cascades', surfaced once more in the anonymously written *Companion to the Leasowes, Hagley and Enville*, where, again, the shaping of the gloomy hollow's appearance is seen to be a ferocious force of nature:

> From Hence we are conducted through a narrow pass, along the lawn by the margin of a murmuring rill, whose steepy banks, composed of large rocky substances, seem as if rent asunder by some subterraneous irruption of nature, whilst on either side a gushing cascade adds to the solemnity of the whole.[35]

By 2012 a single cascade with a stepped race passing below two drystone walls recessed into the northern bank was the only obvious outlet from the pool above; it was the single source of the eighteenth-century 'pebbly chirping rill' that ran toward the church. This outfall, however, was hardly the 'rude cascade' described by Maurice. Rather than having any rude or natural appearance, its design was of a practical, utilitarian nature. Such water management down a long, evenly stepped race, with its stones set horizontally to the water's flow, was designed as a braking mechanism to prevent the effects of scouring from the force of seasonal inundations of water.[36] A cylindrical ceramic pipe at the head of the cascade's race showed that the supply to this cascade had been repaired in the more recent past, suggesting the likelihood of a redesign to the original outflow (Figure 9.8).

In 2013 excavations to repair these ceramic drains, possibly broken or at least provoked in their decline by the falling yew, revealed that they had been laid in part over a substantial stone foundation. This was probably that of a blade-mill similar to others sited adjacent to the region's watercourses from the fourteenth to the sixteenth centuries; Hagley's was swept away in a flood of 1698.[37] The substantial flagstone floor included a deep circular recess that would have held an upright pillar which probably supported the wheel mechanism. What was until recently thought to be a secondary supply of water from the hollow-way followed the path of a higher narrow leat, now covered and lying just below today's ground level. Such a flow of water was ideal for powering an undershot waterwheel, and the discovery of a well-worn millstone nearby supports this interpretation. This feature provides evidence that the Palladian pool was much older than any post-re-emparkment construction.

The clearance of vegetation on the opposite side to the extant cascade revealed another ceramic pipe sited at the top of the southern steep bank. The pipe's diameter suggested a reasonable outflow point and provided a first clue to the missing cascade's position. After the probing of the ground with a pitchfork revealed the presence of stone beneath the surface, archaeologists were called in to explore and uncover trial areas. The removal of decades of overburden (soil, decayed leaf litter and other organic detritus) exposed an array of carefully placed undressed stones which, although of natural appearance, were not local to the area. Further enquiry showed this stone to be present throughout the surrounding banks. Maurice's rude cascade had been found and, although it was among Heely's 'huge stones, seemingly rolled or driven there, by some violence, in the utmost disorder', it was in fact an eighteenth-century intervention created by George Lyttelton.[38]

Arthur Young's tour of 1768, which preceded those of both Heely and Maurice, gives the first mention of the rill, the appearance of the hollow and one of the cascades and adds a wooded aspect to the approach: 'the Walk from the house leads through a wood, by the side of a purling stream, which meanders over grass from out a dark hollow; you pass a gush of water, which falls into it.'[39] Following this route today through a largely imagined wood, along Maurice's narrow lawn, accompanied by Heely's pebbly rill, the path rises gently towards the site of the Palladian bridge (Plate 9.3), and it becomes evident that the newly recovered rude cascade would have been the only directly visible water feature from the visitor's vantage point (Figure 9.9). The gushing recessed cascade on the northern side, although contributing to the aural dynamic and enhancing the wild nature of the scene, was much less visible. Heely was the first to recognise the hand of art in the creation of this 'wild' scenery, remarking, 'this place, though perhaps but cursorily attended to, is capital; – and no one part of the park shows a greater exertion of genius.'[40]

Figure 9.9 The 'rude cascade' fully restored at Hagley Park. © Joe Hawkins

The numerous weighty stones that decorated the banks were intended to create a 'natural' scene, but as they had no relationship to the immediate topography they were probably quarried from elsewhere in the park and would have taken considerable industry to put into place. The local response by those who knew of this artifice was perhaps recognised by George Lyttelton in his letter to historian Archibald Bower while on his extended Welsh tour of 1756, when he related an exchange whilst visiting Vaynor Park:

> but, to let you see how vulgar minds value such improvements, I must tell you an answer made by our guide, who was servant to Lord Powis's steward, and spoke, I presume, the sense of his master, upon our expressing some wonder that this Gentleman had been able to do so much with so small a fortune; 'I do not, said he, know how it is, but he is always doing some nonsense or other.' I apprehend, most of my neighbours would give the same account of my improvements at Hagley.[41]

Whatever the local perception, and assisting in guiding our understanding of the inspiration behind his design, there is evidence to show that a deeply contemplative response to nature had been part of George Lyttelton's thinking since his youth. In a letter written at the age of 19 to his father he discussed the merits of John Milton's descriptions in *Paradise Lost*, remarking: 'Nature is very strictly observed, the boldness of his genius appears without shocking us with the least impropriety: we are surprised, we are warmed, we are transported; but we are not hurried out of our senses, or forced to believe impossibilities.'[42]

Lyttelton's contemplation and endorsement of the poet's verse suggests an eye for detail that can be ascribed only to an understanding that stems from being in a landscape. He then presented proof that this was no naive critical analysis by adding, 'the sixth book is, I fear, in many places an exception to this rule; the *poetica licentia* is stretched too far, and *the just* is sacrificed to *the wonderful*.'[43] He concluded 'you will pardon me, if I talk too much in the language of the schools'.[44] Milton's descriptions of nature were integral in the development of the English landscape style. Stephen Switzer's influential *Iconographia rustica* of 1718 embedded Milton's literary descriptions into garden culture and he considered the poet's 'inimitable description of Paradise' worthy of a place among the directives for the creation of 'rural landskips'.[45] Earlier still, 18 issues of Joseph Addison's *The Spectator* had guided readers through the sublimity of Milton's *Paradise Lost*, encouraging his audience to take an interest in themes with which Lyttelton was no doubt conversant: 'Milton's chief Talent, and indeed his distinguishing Excellence, lies in the Sublimity of his Thoughts.'[46] Lyttelton's critical commentary on Milton was written just prior to him embarking on a grand tour that would take him, after a long stay in France, across the Alps to Geneva.[47] Writing to his father following his passage, he described in lengthy detail the awesome scenes of nature experienced *en route* over Mont-Cenis.[48]

Lyttelton's continued interest in the effects of sublimity reappeared during his extended Welsh trip of 1756, where he witnessed:

> the formidable mountains of Snowdon, black and naked rocks, which seemed to be piled one above the other. The summits of some of them are covered with clouds, and cannot be ascended. They do altogether strongly excite the idea of Burnet, of their being the fragment of a demolished world.[49]

His commentary revealed a familiarity with Thomas Burnet's controversial *Sacred theory of the earth* (1684), an epic narrative that attempted to bring a geological concept to the fall of Paradise by attributing the deluge and conflagration to natural causes. Although Burnet's quest to unite science and theology failed, his descriptions of 'a broken globe' and 'wild, vast and indigested heaps of stones and earth' gripped the imagination of the reader, raising an awareness of nature and assisting in the creation of a taste for the sublime experience.[50] Maurice's and Heely's accounts of the gloomy dell behind the Palladian bridge were couched in language similar to that used by Lyttelton on his Welsh tour.

From these accounts Lyttelton's creation at Hagley can be read as a three-dimensional translation of Milton's postlapsarian world and Burnet's ruined earth. The rude cascade, rock-strewn environs and pervading gloom presented a physical rendition of sublimity, here hewn in miniature: a poetic interlude drawn upon the landscape. Describing his own experience of Lyttelton's scene, Heely stepped 'into the midst of it, to a simple bench under a tree; and from the gaiety of the park, open and filled with cheerful objects, found myself immersed in a wild disordered and savage solitude'.[51] Encouraged by a convenient seat and the thought-provoking opportunity afforded by his own solitude, Heely's contemplative reflection not only feels the sublimity portrayed but also explores its context within the wider park. His identification of 'the gaiety of the park, open and filled with cheerful objects' and his subsequent transportation into 'the roseate bowers of Paradise' allows us to recognise the gloomy hollow as a contrasting episode in the landscape's series of moods or atmospheres, each artfully designed to arouse the visitor's imagination.

One of the earliest visitors to record the improvements in the park was Daniel Defoe, who, reflecting on George Lyttelton's endeavours in its development, saw a

> beautiful Spot of Ground having as great a variety of Hills, Valleys, and Wood, as can be imagined in such a Space of Ground; and the present Possessor is constantly improving and helping Nature; so that it may be esteemed one of the finest Seats in this County.[52]

Defoe's emphasis on the park's variety and his observation of the assisted cultivation of nature portrayed a design scheme assiduously adhering to the tenets that informed the English landscape garden. Switzer presented both aspects in *Iconographia rustica*: 'Variety is the most distinguishing Characteristick in any country-Seat or Garden' and 'the natural Gardener [is he who will make] his design submit to Nature and not Nature to his Design.'[53]

This chapter has reflected on contemporary descriptions of one small region of the park, setting them in their time and place. By studying these descriptions in the physical landscape and seeking past sensory impressions in the present, they allow the viewer to perceive the 'genius of the place'.[54] To understand a landscape, the imperative remains: you must experience a place to know it.

## Notes

1. H. Walpole, *Private correspondence Of Horace Walpole, Earl Of Orford: now first collected*, 1st edn, 4 vols (London, 1820), vol. i, p. 307.
2. M. McCarthy, 'The building of Hagley Hall, Worcestershire', *Burlington Magazine*, 118/877 (April 1976), pp. 214–25; M. Droth and P. Curtis (eds), *Taking shape: finding sculpture in the decorative arts* (Leeds and Los Angeles, 2009).
3. Historic England's *Register of parks and gardens of special historic interest in England* celebrates designed landscapes of note and encourages appropriate protection to safeguard their features and qualities for the future. The National Heritage List for England is the official database of all nationally protected historic sites and buildings. See <http://www.historicengland.org.uk/listing/the-list/>, accessed 5 November 2017.
4. C. Gerrard, 'Lyttelton, George, first Baron Lyttelton (1709–1773)', *Oxford Dictionary of National Biography* (*Oxford DNB*) (Oxford, 2004); online edn <http://www.oxforddnb.com/view/article/17306>, accessed 17 January 2017.
5. G. Sherburn (ed.), *The correspondence of Alexander Pope*, 5 vols (Oxford, 1956), vol. iv, pp. 185, 190.
6. J. Thomson, *The works of James Thomson. In four volumes complete. With his last corrections, additions and improvements* (London, 1757), pp. 36–8.
7. Walpole, *Private correspondence*, vol. i, p. 307.
8. Rev. Luke Booker, 'To the groves of Hagley', in *Miscellaneous poems* (Stourbridge, 1789), p. 83.
9. Christopher Lyttelton (b. 1947), inherited the title of Viscount Cobham on 13 July 2006 following the death of his elder brother John Lyttelton, 11th Viscount Cobham.
10. M. Cousins, 'Hagley Park, Worcestershire', *Garden History*, 35/Supplement 1 (2007), pp. 1–152. The article was researched with the co-operation of the 11th Viscount Cobham and published post-succession. This was followed by M. Symes and S. Haynes, *Enville, Hagley and the Leasowes: three great eighteenth-century gardens* (Bristol, 2010), which considered the rise and relationship of three landscapes in close proximity and their draw to contemporary tourists; A. Nelson, *Hagley Park conservation management plan*, commissioned by the 12th Viscount Cobham and Natural England (York, 2011).
11. The project's initial funding came from Natural England, English Heritage and Viscount Cobham.
12. T. Maurice, *Hagley. A descriptive poem* (Oxford, 1776), p. 4.
13. W. Scott, *Stourbridge and its vicinity* (Stourbridge, 1832), p. 258.
14. The British Library (BL), Add. MS 163, Hatton – Finch Correspondence, vol. iii.
15. Library of Birmingham, MS 3279/351588, Lease for fifty years from John Seynteleger, esq., to Richard Smythe of Hagley, laborer, of a cottage, a little close called the Horse Pool adjoining the

Churchyard of Hagleye and common of fifteen sheep in and upon the common of Hagley, 28 August 30 Hen. VIII. [1538].
16   *Select letters between the late Duchess of Somerset, Lady Luxborough, Mr. Whistler, Miss Dolman, Mr. R. Dodsley, William Shenstone, Esq. and Others … the whole now published by Mr. Hull*, 2 vols (London, 1778), vol. i, Letter XI, W. Shenstone, Esq. to the Rev. Mr. Jago, 1747. For Shenstone see John Hemingway's chapter in this volume.
17   The original Hall was a hunting lodge extended first by Sir John Lyttelton in 1564 and again by Sir Charles during his re-emparkment begun in 1693.
18   J. Cartright (ed.), *The travels through England of Dr. Richard Pococke*, 2 vols (London, 1889), vol. i, pp. 225–6.
19   R. Thorne, 'Pitt, Thomas, first Baron Camelford (1737–1793)', *Oxford DNB* (Oxford, 2004); online edn <http://www.oxforddnb.com/view/article/22335>, accessed 29 March 2017.
20   R. Patching, *Four topographical letters, written in July 1755* (London, 1757), p. 60.
21   W. Toldervy, *England and Wales described. In a series of letters* (London, 1762), p. 343.
22   Sherburn, *The correspondence*, vol. iv, pp. 185, 190.
23   B. Schnorrenberg, 'Montagu, Elizabeth (1718–1800)', *Oxford DNB* (Oxford, 2004); online edn <http://www.oxforddnb.com/view/article/19014>, accessed 29 March 2017.
24   Huntington Library, CA, Montagu correspondence, iv MO 1302 [Hagley Park, 15 Oct. 1762].
25   J. Heely, *A description of Hagley, Envil and the Leasowes: wherein all the Latin inscriptions are translated, and every particular beauty described. Interspersed with critical observations* (London, 1775), p. 86.
26   E. Burke, *A philosophical enquiry into the origin of our ideas of the sublime and beautiful*, 4th edn (London, 1764), p. 127.
27   Heely, *A description*, p. 85.
28   J. Heely, *Letters on the beauties of Hagley, Envil and the Leasowes etc.*, 2 vols (London, 1777).
29   Heely, *A description*, p. 85.
30   Heely, *Letters*, vol i, pp. 127–128.
31   Hagley Archive, Folio 81, June 13 1748, Letter from Sir Thomas Lyttelton to Charles Lyttelton.
32   Heely, *A description*, p. 85.
33   Heely, *Letters*, vol i, p. 129.
34   Maurice, *Hagley*, p. 19.
35   Anon., *A companion to the Leasowes, Hagley and Enville* (Birmingham, 1789), p. 72.
36   Such a recessed outfall is also commensurate with a fish management system where a pool could be drained and the fish caught in woven baskets prior to transfer to other ponds.
37   BL, Add MSS 29579 fol. 53i Letter from Sir Charles Lyttelton to Christopher Hatton, Dated 5 November 1698.
38   Heely, *Letters*, vol. i, p. 129.
39   A. Young, *A six months tour through the north of England*, 2nd edn (London, 1771), vol. iii, p. 264.
40   Heely, *A description*, p. 86.
41   G. Ayscough (ed.), *The works of George Lyttelton* (London, 1774), p. 741.
42   Hagley Archive, Letter to Sir Thomas Lyttelton, February 4, 1728. The letter was written from London prior to the 19-year-old embarking on a grand tour that would take him after a lengthy stay in France, across the Alps and on to Italy.
43   *Ibid*.
44   *Ibid*.
45   S. Switzer, *Ichnographia rustica: or, the nobleman, gentleman, and gardener's recreation*, 3 vols (London, 1718), vol. i, p. 344.
46   J. Addison, *The Spectator*, 279 (19 January 1712) (4): '*Milton's* chief Talent, and indeed his distinguishing Excellence, lies in the Sublimity of his Thoughts'.

47  Hagley Archive, Letter to Sir Thomas Lyttelton, Letter XXV Lions [sic], October 16, 1729: 'I set out for Geneva tomorrow with Sir William Wyndham's son Charles Wyndham (1710–1763), and shall go from thence to Turin.'
48  Hagley Archive, Letter to Sir Thomas Lyttelton, October 26, 1729.
49  Ayscough, *The works*, p. 752, George Lyttelton to Archibald Bower, Brynker, in Carnarvonshire, July 6, 1756.
50  T. Burnet, *The sacred theory of the earth* (London, 1816), pp. 174, 159.
51  Heely, *A description*, p. 32.
52  D. Defoe, *A tour through the whole island of Great Britain: divided into circuits or journeys*, 4th edn, 4 vols (London, 1748), vol. ii, p. 338.
53  Switzer, *Ichnographia rustica*, vol. ii, pp. 196, 201.
54  A. Pope, *Epistles to several persons: Epistle iv, to Richard Boyle, Lord Burlington* (London, 1731).

# Bibliography
*Primary sources*
British Library (BL)
 Add. MS 163, Hatton – Finch Correspondence, vol. iii
 Add. MSS 29579 fol. 53i, Letter Charles Lyttelton to Christopher Hatton, 5 November 1698
Hagley Archive
 Folio 81, June 13 1748, Letter from Sir Thomas Lyttelton to Charles Lyttelton
 Letter to Sir Thomas Lyttelton, February 4, 1728
 Letter to Sir Thomas Lyttelton, Letter XXV Lions [sic], October 16, 1729
Huntingdon Library, CA
 Montagu correspondence, iv MO 1302 [Hagley Park, 15 Oct. 1762]
Library of Birmingham
 MS 3279/351588, Lease for fifty years from John Seynteleger, esq., to Richard Smythe of Hagley, laborer, of a cottage, a little close called the Horse Pool adjoining the Churchyard of Hagleye and common of fifteen sheep in and upon the common of Hagley, 28 August 30 Hen. VIII. [1538]

*Printed primary sources*
Anon., *A companion to the Leasowes, Hagley and Enville* (Birmingham, 1789).
Addison, J., *The Spectator*, 279 (19 January 1712).
Ayscough, G. (ed.), *The works of George Lyttelton* (London, 1774).
Booker, Rev. L., 'To the groves of Hagley', in *Miscellaneous poems* (Stourbridge, 1789).
Burke, E., *A philosophical enquiry into the origin of our ideas of the sublime and beautiful*, 4th edn (London, 1764).
Burnet, T., *The sacred theory of the earth* (London, 1684, repr. 1816).
Cartright, J. (ed.), *The travels through England of Dr. Richard Pococke*, 2 vols, vol. i (London, 1889).
Defoe, D., *A tour through the whole island of Great Britain: divided into circuits or journeys*, 4th edn, 4 vols, vol. ii (London, 1748).
Heely, J., *A description of Hagley, Envil and the Leasowes: wherein all the Latin inscriptions are translated, and every particular beauty described. Interspersed with critical observations* (London, 1775).
Heely, J., *Letters on the beauties of Hagley, Envil and the Leasowes etc.*, 2 vols (London, 1777).

Maurice, T., *Hagley. A descriptive poem* (Oxford, 1776).
Patching, R., *Four topographical letters, written in July 1755* (London, 1757).
Pope, A., *Epistles to several persons: Epistle iv, to Richard Boyle, Lord Burlington* (London, 1731).
Scott, W., *Stourbridge and its vicinity* (Stourbridge, 1832).
*Select letters between the late Duchess of Somerset, Lady Luxborough, Mr. Whistler, Miss Dolman, Mr. R. Dodsley, William Shenstone, Esq. and Others ... the whole now published by Mr. Hull*, 2 vols, vol. i (London, 1778).
Sherburn, G. (ed.), *The correspondence of Alexander Pope*, 5 vols, vol. iv (Oxford, 1956).
Switzer, S., *Ichnographia rustica; or, the nobleman, gentleman, and gardener's recreation*, 3 vols, vol. i (London, 1718).
Thomson, J., *The works of James Thomson. In four volumes complete. With his last corrections, additions and improvements* (London, 1757).
Toldervy, W., *England and Wales described. In a series of letters* (London, 1762).
Walpole, H., *Private correspondence of Horace Walpole, Earl of Orford: now first collected*, 4 vols, vol. i (London, 1820).
Young, A., *A six months tour through the north of England*, 2nd edn, vol. iii (London, 1771).

*Secondary sources*

Cousins, M., 'Hagley Park, Worcestershire', *Garden History*, 35/Supplement 1 (2007), pp. 1–152.
Droth, M. and Curtis, P. (eds), *Taking shape: finding sculpture in the decorative arts* (Leeds and Los Angeles, 2009).
Gerrard, C., 'Lyttelton, George, first Baron Lyttelton (1709–1773)', *Oxford Dictionary of National Biography* (*Oxford DNB*) (Oxford, 2004); online edn <http://www.oxforddnb.com/view/article/17306>, accessed 17 January 2017.
Historic England, *Register of parks and gardens of special historic interest in England*, <http://www.historicengland.org.uk/listing/the-list/>, accessed 5 November 2017.
McCarthy, M., 'The building of Hagley Hall, Worcestershire', *Burlington Magazine*, 118/877 (April 1976), pp. 214–25.
Nelson, A., *Hagley Park conservation management plan, commissioned by the 12th Viscount Cobham and Natural England* (York, 2011).
Schnorrenberg, B., 'Montagu , Elizabeth (1718–1800)', *Oxford DNB* (Oxford, 2004); online edn <http://www.oxforddnb.com/view/article/19014>, accessed 29 March 2017.
Symes, M. and Haynes, S., *Enville, Hagley and the Leasowes: three great eighteenth-century gardens* (Bristol, 2010).
Thorne, R., 'Pitt, Thomas, first Baron Camelford (1737–1793)', *Oxford DNB* (Oxford, 2004); online edn <http://www.oxforddnb.com/view/article/22335>, accessed 29 March 2017.

# Index

Adam, Robert 24
Adams, John 189
Addison, Joseph 64, 202
Allen, Ralph 189
Allensmore Court, Herefordshire 24
Amyand, George, later Cornewall, Sir George 23–4
Apollo Gardens, Birmingham 82
Aramstone, Herefordshire 19
Ashbourne, Derbyshire 108
Aston Hall, Birmingham 80
Ayres, Mary and Thomas 109–10

Bach, John 18–19, 20
Backbury Hill, Herefordshire 13
Barlow, Sir Thomas 165
Barrell, John 14, 16
Baskerville, John 44
Bateman, Richard 18
Beale, John 12–14
Belmont, Herefordshire 28, 32
Berg, Maxine 2
Berrington, Herefordshire 10, 19, 21–4, 28, 31
Biddulph, John 25
Birmingham Botanical Gardens 122
Blomfield, Reginald 155
Borsay, Peter 76, 77, 83
Boulton, Matthew 2, 79, 87
Bournville, Birmingham 171
Bower, Archibald 202
Brampton Bryan, Herefordshire 12, 18, 22
Bridgeman, Holte 82
Brinsop Court, Herefordshire 15
Bristowe, John Syer 167
Brobury Scar, Herefordshire 21, 30
Bromsgrove, Worcestershire 160

Brookes, Mrs 114–15
Brown, Lancelot 'Capability' 1, 10, 21–8, 31, 32
Burke, Edmund 26, 195
Burlton, Herefordshire 15
Burnet, Thomas 203
Burnett, Frances Hodgson 176
Butler, Andrew 82

Cadbury, Elizabeth Taylor 171
Cadbury, Geraldine 152, 160, 165, 171–2, 175, 177
Cadbury, Helen 142, 148, 150
Cadbury, Paul 165
Camden, William 12
Chamberlain, Austen 146–8
Chamberlain, Beatrice 148, 150, 154
Chamberlain, Caroline 143–4
Chamberlain, Ethel 148, 154, 155
Chamberlain, Hilda 152, 154–5
Chamberlain, Mary née Endicott 146, 148, 154–5
Chatsworth, Derbyshire 104, 112, 123, 145
Chowry-Muthu, David 176
Clark, John 18
Clent, Worcestershire 44, 186, 189
Cobham, 12th Viscount (Lyttelton, Christopher) 6
Conlin, Jonathan 77, 87
Constable, John 28
Corfield, Penelope 92
Cornewall, Catherine 23
Cornewall, Velters 20–1
Court of Noke, Herefordshire 12
Croft Castle, Herefordshire 19–20, 27, 32
Currie, Christopher 46, 47, 49, 50

Dale Coppice, Coalbrookdale 59
Dale House, Shropshire 60
Darby, Abraham I 56, 59–60

Darby, Abraham II 60
Darby, Abraham III 56
Darwin, Erasmus 2
Davenport, John 24
Defoe, Daniel 203–4
Delany, Mary 76, 78, 84, 87, 89
Derrick, Samuel 78
Digby, Lord 14
Dodsley, Robert 47, 48
Dolman, Maria 40, 46
Downton, Herefordshire 17, 25, 27, 28, 29, 30
Duddeston (Dudston), Birmingham 76, 80, 81, 82, 93
Duff Cooper, Caroline née Cornewall 30
Duffield, Derbyshire 109, 110

Eau Withington, Herefordshire 15
Elton Hall, Herefordshire 28
Emes, William 24, 27, 65
enclosure 10–11, 22–3
Evelyn, John 12–13
Eversmann, John 84
exhibitions and trade fairs
   Great Exhibition of the Works of Industry of all Nations, London 128, 133
   Royal Agricultural Show Wolverhampton 131
   Wolverhampton Art and Industrial Exhibition 125, 133
Eye Manor, Herefordshire 19, 22, 23
Eywood, Herefordshire 10, 19, 21–2

Ferme ornée 14, 20, 30, 41, 65
Firs estate, Moor Green, Birmingham 148
Foley family 12, 19, 21
Ford, Richard 60
Fothergill, Patty 87
Foxley, Herefordshire 3, 16, 17
Frances, Lady Scudamore 14
Freen's Court, Herefordshire 12

Gainsborough, Thomas 16, 17, 28
Garden history, methodologies 1, 3–7
Garnons, Herefordshire 26, 32
Gay, John 14
Gilpin, Revd William 16, 26
Gilpin, William Sawrey 29, 30
Goldney, Thomas III 61–2
Gorge, Henry 19
Gough, Walter 81, 82

Grange estate, Kings Heath, Birmingham 151, 153
Gray, Thomas 17
Greening, Thomas, 18
Greenly, Elizabeth 30
Grevis (Greaves) family 139

Hampton Court, Herefordshire 12, 18, 20, 23
Harley, Edward, 4th earl of Oxford 21
Harley, Thomas 22, 23
Harrington, Ralph 45
Hartlibb, William 12, 13
Harvey, John, author 102
Harvey, John, land agent 25
Haywood Lodge, Herefordshire 19
Hearne, Thomas 17, 27
Heely, Joseph 50, 195, 197, 198, 200, 203
Hill, Leonard 179
Holme Lacy, Herefordshire 14, 18, 19, 30–1, 32
Holte, Sir Thomas 80
Holte, Dowager Lady 81
Horne, Edward 45
Horwood, Catherine 3
Howard, Charles, 11th duke of Norfolk 30, 31
Hulbert, Charles 56
Hull, Thomas 47
Hutton, William 80, 82

Ironbridge, Shropshire 56, 58

Jacson, Maria 3
Jago, Richard 193
Jefferson, Thomas 189

Keck, Anthony 24
Kent, Nathaniel 17
Kent, William 49
Kentchurch Court, Herefordshire 15, 32
Kilpeck Castle, Herefordshire 19
Kipling, Rudyard 175
Knight, Henrietta (Lady Luxborough) 3
Knight, Richard Payne 17, 20, 25–30, 32
Knight, Thomas Andrew 28
Koch, Robert 166
Kyre Park, Worcestershire 24
Kyrle, John 14

Ledbury Park, Herefordshire 25
Leggett, Thomas 24
Lincoln Hill, Shropshire 62–3, 66, 69–70

# INDEX

Lipscomb, George 17
Littler, Joseph and Martha 113–4
Lockman, John 21
Longworth, Herefordshire 19
Loudon, Jane 3
Loudon, John Claudius 2, 30, 92, 145
Lowe, William 44–5
Luxborough, Lady *see* Knight, Henrietta
Lyndon, George 151, 153
Lyndon, Walter 151
Lyttelton, Christopher *see* Cobham, 12th Viscount
Lyttelton, George, 1st Baron 188
Lyttelton, Lucy 188
Lyttelton, Sir Charles 186, 188, 192
Lyttelton, Sir Thomas 197–8

Malden, Lord 23
Manor House, Northfield, Birmingham 153
Maurice, Thomas 192, 194, 195, 197, 198–9, 200
Milner, Edward 144–5, 146
Milner, Henry Ernest 145, 151–2, 154, 155, 156
Milton, John 202, 203
Moccas Court, Herefordshire 12, 17, 20–1, 23, 30, 32
Money, John 79
Moor Green Hall, Birmingham 143, 144, 154
Moore, Mrs 114
More, Samuel 62
Morris, William 178–9
Murchison, Sir Roderick 16
Mynde, The, Herefordshire 19, 25

Newport Almley, Herefordshire 19
Nightingale, Florence 166

Palmer, Mrs 115
Parkes, David 49
parks
  Addlerley Park, Birmingham, 92
  Burslem Park, Stoke on Trent 120, 122, 123, 129, 134
  Cannon Hill Park, Birmingham 129
  East Park, Wolverhampton 124
  Handsworth Park, Birmingham 125, 127, 130, 134
  Hanley Park, Stoke on Trent 127, 131, 133
  Hickman Park, Bilston 127
  Small Heath Park, Birmingham 124
  Sutton Park, Sutton Coldfield 130
  West Park, Wolverhampton 124, 125, 127, 128, 130, 131
Parnell, Sir John 48
Patching, Resta 78, 84, 194
Pateshall, Edmund Lechmere 24
Paxton, Joseph 2, 145
Peacock, Barry 165
Pemberton, Abraham 82
Perry, George 60, 62, 71
Philips, John 15
Phipps, Samuel 25
Pitt, Thomas 194, 195
Plymley, Katherine 70
Pococke, Revd Richard (Bishop Pococke) 21, 62, 194, 198
Pope, Alexander 14, 30, 44, 188, 189, 194
Pope, Mary 115
Price, John 17
Price, Robert 16, 17
Price, Uvedale 10, 17, 25–31, 32
Price, Uvedale Tomkyns 16
Prospect, The, Ross-on-Wye 14
Pye, Elizabeth 19
Pytts, Edward 24

Repton, Humphry
  Herefordshire 10, 23, 25–6, 28, 30, 32–3
  Moseley Hall, Birmingham 139–42, 156
Reynolds, Hannah Mary 66
Reynolds, Richard 58, 61, 65–6, 68, 70–1
Richardson, Benjamin Ward
Rogers, George and Mary 113
Rosehill House, Shropshire 60, 61
Rushbrooke, Frederick 165–6, 169
Ruskin, John 178, 179
Ryland, Clara *née* Chamberlain 143–4

Sandys, Anne 108–9
Saul, Pauline 163, 174
Seward, Anna 63–4
Shobdon Court, Herefordshire 18
Shteir, Ann 2
Sleigh, Bernard 171, 172
Small, Dr William 44
Somerville, William 50
Southcote, Philip 45
Spinks, Frances 102–6
Spinks, Thomas 105

Stamford, earl of 48
Stebbing Shaw, Revd 39
Stobart, Jonathan 77, 78
Stoke Edith, Herefordshire 18, 20, 21, 26, 32
Stuart, James 'Athenian' 65
Sunniside, Shropshire 60, 61, 62
Switzer, Stephen 202, 204

Taylor, John 139
Taylor, John II 140, 141, 156
Thomson, James 51, 188, 189
Toldervy, William 194, 195
Tyers, Jonathan 82

Vaughan, Francis 12
Virgil 44, 49, 188
Vivares, Frances 60, 61, 62, 63

Walpole, Horace 189
Warner, Richard 70
Wathen, James 17
Weaver, Hannah 9
West, Benjamin 31
Westonbury, Herefordshire 12
Wheeler, Edward 24–5
Whitfield, Herefordshire 19
Whitney, Jane 160
Williamson, Tom 1
Wilmot, Frances 163, 174
Wilson, Joseph, Joshua and Mary 110, 112
Withering, Dr William 2
Woodhouse, Francis 19
Wyatt, James 65
Wye, river, Herefordshire 16–18

Yates, Lydia 110, 112
Young, Arthur 63, 200